The Rural South Since World War II

The Rural South Since World War II

Edited by R. DOUGLAS HURT

LOUISIANA STATE UNIVERSITY PRESS
Baton Rouge

Designer: Melanie O'Quinn Samaha
Typeface: Sabon
Typesetter: Wilsted & Taylor Publishing Services
Printer and binder: Edwards Brothers, Inc.

Library of Congress Cataloging-in-Publication Data

The rural South since World War II / edited by R. Douglas Hurt.
    p. cm.
    Includes bibliographical references and index.
    ISBN 0-8071-2289-0 (cloth : alk. paper)
    1. Southern States—History—1951–   2. Southern States—
History—1865–1951.   3. Southern States—Rural conditions.
I. Hurt, R. Douglas.
F216.2.R87   1998
975'.04—dc21   98-22263
                                                   CIP

Contents

Illustrations

Acknowledgments

During the course of this project, I had the pleasure of working with three excellent archivists. Gail Miller Deloach at the Georgia Department of Archives and History, Dennis S. Taylor at Special Collections in the Clemson University library, and John Medley at the Country Music Hall of Fame and Museum provided essential help with the illustrations from their superb collections. I am grateful for the help of everyone who assisted with this collection of essays on the rural South.

The Rural South Since World War II

Introduction

R. DOUGLAS HURT

Without question the South has received more attention from American historians, political scientists, sociologists, and economists than any other region. A host of books and articles have attempted to explain the South's historical significance as well as its influence on people and institutions far beyond the borders of the old Confederacy. Yet most of these studies, especially for the rural South, have not ventured beyond World War II. Although the New South, that is, the urban, industrial, Sunbelt South, has received increasing scholarly attention during the last decade, the rural South has been largely forgotten, or at least overlooked. The reason for this scholarly neglect, at least compared to the past, when slavery, sharecropping, and tenancy dominated thoughts about the region, is that agriculture no longer reigns supreme. Indeed, the cotton South has been gone for a long time. By 1980 cotton was no longer the leading cash crop in any southern state, and few people have given much thought to the social, economic, and political consequences of the cotton culture's decline since 1945. This is not to say that cotton is unimportant in the Mississippi Delta and eastern Texas or that tobacco no longer remains vital to the economy of North Carolina, but any traveler passing through the region today will see more fields in soybeans and pastures with grazing cattle than cotton fields. Tractors and mechanical pickers, along with government programs that reduced cotton acreage, replaced sharecroppers and tenants long ago. The radical decline in the number of farms, tenants, and sharecroppers, as well as the extraordinary diversification of southern agriculture, brought a way of life to an end. Moreover, when those sharecroppers and tenants, both black and white, left the land, they were quickly forgotten, as were the people who remained in the countryside. As many fled the poverty and drudgery of the farm for the promise of a better life in the cities, the interests of scholars followed them.[1]

In 1940 nearly 16 million southerners, or about 43 percent of the population, lived on 2.9 million farms, while a total of 65 percent of the people could be classified more generally as rural residents. Flight from the land began in earnest during World War II and reduced the farm population by approximately 3.2 million, or about 22 percent, by 1945. In 1950 only 11 million people remained on southern farms, and a decade later their number had declined to 7 million, or 15 percent of the regional population, while the rural population had fallen to 58 percent of the total. In 1969, the Bureau of the Census ceased recognizing sharecroppers as a distinguishable population and stopped counting them.[2]

Many southerners who fled the land after 1940 sought jobs in defense-related businesses located in cities. In 1940, for example, approximately 8 million southerners, or 20 percent of the region's population, lived in urban areas. After World War II the southern states actively recruited northern industries with the lure of a moderate climate, incentives that reduced or deferred taxes, and a cultural opposition to unionization. Southern states also expanded already established enterprises such as furniture making and paper milling. Wages higher in urban than in rural areas nearly doubled the bank deposits of southerners by 1950, while individual income increased by 223 percent. By the early 1960s, the southern states issued 87 percent of the industrial development bonds in the nation. In response to these initiatives, rural southerners flocked to the cities in search of jobs and a better life. By 1960 21 million people, or 43.5 percent of the South's population, lived in metropolitan areas, and only 10 percent still worked in agriculture. During the next decade, the farm population declined by another 50 percent. Moreover, by the late 1960s mechanical harvesters picked nearly the entire cotton crop, which further contributed to the decline of the rural population, particularly African Americans. The automobile and the federal and state highway systems aided migration and urban growth, and the civil rights legislation of the 1960s encouraged the expansion of suburbs as whites began fleeing the cities. By 1970 only 6.9 percent of the population remained engaged in agriculture.[3]

1.   William J. Cooper, Jr., and Thomas E. Terrill, *The American South: A History* (New York: McGraw-Hill, 1991); Gilbert C. Fite, *Cotton Fields No More: Southern Agriculture, 1865–1980* (Lexington: University Press of Kentucky, 1984); Jack Temple Kirby, *Rural Worlds Lost: The American South, 1920–1960* (Baton Rouge: Louisiana State University Press, 1987).

2.   Pete Daniel, "Going Among Strangers: Southern Reactions to World War II," *Journal of American History* 77 (December 1990): 886–911; Pete Daniel, "The Transformation of the Rural South: 1930 to the Present," *Agricultural History* 55 (July 1981): 231–48; Gavin Wright, *Old South, New South: Revolutions in the Southern Economy Since the Civil War* (New York: Free Press, 1986), 241, 245–46; Dewey W. Grantham, *The South in Modern America: A Region at Odds* (New York: Harper/Collins, 1994), 261; David R. Goldfield, *Promised Land: The South Since 1945* (Arlington Heights, Ill.: Harlan Davidson, 1987), 24; Cooper and Terrill, *American South*, 738.

3.   Numan V. Bartley, *The New South, 1945–1980* (Baton Rouge: Louisiana State University

In addition, by 1970, more than half of all southerners were employed by service industries, such as banking, insurance, and government, rather than rural-based manufacturing firms, and their places of work were often located in the suburbs. As urban areas became more populated, public demands for other services increased. Jobs in urban service industries, such as chemicals, electronics, and transportation equipment, developed and existed independently from the needs of the rural South, and the suburbs became increasingly self-sustaining by generating jobs independent of either the cities or the countryside. The colonial economy based on the rural extractive industries of agriculture, forestry, and mining no longer reigned supreme. By 1970, southern states, especially North Carolina, had begun recruiting high-technology industries and think tanks for urban areas. In addition, the term *Sunbelt* emerged, and the American people began associating the South with golf courses, retirement communities, and vacation spots, rather than with cotton fields, sharecroppers, and poverty. Two out of three southerners now lived in cities of between fifty thousand and one hundred thousand.[4]

Indeed, by the 1970s, the urban Sunbelt South eclipsed the rural South in economic significance, while the white suburban middle class replaced the rural county-seat political elite as the foundation of southern consciousness. From 1950 to 1975, the number of southern farms declined from 2.1 million to 720,000. Five years later, nearly 14 million people had left southern farms since 1940. Only 8 percent of southern farmers remained tenants; owners and part-owners characterized farm tenure in the region. By the mid-1990s, farmers composed only 2 percent of the southern population, and the number of farms had declined to about 500,000. Although southern farmers were more prosperous than before, they had converted much of the land from cotton to pasture for livestock and to soybeans. Poultry houses, where farmers raised chickens on contract for processors, rather than cotton warehouses, rose from the land in many areas. All agricultural endeavors now required relatively few laborers, so that little opportunity for personal economic improvement remained in the countryside. Sophisticated Atlanta, sprawling Charlotte, bustling Nashville, and zone-free Houston lured the hopeful, both southerners and northerners, with employment. Northern-based and financially capitalized corporations offered many new opportunities, provided the job seekers had educational credentials and the necessary skills.[5]

By 1980, approximately 75 percent of the South's population lived in cities,

Press, 1995), 134, 430; Grantham, *The South in Modern America*, 260–61; Goldfield, *Promised Land*, 28–30, 34, 39, 146; Wright, *Old South, New South*, 243–44.

4. Bartley, *New South*, 436; Grantham, *The South in Modern America*, 259; Wright, *Old South, New South*, 264; Goldfield, *Promised Land*, 136, 152–53.

5. Bartley, *New South*, 448; Grantham, *The South in Modern America*, 260–61; Goldfield, *Promised Land*, 139–40, 146–53.

and southerners enjoyed a standard of living little different from that of urbanites in other regions of the nation. Moreover, approximately one-quarter of southern workers were well-educated and held professional and white-collar jobs. Blue-collar workers made up only 46 percent of the southern work force, while pink-blouse clerical and sales employees composed about 25 percent of the laboring population. More people now moved to the South from other regions than left this portion of the Sunbelt for a net gain of more than 1.6 million residents. Moreover, African Americans began moving into the urban areas of the region in search of economic opportunities and an improved standard of living.[6]

Not everyone, of course, left the rural South after World War II, either forced off the land by New Deal programs or lured by wartime employment and peacetime service industries in the cities. Many stayed, black and white, and they continued to work the land, lived in rural areas, addressed new political concerns while making accommodations for old grievances, maintained traditional cultural practices, and remained the most Protestant and churchgoing people in the nation. While most southerners had opted for an urban lifestyle that provided a standard of living comparable to that in cities across the country, as late as 1980 rural southerners composed 55 percent of the region's poor. Hunger was still a common experience for many in the rural South. In addition, post–World War II changes sometimes came hard for the South and the nation, especially regarding the constitutional and statutory guarantees of civil rights. Often, these changes were subtle and carried a rhythm and melody that others heard over the radio and soon took for granted as a part of American folk culture. As always, the men and women who lived in the rural South after World War II made economic, social, and political accommodations based on race, class, and gender and thereby contributed to a culture that remained distinctive in American life.[7]

This book is intended to provide a road map for the most important concerns, issues, and developments in southern rural life since 1945. The contributors are authorities on the South whose expertise in history, sociology, and political science provides a new and important look at the manner in which economic, social, political, and cultural changes in the rural South have affected the region in its transition to an urban and industrialized society. Each author was asked to consider a specific topic in the context of the South as defined by the Confederacy, with the exception of Florida. The heavy migration of northerners and people from the Caribbean arguably has made Florida something other than a southern state; consequently, the contributors were asked to exclude Florida from their analyses unless they could not avoid it. The result is a wide-ranging discussion of the economic, social, political, and cultural changes in the rural South since World War II.

6. Bartley, *New South,* 449, 451; Grantham, *The South in Modern America,* 264–65.
7. Goldfield, *Promised Land,* 141–44, 220; Cooper and Terrill, *American South,* 738.

To begin, Donald L. Winters discusses the revolutionary transformation of southern agriculture after World War II. Technological improvements in the form of mechanical pickers changed the labor requirements for cotton production, while competition from California and Arizona and government programs encouraged diversification. As cotton acreage declined, southern farmers expanded their soybean acreage and grazed more cattle, both of which changed the face of the countryside. The poultry industry became a vertically integrated agribusiness and fish farming grew in importance. As southern farms increased in size, farmers needed more technical knowledge, increased capital, and better managerial ability to succeed in a market economy. Often they had to take off-the-farm employment. As the cotton South disappeared, farming became a business rather than a way of life. But, Winters observes, while farm men and women often left the land for better-paying jobs and a higher standard of living in the cities and towns, many yearned for a bygone way of life in which they were close to nature, the soil, and their families.

Anyone who studies twentieth-century American history will confront turbulent race relations and a civil rights movement born from hate, repression, and violence as well as love, liberation, and nonviolence. Yet studies of the civil rights movement invariably focus on urban areas and ignore the countryside. Orville Vernon Burton provides a new look at race relations in the South by analyzing the effect of the civil rights movement on rural areas, where school desegregation, civil liberties, and voting rights did not come easily. Burton notes that although significant problems remain, race relations in the rural South have undergone dramatic change for the better since World War II.

Sally McMillen discusses the role of women in the rural South during the war years and beyond. She analyzes the social implications of midwifery, health care, and child raising as well as the impact of electricity and child care centers on women's lives. McMillen comments in particular on the changes that have affected Appalachian women, such as improved roads and communication and consumer demand for their handicrafts. She also poignantly traces the decline in the number of women (black and white) on the farms, their increasing employment in low-wage industries, and the effects of these changes, both good and ill, on family life. In addition, McMillen notes the role of southern women as activists in the civil rights movement and union organizational work.

By the late twentieth century, many people identified country music with the South as much as others traditionally associated cotton with the region. Bill C. Malone cogently traces the increasing popularity of that musical genre and its spread beyond the South. Country music traditionally has portrayed the often hard realities of life, particularly among the working class. It remains distinctive for its regional and rural themes, but it has also undergone considerable change since World War II, becoming as much American as southern music. Malone analyzes the influence of artists such as Eddy Arnold, Elvis Presley, Hazel Dickens, Bill Monroe, Hank Williams, and Emmylou Harris in the transformation of country music from regional and class appeal to a national audience that cuts across class and, to an extent, race. Malone also notes the effects of rock-and-roll, bluegrass, and folk in country music. Although many country musicians today are neither southern nor rural, they continue to make music that appeals to rural southerners as well as to those who have their roots in the region. At the same time, country music provides meaning to others far beyond the South.

Religious fundamentalism often is associated with southerners, usually in a negative sense. Ted Ownby takes a different tack, however, as he discusses the significance of religion in the rural South and the sense of crisis that concerns many members of the evangelical and Pentecostal churches. He notes that while the members of the evangelical and Pentecostal denominations remain well-known for their reliance on the Bible as the sole reference point in life, they confront a host of problems such as wealth, large memberships, and church construction that threaten to depersonalize worship services and challenge traditional beliefs. Ownby also analyzes the significance of the African American evangelical churches to the civil rights movement and the interests of white evangelicals in social issues that can be addressed through politics. The result is a wide-ranging study of the place of evangelical religion in the rural South.

Since World War II, southern politics also has undergone fundamental change as the Republican party has captured many of the traditional supporters of the Democratic party. Political scientists Wayne Parent and Peter A. Petrakis discuss political issues in the postwar South in the context of populist change. They analyze the mobilization of African American voters, partisan change, and the emergence of the Republican party. They note that the politics of race remains important and that urban and white-collar workers have used it to strengthen the Republican party and make the South a two-party region. Parent and Petrakis emphasize the influence of social issues such as gun control, abortion, school prayer, gay rights, affirmative action, and welfare rather than economic issues on the political behavior of rural whites and Republican ascendancy, and they find much of that behavior rooted in the Populist movement of the 1890s. Moreover, by blaming economic problems on technocrats, the Republican party has appealed to the middle class without alienating the wealthy. As a result, the Republican party has won the support of many rural, white, low-income southerners who traditionally supported the Democrats. Parent and Petrakis see the politics of the New South as a new populism.

The distinctiveness of the South has been a matter of debate for a long time. Sociologists Jeanne S. Hurlbert and William B. Bankston conclude this collection of essays by considering southern cultural distinctiveness vis à vis the use of violence, conservative political issues, racial attitudes, and religious beliefs. Although they note differences between southerners and nonsoutherners as well as variations within the South, they have found less regional distinction than in the past. In the case of gun control legislation, for example, the views of southerners have drawn closer to those of nonsoutherners, although southerners still strongly support the right to own guns. In other cases, such as interracial marriages, southerners remain distinctive in their opposition. In general, Hurlbert and Bankston contend that the social and political attitudes and behavior of nonsoutherners have converged with those of southerners since World War II. Nevertheless, a certain southern cultural identity remains a fundamental part of American life.

These essays, then, will introduce students of southern history to an important and largely forgotten part of the American past. Moreover, each essay should prove suggestive for further study and research on a variety of topics concerning the rural South since World War II.

Agriculture in the
Post–World War II South

DONALD L. WINTERS

Agriculture, from the beginnings of colonial settlement, has played a central role in the lives of southern people. It has provided subsistence for rural households and supplied marketable goods to urban businesses and residents. It has generated money income, either directly or indirectly, for a wide segment of the region's population and contributed vastly to its wealth. It has shaped values, ideas, and attitudes and influenced the behavior of successive generations of southerners. Throughout most of the South's history—the Civil War era was a significant exception—stability and gradual transformation typified agricultural activities. Such has not been the case over the past half-century. Since 1945, the pace of change has quickened, affecting the structure, organization, and production patterns of southern agriculture.

One of the most remarkable developments has been the sharp drop in the proportion of southerners living on farms and depending on agriculture for their livelihood. From the beginning of World War II to the mid-1990s, farm households declined from over 40 percent to less than 5 percent of the region's population. Farmers represented approximately a third of the South's labor force in 1945; fifty years later, they made up barely 2 percent. Over the same period, the number of farms dropped by nearly 80 percent, from 2.3 million to about half a million. Clearly, farmers have occupied a rapidly shrinking position in the South's population in the years since World War II.[1]

I wish to thank Jimmie L. Franklin and V. Jacque Voegeli for their suggestions on revising this essay.

1. All quantitative evidence has been drawn from the appropriate volumes of the federal agricultural census, 1945 to 1992, unless otherwise indicated.

Changes in the rural population and labor force reflect two reinforcing trends. Opportunities outside of agriculture drew large numbers of rural southerners, especially the young and the landless, into urban occupations. The growth of manufacturing and construction in the postwar years, much of it occurring in the South, provided alternative employment that attracted many unskilled and semiskilled farmers and farm laborers to the cities. Expanded access to higher education enabled others to pursue more lucrative urban careers in business, administration, and the professions. At the same time, employment opportunities in the rural South contracted. Changes in agriculture often brought greater efficiency, but they also reduced the number of farmers and farm laborers required to meet the growing demand for southern farm goods. Shifts from relatively labor-intensive to relatively labor-extensive production also eroded the need for farmhands. These concurrent developments in urban and rural employment combined to bring about momentous changes in southern rural population patterns.[2]

Those who elected to remain in or enter farming as their source of livelihood encountered a rapidly transforming economic sector. Nothing epitomizes the profound changes occurring in southern agriculture better than the cultivation of cotton, the crop with which the region has been historically identified. Coming out of World War II, the southern states produced almost 11 million bales of the fiber, accounting for 90 percent of the nation's total output. Texas led the country with 2.5 million bales, followed by Mississippi with 1.9 million and Arkansas with 1.4 million bales. By 1982, southern cotton production had fallen to 6.8 million bales, barely 60 percent of national output, and Texas and Mississippi had slipped to second and third place behind California. Southern cotton production reversed its postwar trend and rose in the late 1980s, returning to its 1944 level of 11 million bales by the early 1990s, and Texas had regained its lead. Still, the region's output in 1992 was only about 70 percent of the nation's, well below its proportion in the immediate postwar period.

The trend in cotton production in the four decades following the war was, in some respects, the continuation of a longer trend reaching back to the 1920s. Cotton acreage declined steadily from the mid-1920s through World War II. Production also declined through the 1930s, but higher yields, resulting largely from improved varieties and greater application of fertilizers, permitted a modest increase during the war. Overproduction and competition from synthetic fibers depressed cotton prices and discouraged cultivation throughout the prosperous 1920s. The devastating economic crisis and government schemes to control production during the following decade brought sharp drops in acreage and output. Despite increased demand and higher prices during World War II, labor shortages and more profitable alternatives deterred southern farmers from renewing their commitment to cotton production.[3]

2.   Louis Ducoff and Joe R. Motheral, "The Manpower Situation in Southern Agriculture," *Journal of Farm Economics* 36 (February 1954): 52–65.

3.   John Leonard Fulmer, *Agricultural Progress in the Cotton Belt Since 1920* (Chapel Hill: Uni-

For a time in the postwar period similar circumstances prevailed, continuing to discourage the revival of a regional specialization in cotton. Heavy production, now exacerbated by foreign competitors, and newly improved synthetic fibers once again depressed world prices, except for a brief period during the Korean War. Federal acreage allotments and price controls and the high costs of labor, caused in large part by competing alternatives in urban employment, limited the profitability of cotton production. Much of the country's cotton cultivation shifted to more efficient producers in the West, who employed sophisticated irrigation systems and exploited the latest agricultural technology. Small wonder, then, that many southern farmers chose to devote their resources to the production of commodities other than cotton.[4]

Shifting market conditions in the 1980s and 1990s created a more favorable environment for southern cotton producers. Growth in demand for the fiber accelerated following the development of versatile cotton blends and modifications in consumer preference. Cotton, Inc., a trade association for the textile industry, capitalized on new attitudes among consumers and aggressively promoted the fiber. More recently, Asian producers, the chief competitors of United States producers, have experienced sharp declines in yields because of insect infestations; ironically, the principal menace has been the boll weevil, the nemesis of southern cotton farmers earlier in the twentieth century. These developments created a disparity between worldwide supply and demand that pushed prices to unprecedented levels. The use of sprinkler irrigation, moreover, improved cotton yields in the South and narrowed the competitive advantage of producers in the West. All of these factors joined to reverse the long-term decline in southern cotton cultivation.[5]

Accompanying the revival of interest in cotton production was a revolution in cotton cultivation. The fiber had traditionally been a highly labor-intensive crop. Farmers prepared the ground with animal-drawn plows and seeded, cultivated, and picked the fields by hand. Because of the physical effort required, cultivation usually occurred on a relatively small scale. The development of mechanized

---

versity of North Carolina Press, 1950), 5–6; Walter W. Wilcox, *The Farmer and the Second World War* (Ames: Iowa State College Press, 1947), 64–65, 218–19; James H. Street, *The New Revolution in the Cotton Economy: Mechanization and Its Consequences* (Chapel Hill: University of North Carolina Press, 1957), 72–73; Gilbert C. Fite, *Cotton Fields No More: Southern Agriculture, 1865–1980* (Lexington: University Press of Kentucky, 1984), 164.

4. Street, *New Revolution in the Cotton Economy*, 85–86; Fulmer, *Agricultural Progress in the Cotton Belt Since 1920*, 8–9; Fite, *Cotton Fields No More*, 194–95.

5. J. Nicholas Hahn, "Consumers 'Take Comfort in Cotton,'" in *Marketing U.S. Agriculture, USDA Yearbook of Agriculture, 1988* (Washington, D.C.: U.S. Department of Agriculture, 1988), 283–84; Mark L. Gardner and Ronny Richardson, "Factors Affecting the Resurgence of Cotton Production in Georgia During the 1980s," *Agricultural History* 68 (Spring 1994): 243–45; *Georgia Agricultural Experiment Stations, Annual Report, 1961* (Athens: University of Georgia College of Agriculture, 1961), 9; *Nashville Tennessean*, April 10, 1995, Section E, 2.

equipment and scientific agriculture since 1945, however, vastly altered traditional methods.

Even before World War II, the internal combustion engine tractor had begun gradually replacing the mule as the primary source of nonhuman power in southern agriculture. Its adoption accelerated in the postwar years. In 1945, roughly 10 percent of southern farms used tractors; thirty years later the share had increased to three-quarters. By the end of the 1980s, draft animals had largely disappeared from southern farms. Animal-drawn implements used for such tasks as plowing, disking, harrowing, and cultivating were, with minor adjustments, well suited to the tractor. In time, tractor-propelled machines for planting, harvesting, and threshing also appeared. Although the initial investment was greater, tractors cost less to maintain, delivered more power, and were more dependable than mules. Most important, tractors substantially reduced the need for farmhands, a critical factor in the period of rising labor costs following World War II. Farmers eventually used tractors for a wide variety of operations, none more important to southern agriculture than cotton cultivation.[6]

Harvesting had always created the greatest constraint on improved efficiency in cotton cultivation. Well after farmers began using animal-powered equipment for many other tasks, this phase of cotton production defied mechanization. A variety of mechanical picking devices appeared in the late nineteenth and early twentieth centuries, but none offered a satisfactory alternative to hand picking. Beginning in the 1920s, commercial manufacturers introduced improvements that addressed some of the technical problems. By the early 1940s, two types of machines had come into limited use. The stripper harvester, which removed all the fiber in a single run through the field, was well adapted to irrigated cotton production in the West, where the entire crop matured at approximately the same time. The spindle harvester removed only the lint from open bolls, but it damaged the immature plants until scientists developed varieties that matured uniformly.[7]

Western cotton producers eagerly adopted the stripper harvester after World War II, but southern producers took up the spindle harvester at a far slower pace. One deterrent was that a large amount of trash was introduced into fiber picked by machine, which lowered the market grade and price. Most of the trash consisted of weeds, dirt, and plant leaves. Southern farmers experimented with flame weeders and rotary hoes for weed control, but with limited success. Herbi-

6.   Charles P. Butler, "Cotton Production Practices and Requirements in South Carolina," *South Carolina Agricultural Experiment Station, Bulletin 387* (1950), 24–29; Charles P. Butler and D. E. Crawford, "Economics of Tractor Farming in the Piedmont Area of South Carolina," *South Carolina Agricultural Experiment Station, Bulletin 377* (1948), 46–47; David R. Goldfield, *Promised Land: The South Since 1945* (Arlington Heights, Ill.: Harlan Davidson, 1987), 26.

7.   Fulmer, *Agricultural Progress in the Cotton Belt Since 1920*, 87–88; Street, *New Revolution in the Cotton Economy*, 92–93, 107–34.

cides and defoliants developed in the 1950s more effectively controlled weeds and leaves. Also, changes in gins improved their cleaning capacity, at least partially alleviating the problem of trash. Another disadvantage of mechanical harvesting was cotton loss. Because plants varied in height, the machine was unable to reach all of the bolls and left about 10 percent of the lint in the field. Improvements in the spindle harvester and genetically designed plants with greater uniformity in height mitigated, but failed to resolve, the problem of crop loss.[8]

Despite the lingering drawbacks of mechanized cotton harvesting, it offered one enormous advantage: vastly improved labor productivity. Once the harvester's technical problems had been partially remedied, reducing labor costs became the driving force behind its adoption by southern producers. A machine required only one driver but accomplished the work of roughly forty hands. Traditional methods of cotton cultivation required about 155 hours per bale for the entire process. Using a tractor to prepare the land reduced the time to 132 hours. Adding a machine to pick the fiber reduced the time to 10 hours. With the harvester offering such dramatic benefits, the pace of adoption rapidly accelerated. In 1950, practically all southern cotton was picked by hand; by the end of the 1960s, over 90 percent was picked by machine.[9]

At the end of World War II, although some large-scale enterprises employing hired labor existed, primarily in the Mississippi Delta, cotton was cultivated primarily on small farms. The typical unit devoted approximately fifteen acres to cotton and produced fewer than ten bales per year. Investment in machinery and the resulting improvement in labor productivity placed a premium on larger-scale production. The harvester in particular created significant economies of scale. Full mechanization required production of at least one hundred bales per year to turn a profit on the investment and much more to realize optimal returns. By 1992, accordingly, the typical cotton operation had grown significantly. It now placed about three hundred acres in cotton and marketed almost four hundred bales per year.[10]

8.   Glenn H. Glover, "An Economic Analysis of Selected Cotton Production Practices Used in Tennessee," Tennessee Agricultural Experiment Station, *Bulletin 458* (1969), 45; Daniel F. Capstick, "Economics of Mechanical Cotton Harvesting," Arkansas Agricultural Experiment Station, *Bulletin 622* (1960), 7–8; Gale E. Peterson, "The Discovery and Development of 2,4-D," *Agricultural History* 41 (July 1967): 249–53; Gilbert C. Fite, "Mechanization of Cotton Production Since World War II," *Agricultural History* 54 (January 1980): 194–96; Charles R. Sayre, "Cotton Mechanization Since World War II," *Agricultural History* 53 (January 1979): 111–15.

9.   James L. Novak, Greg Traxler, Max Runge, and Charles Mitchell, Jr., "The Effect of Mechanical Cotton Harvesting Technology on Southern Piedmont Cotton Production, 1896–1991," *Agricultural History* 69 (Spring 1995): 361; Reynold M. Wik, "Mechanization of the Farm," in *Technology in Western Civilization*, ed. Melvin Kranzberg and Carroll W. Pursell, Jr. (New York: Oxford University Press, 1967), 2:365; Street, *New Revolution in the Cotton Economy*, 170–71; Fulmer, *Agricultural Progress in the Cotton Belt Since 1920*, 88, 97.

10.   Grady B. Crowe, "Mechanical Cotton Picker Operation in the Yazoo-Mississippi Delta," Mississippi Agricultural Experiment Station, *Bulletin 465* (1949), 10; Fite, "Mechanization of Cotton Production Since World War II," 202–3.

Tobacco, the other cash crop long associated with the South, also went through a period of transition after World War II. Acreage and production had declined modestly in the 1920s and 1930s in response to low prices brought on by worldwide increases in production and to federal controls implemented during the Great Depression. Prices dropped even further with the loss of European exports at the outbreak of the war, but they rebounded and remained high when the domestic economy recovered following the entry of the United States into the conflict. More intensive cultivation, increased fertilization, and ideal weather conditions contributed to a notable increase in production with only a small change in acreage in the first half of the 1940s. After World War II, the number of farms and amount of acreage in southern tobacco cultivation resumed their prewar trend, but at an accelerated pace. North Carolina, which led the nation in production and accounted for over half of the South's total output, illustrates the postwar developments. The number of the state's tobacco farms dropped by nearly 90 percent and its tobacco acreage by more than 50 percent between 1945 and 1992. Improving yields per acre, however, limited the decline in total production to about 11 percent.[11]

Postwar trends in tobacco production, like those in cotton cultivation, resulted from changes in the market, consumer attitudes, federal programs, and technology. Prices declined and remained relatively low after the war in large part because of expanding production elsewhere in the world. At the same time, higher labor expenses pushed up production costs in the United States. Beginning in the 1980s, increasing realization of the detrimental effects of tobacco on personal health and well-publicized campaigns to limit and control its use eroded domestic demand, exacerbating the effects of worldwide overproduction. Moreover, federal price-support programs were coupled with production allotments, placing constraints on output. Under these conditions, farmers had little incentive to maintain their levels of tobacco cultivation.

Such an environment understandably encouraged tobacco farmers to search for ways to improve efficiency. Tractors, which had been so beneficial to cotton farmers, proved advantageous in preparing tobacco fields and in cultivating young plants. In the 1960s, many operators began to use mechanical transplanters and mechanical toppers, which also applied chemicals for control of suckers. These machines reduced the labor needed for preharvest tasks by over 50 percent. Yet, as with cotton, the major bottleneck in tobacco production was harvesting. At the end of World War II, farmers still picked the crop by hand, just as they had since the seventeenth century. Carts—some tractor-drawn, others self-propelled—from which farmhands picked tobacco as they rode through the fields only modestly improved labor productivity in the 1950s. The real technological breakthrough came in the early 1970s, with the development of a mechanical harvester that stripped the leaves from tobacco stalks. This device cut

---

11. Wilcox, *The Farmer and the Second World War,* 238–41; Fite, *Cotton Fields No More,* 166.

the labor required for harvesting by almost 40 percent. By 1980, nearly 50 percent of the nation's tobacco was picked by machine. Adoption of loose-leaf marketing for flue-cured varieties, beginning in 1968, eliminated the need to tie tobacco into bunches for sale and curing, greatly reducing the time for market preparation. According to one estimate, the new technology and marketing procedures cut the total labor requirements for flue-cured tobacco, the varieties for which they were most adaptable, from 425 hours per acre in 1965 to 172 in 1979.[12]

Because tobacco was so labor-intensive, farmers had traditionally planted only a very few acres in the crop. Much of the new labor-saving technology, however, required production on a larger scale. For farmers to realize a profit on investments in the new machinery, they had to devote considerably more of their land to the crop. At first, government support programs severely limited the amount of tobacco individual farmers could produce. Federal allotments applied to specific farms and were nontransferable, which essentially froze the amount of acreage a participant could plant or, after the government switched to a poundage basis, the amount of tobacco a participant could market. Beginning in 1961, the government allowed the intracounty lease and transfer of flue-cured allotments; ten years later it extended the authorization to burley allotments. Considerable consolidation of tobacco cultivation occurred in the wake of these changes, significantly increasing the size of a typical operation. Larger, more efficient farmers began leasing the allotments of their smaller, less efficient neighbors. From 1974 to 1992, the average acreage and poundage of flue-cured farms in North Carolina and of burley farms in Tennessee more than doubled.[13]

As many farmers abandoned cotton and tobacco production in the years following World War II, they moved into other areas of agricultural activity. One of the most lucrative was soybean production. Before the 1940s, southern farmers grew soybeans almost exclusively for forage or green manure, which they plowed under to replace soil nitrogen. A few sold the beans to processors of meal for

---

12. Verner N. Grise, "Trends in Flue-Cured Tobacco Farming," USDA, *Agricultural Economics Report 470*, 1981, 12–15; Gig Beradi, "Can Tobacco Farmers Adjust to Mechanization? A Look at Allotment Holders in Two North Carolina Counties," in *The Tobacco Industry in Transition*, ed. William R. Finger (Lexington, Mass.: Lexington Books, 1981), 47–49; Jerry R. Skees and Louis E. Swanson, "Farm Structure and Rural Well-Being in the South," in *Agriculture and Community Change in the U.S.*, ed. Louis E. Swanson, Congressional Research Reports (Boulder, Colo.: Westview Press, 1988), 279; *Georgia Agricultural Experiment Stations, Annual Report, 1962* (Athens: University of Georgia College of Agriculture, 1962), 9.

13. Luther H. Keller and James A. Culver, "Economic Aspects of Permitting Intercounty Transfer of Burley Tobacco Quotas," Tennessee Agricultural Experiment Station, *Bulletin 589* (1979), 3–4; Beradi, "Can Tobacco Farmers Adjust to Mechanization?," 48–49; James A. Seagraves, "Capitalized Values of Tobacco Allotments and the Rate of Return to Allotment Owners," *American Journal of Agricultural Economics* 51 (May 1969): 321–22. North Carolina was the leading national producer of flue-cured tobacco. Tennessee was the leading southern producer of burley tobacco but ranked second to Kentucky in the nation.

high-protein animal feed or oil for soaps, paints, varnishes, and other industrial products. With the development in the late 1930s of a method to remove its unpalatable flavor and disagreeable odor, soybean oil became an ingredient in margarine, shortening, and other goods for human consumption. Shortages of both industrial and edible oils during World War II raised prices and stimulated interest in soybean production. The oil found other uses over time, most recently as the main component of a biodegradable ink for newspapers. The new uses greatly expanded the demand for soybeans in both the domestic and export markets. In 1956, the American Soybean Association, an organization representing producers and processors, opened its first foreign office in Japan and began to develop the export market. Already the country's largest customer abroad, Japan purchased 26 million bushels of soybeans from the United States that year. Thirty years later it imported six times that amount. The association has also built substantial markets in several other Asian countries, most notably the People's Republic of China, and in European countries.[14]

The conditions and changing circumstances in the South well suited the growth of soybeans after World War II. Land taken out of cotton production, often fertile and relatively flat, was ideal for soybean cultivation. The South's abundant clay soils, normally poorly suited to cotton, were also satisfactory for soybeans. In the lower South with its longer growing season, the crop offered the possibility of double-cropping the land, planting winter wheat followed by soybeans in the late spring. Soybean cultivation profited from the widespread adoption of new technology that occurred in southern agriculture. Tractors prepared the soil and cultivated the plants, herbicides controlled the weeds, and combines harvested the crop. Those same combines—multipurpose machines that were greatly improved in the postwar period—also harvested winter wheat under double-cropping systems. Furthermore, soybean production required relatively little labor, thus mitigating increasing labor costs. Screw-press crushing mills, already in existence throughout the South for processing cottonseed, were also capable of processing soybeans. Soybeans, for a variety of reasons, fit well the South's need for alternatives to cotton and tobacco.[15]

The southern states, which more than doubled their output of soybeans during World War II, expanded cultivation of the crop at a phenomenal rate over the next four decades. Immediately after the war, the South produced about 9 mil-

14. Wayne Bennett, "Opening New Markets for U.S. Soybeans," in *Marketing U.S. Agriculture,* USDA Yearbook of Agriculture, 1988 (Washington, D.C.: U.S. Department of Agriculture, 1988), 230–33; Harry D. Fornari, "The Big Change: Cotton to Soybeans," *Agricultural History 53* (January 1979): 246–47.

15. S. Darrell Mundy and Morgan D. Gray, "Types of Farming in Tennessee," Tennessee Agricultural Experiment Station, *Bulletin 646* (1986), 30; Morton D. Winsberg, "Agricultural Specialization in the United States Since World War II," *Agricultural History 56* (October 1982): 699; Fornari, "The Big Change," 251–52; *Georgia Agricultural Experiment Stations, Annual Report, 1950–1951* (Athens: University of Georgia College of Agriculture, 1951), 9.

lion bushels. In 1982, it produced almost half a billion bushels. Land under soybean cultivation increased from 1 million to 20 million acres during the same period. As cotton returned to favor as a cash crop in the late 1980s and early 1990s, many southern farmers reduced their commitment to soybeans. Production declined to 300 million bushels and acreage to a little over 10 million by 1992. Arkansas led the southern states, producing a fifth of the region's output on 4 million acres in 1982 and a third of its output on 3 million acres in 1992.

Some farmers shifted from cotton to another oil-producing crop—peanuts. Their cultivation increased during and for several years following the war, but peanuts never approached soybeans in their importance to southern agriculture. For one thing, they were considerably more labor-intensive. Farmers harvested peanuts by hand through the 1940s. A machine for removing the plants from the soil, shaking off the excess dirt, and placing them in windrows across the field became available in the 1950s. Tractor-drawn combines threshed the crop after it had dried. This process left about 10 percent of the peanuts in the field and was, at best, only moderately more efficient than hand methods. Although improvements in the machinery reduced crop loss and expanded capacity by the 1970s, high labor costs continued to discourage extensive cultivation. Moreover, since peanut oil was not as versatile as soybean oil, the demand grew at a less robust pace. Georgia, with an output of 1.7 billion pounds on 630,000 acres in 1992, was the country's major producer.[16]

The South produced a variety of other commercial crops. Arkansas led the nation in rice cultivation and Louisiana in sugarcane cultivation. Because these crops required substantial investments in machinery and irrigation facilities, farmers normally operated on a large scale. In 1992, the typical Arkansas producer placed about three hundred acres in rice, and the typical Louisiana producer placed about five hundred acres in sugarcane. Cultivated acreage in excess of a thousand acres, however, was not uncommon. The South became a major source of fresh and processed fruits and vegetables, mainly because improvements in packaging and in the transportation and distribution system extended the produce market well beyond the region. The main commodities were peaches, apples, strawberries, tomatoes, beans, peas, and melons. Large-scale farmers handled their own marketing, but small-scale farmers normally contracted to sell their goods to handlers or processors.[17]

16. Fite, *Cotton Fields No More*, 165, 190; *Georgia Experiment Stations Annual Report, 1950–1951*, 13–14; Harold L. Streitman, "Costs and Practices in Producing Peanuts in South Carolina," South Carolina Agricultural Experiment Station, *Bulletin 424* (1955), 25.

17. Troy Mullins, Warren R. Grant, and Ronald D. Krenz, "Rice Production Practices and Costs in Major U.S. Rice Areas, 1979," Arkansas Agricultural Experiment Station, *Bulletin 851* (1981), 3–6, 28; Leo Popolous, "Louisiana Agriculture: Economic Trends and Current Status," Louisiana Agricultural Experiment Station, *Bulletin 550* (1962), 54–55; Geoff Burrows and Ralph Shlomowitz, "The Lag in the Mechanization of the Surgarcane Harvest: Some Comparative Perspectives," *Agricultural History* 66 (Summer 1992): 65–75; Fite, *Cotton Fields No More*, 203.

Farmers across the South continued to produce a variety of grains after World War II, principally corn and wheat. They grew corn in large quantities, as they had for over three hundred years. It was sold as a cash crop or fed to the farmers' own livestock. Although corn no longer held the predominance it once had, it remained a central part of southern farming. Earlier in the century, wheat had been of minor commercial importance. New varieties better adapted to southern conditions were developed after the war, making the crop more attractive particularly to farmers using small grain for crop rotation or double-cropping. Corn and wheat offered other advantages: they demanded relatively little labor, accommodated well to tractor technology, and usually returned a profit even when cultivated on modest scale. In 1992, Texas led in the production of both corn and wheat; North Carolina ranked second in corn, Arkansas second in wheat.[18]

The South's natural forested areas and exhausted cotton lands replanted in trees provided yet other commercial opportunities. Large tree plantations, which farmers began to develop in the 1940s, sold timber for lumber and pulpwood on a contract basis to local firms. The companies, many of which moved to the South after World War II, harvested and removed the trees. Indigenous pines were the preferred variety because they matured rapidly and flourished under southern conditions. Some farmers experimented with more valuable northern hardwoods, but the rate of failure was often unacceptably high. A few found another profitable use for their forested areas. By the 1970s, all southern states had legalized the selling of hunting privileges on private property, and large landowners established commercial preserves for hunting such animals as deer, quail, and turkey. Virginia, Mississippi, and Alabama saw the most extensive development of this commercial activity.[19]

Even though field crops had historically constituted the major source of agricultural income in the South, livestock and livestock products had always provided a substantial supplement. As farmers reduced or eliminated their cotton and tobacco acreage, the importance of animals in the rural economy grew substantially. The expansion of livestock production made sense for several reasons. Much of the land formerly in cotton was eroded or exhausted, but it was still well suited to grass for feeding beef or dairy cattle. The development of coastal Bermuda grass in the early 1940s provided a powerful incentive for the produc-

18.   Dana G. Dalrymple, "Changes in Wheat Varieties and Yields in the United States, 1919–1984," *Agricultural History* 62 (Fall 1988): 21–32.

19.   J. Reid Parker and G. H. Aull, "Farm Marketing Saw Timber and Pulpwood in a Selected Area of South Carolina," South Carolina Agricultural Experiment Station, *Bulletin 403* (1953), 9–10, 19; Fayette M. Meade, "Forest Plantations in Arkansas," Arkansas Agricultural Experiment Station, *Bulletin 512* (1951), 49; Jack Temple Kirby, "The Transformation of Southern Plantations ca. 1920–1960," *Agricultural History* 57 (July 1983): 275; B. L. Dillman and J. S. Jordan, "Costs and Returns of Commercial Quail Shooting Preserves in the Southeast," South Carolina Agricultural Experiment Station, *Bulletin 556* (1971), 1–4; Leonard J. Kouba, "The Evolution of Hunting Preserves in the United States," *Professional Geographer* 28 (May 1976): 145.

tion of livestock. It yielded twice as much as common varieties of grass, offered greater nutritional value, and accommodated either grazing or haymaking. Better machinery for mowing, raking, and baling made haymaking less arduous and less time-consuming. After some initial resistance among farmers, who had long considered the ordinary strain of Bermuda grass an unwanted weed, the new variety became the principal plant for pasture and hay. Corn, however, remained the major source of nourishment for both cattle and swine.[20]

Improvements in the quality of animals and changes in the market provided additional incentives to adopt livestock production. The development of animals better adapted to the southern environment, a process that had been occurring for well over a century, continued after the war. Moreover, livestock required less work than field crops, a crucial factor as labor costs rose. Several decades of national prosperity and economic expansion increased the nation's personal income and, along with it, the demand for livestock products. Per capita food consumption remained fairly stable, but as consumers could afford more expensive diets, their purchase of meat and dairy products increased proportionately. Modernization of distribution and merchandising enhanced the ability of processors and marketers to exploit the rising demand, which, of course, benefited livestock producers as well.

The quality of beef and dairy cattle improved markedly in the postwar period. Cattle varieties available in 1945 derived, for the most part, from bloodlines imported from Great Britain in the nineteenth century. Low toleration of the heat and susceptibility to insect-borne diseases made some beef cattle lines unsatisfactory for parts of the South. The crossbreeding of established bloodlines with new bloodlines, introduced primarily from India and mainland Europe, created several new strains better adapted to southern conditions. Among the most successful were the American Brahman, Brangus, Charbray, and Charolais. Widespread use of artificial insemination achieved remarkable improvements in dairy cattle. The process allowed far more extensive use of sires with records of superior productivity than was possible through selective breeding. A preferred bull could normally service about forty cows a year; with artificial insemination, as many as two thousand a year. Tests in 1964 estimated that artificially inseminated cows were 50 percent more productive than normally bred cows. Milk output per cow in Tennessee grew by 125 percent between 1960 and 1984, largely because of the application of this procedure.[21]

20.   Glenn W. Burton, "Coastal Bermuda Grass for Pasture, Hay and Silage," Georgia Agricultural Experiment Station, *Bulletin 2*, n.s. (1955); Glenn W. Burton, "A Geneticist's Early Years in South Georgia," *Agricultural History* 60 (Spring 1986): 63–64; Robert E. Coats, "Coastal Bermuda Grass in Mississippi," Mississippi Agricultural Experiment Station, *Bulletin 549* (1957), 9–10.

21.   Wayne D. Rasmussen, "Scientific Agriculture," in *Technology in Western Civilization*, ed. Melvin Kranzberg and Carrol W. Pursell, Jr. (New York: Oxford University Press, 1967), 2:346–47; *Georgia Agricultural Experiment Stations, Annual Report, 1960* (Athens: University of Georgia Col-

Swine benefited less from scientific advancements than either beef or dairy cattle. Still, experiments in interbreeding generated lines that gave faster weight gain and larger litters; they also resulted in animals with leaner meat, which consumers had come to prefer. Advanced methods of feeding and animal disease control also improved productivity and meat quality in both beef cattle and swine.[22]

Texas led the country in the production of beef cattle, raising over 5 million head in 1992. Tennessee was a distant second among southern states with about 1 million head. The two states also ranked first and second in the South, respectively, in dairy cattle and dairy products. North Carolina, with 2.5 million head in 1987 and over 5 million in 1992, led the South in raising swine. Georgia, Tennessee, and Arkansas were also major producers. Although the value of livestock sales remained well below that of crop sales—about 50 percent in 1988—meat and dairy animals became much more important in southern agriculture after 1945.[23]

Of all agricultural activities in the South, poultry production underwent the greatest transformation in the post-1945 period. Before the war, farmers normally raised chickens on a small scale as a supplement to their major source of income from such commodities as cotton, tobacco, swine, or cattle. Roosting facilities were primitive, and the free-range birds scavenged for most of their feed. Farmers usually sold their eggs, fryers, and roasting hens on the local market.

After the war, poultry operations experienced extraordinary changes. Initially, local hatcheries or feed distributors provided farmers with large numbers of chicks and quantities of feed on short-term credit. Farmers raised the birds and sold the mature broilers to dealers or processors, after which they cleared their debt for the chicks and feed. To handle the flocks, they installed heated houses with automatic feeding and watering equipment. The new arrangement required a substantial capital investment and, in most cases, a sizable debt, but it promised rapid returns. The chickens reached market weight in two to three months, which made it possible to raise four broods a year. In time, this scheme took on variations and permutations. Sometimes the local hatcheries or feed dealers purchased and marketed the broilers themselves, in which case farmers received the difference between the purchase price and their debt for the chicks and feed. Eventually, large processors, such as Tyson Foods, and large feed manufacturers, such as Ralston-Purina, completed the postwar transformation of

lege of Agriculture, 1960), 65; Mundy and Morgan, "Types of Farming in Tennessee," 44; *Georgia Agricultural Experiment Stations, Annual Report, 1960,* 71.

22. Rasmussen, "Scientific Agriculture," 346–47; Allen J. Matusow, *Farm Policies and Politics in the Truman Years* (Cambridge, Mass.: Harvard University Press, 1967), 113.

23. "Financial Characteristics of U.S. Farms, January 1, 1989," USDA, *Agriculture Information Bulletin 579* (1989), 100.

poultry raising. The companies set up two kinds of operations. Under one arrangement, the company supplied the farmers with chicks and feed. Farmers, in turn, raised the birds in facilities on their land—which they built, in some cases, with loans from the company—under strict management procedures and specifications. They received a prescribed payment per pound or per broiler. Under the second arrangement, the company owned the land and facilities and ran the entire operation with hired labor.[24]

The new approach to raising poultry proved far more efficient than the traditional one. The sources of this remarkable production advantage were proven technology, economies of scale, and integration of processes. Broiler producers obtained breeds of chicks that had established records of rapid weight gain on a minimal amount of feed. They used scientifically formulated feed to accomplish the same purpose. Carefully designed confinement facilities, which housed each bird in an individual compartment, automatically delivered feed, water, and antibiotics in precisely measured amounts at optimal time intervals. The industry achieved a breakthrough of sorts in the 1970s, when the standard became three pounds of gain in eight weeks on just under six pounds of feed.[25]

The modern poultry complex sustained an enormous capacity, maintaining broods ranging from fifty thousand to one hundred thousand birds. In 1976, the typical Tennessee producer fed more than seventy-three thousand birds at one time. When large processors and feed manufacturers entered the business, they created vertically integrated operations that hatched the chicks, produced the feed, raised the birds, processed the broilers, and marketed the finished product. In merging these functions under single management, the firms were able to reduce costs by eliminating bottlenecks in the production and distribution processes. The structure also enabled them to develop by-products, such as commercial fertilizers, from chicken manure.[26]

Price trends provide the strongest evidence of improving efficiency in the poultry business. While the nominal prices of every other meat rose steadily in the postwar years, those of broilers declined sharply. At one time a luxury food

24.   C. Curtis Cable, Jr., "Growth of the Arkansas Broiler Industry," Arkansas Agricultural Experiment Station, *Bulletin 520* (1952), 8–12; W. E. Christian, Jr., and Paul T. Blair, "Broiler Production, Financing and Marketing in Mississippi," Mississippi Agricultural Station, *Bulletin 514* (1954), 36–37; Fite, *Cotton Fields No More,* 201–2; Skees and Swanson, "Farm Structure and Rural Well-Being in the South," 281; Walter Ebeling, *The Fruited Plain: The Story of American Agriculture* (Berkeley: University of California Press, 1979), 151; Ewell P. Roy and James M. Baker, "The Broiler Enterprise in Louisiana," Louisiana Agricultural Experiment Station, *Bulletin 475* (1953), 3–9, 15–16.

25.   Ebeling, *Fruited Plain,* 149; Fite, *Cotton Fields No More,* 202.

26.   Charles M. Cuskaden and Gary Gene Hunter, "A Perspective of Tennessee Broiler Production," Tennessee Agricultural Experiment Station, *Bulletin 595* (1980), 22; John L. Shover, *First Majority–Last Minority: The Transformation of Rural Life in America* (DeKalb: Northern Illinois University Press, 1976), 144.

reserved for special occasions, chicken became an inexpensive staple of the American diet. Arkansas, Georgia, and Alabama led the South in broiler production, each selling over 700 million birds in 1992.

Although egg producers moved more slowly, some adopted many of the methods that proved so successful for broiler producers. They have set up operations employing new technology, economies of scale, and integration of processes. In time, the egg industry will doubtless become as concentrated and integrated as the broiler industry now is.[27]

Other farmers found raising turkeys to be profitable. The demand for turkeys expanded greatly in the postwar period as a result of innovations in processing and changes in consumer habits. Earlier, the market for turkey meat had consisted almost exclusively of whole, dressed birds sold during the holiday season from Thanksgiving through Christmas. In the 1960s, processors—most notably Louis Rich—began offering uncooked parts and fully cooked products such as bologna, franks, salami, pastrami, and ham made from turkey. The new products won favor among consumers because of high quality and health concerns about eating red meat. Between 1966 and 1988, annual per capita consumption of turkey increased from 6.2 to 15.3 pounds; moreover, it was spread fairly evenly throughout the year. Genetic improvements created turkeys with more rapid weight gain and larger breasts, which provided the meat in greatest demand. Some southern farmers responded to these market and technological changes by increasing their turkey flocks. Arkansas, with sales of 22 million birds in 1992, was the major producer.[28]

One of the more unusual developments in southern agriculture over the past half-century has been the rise of commercial fish operations. Farmers have constructed large water reservoirs and stocked them with catfish, which they feed corn produced on their land. Since raising catfish is far different from any other agricultural activity, it has necessitated considerable experimentation and trial and error in care and feeding. In time, producers have established reasonably successful production procedures, but catfish farming remains a risky enterprise. Still, the mounting demand for fish and the emergence of an efficient distribution system have provided a lucrative opportunity for farmers able to make a substantial investment and willing to assume greater risk. In 1992 Mississippi led the country in catfish production by a wide margin with almost three hundred thousand pounds.[29]

27.   Mundy and Morgan, "Types of Farming in Tennessee," 49; Winsberg, "Agricultural Specialization in the United States Since World War II," 698–99; Gale H. Lyon, "Commercial Chick Hatcheries in South Carolina: Egg Supply, Prices and Practices," South Carolina Agricultural Experiment Station, *Bulletin 392* (1951), 15, 32–34.

28.   Barbara A. Scheulke, "Turkey Anytime," in *Marketing U.S. Agriculture,* USDA Yearbook of Agriculture, 1988 (Washington, D.C.: U.S. Department of Agriculture, 1988), 125–27.

29.   Carroll R. Garner and W. A. Halbrook, "Catfish Production in Southeastern Arkansas: Es-

The postwar transformation of southern agriculture involved more than modification in production and wider use of labor-saving equipment. It also included the adoption and diffusion of new crop strains and chemical fertilizers, which together greatly enhanced soil productivity. Biologists, drawing on the relatively new field of genetic science, created varieties of cotton, tobacco, corn, wheat, grain sorghum, and vegetables that were of higher quality and better ability to adapt to weather and soil conditions. Agricultural scientists fabricated and improved fertilizers. The Tennessee Valley Authority contributed with the development of a method for synthesizing ammonium nitrate and urea nitrate, which replaced nitrogen in deficient soil. These innovations have been largely responsible for the South's phenomenal increases in crop yields per acre since the end of World War II: twofold for cotton and tobacco, fourfold for wheat, and sixfold for corn.[30]

Scientific innovations further revolutionized the way southern farmers dealt with troublesome weeds and insects. Beginning with 2,4-D, developed as part of the government's biological warfare program during World War II, scientists discovered an array of chemicals that selectively controlled unwanted vegetation. At first, total eradication required several applications of different preemergent herbicides, but atrazine, first marketed in 1959, provided a single herbicide that destroyed every species of plant except the crop itself. Defoliants that removed leaves from cotton plants and suckers from tobacco plants were even more selective. The use of herbicides nearly eliminated the need for cultivation during the growing season. It also made possible no-till farming, allowing virtually no field preparation and, therefore, reduced soil erosion, planting time, and labor costs. No-till systems have proven particularly valuable for double-cropping because the shortened planting time improved the yield of the second crop. After the military dropped its monopoly on DDT in 1945, that chemical and related compounds came into wide use as insecticides. The government ban on DDT in 1972 encouraged the development of several other families of chemicals, which proved both more effective and less threatening to the environment. They have largely eliminated crop losses from insect pests such as the boll weevil, corn borer, and armyworm.[31]

---

timated Investment Requirements, Costs, and Returns, for Two Sizes of Farms," Arkansas Agricultural Experiment Station, *Bulletin 203* (1972), 1–16, 23; Ebeling, *Fruited Plain,* 151.

30.   Rasmussen, "Scientific Agriculture," 339–45; *Georgia Agricultural Experiment Stations, Annual Report, 1961,* 9; Dalrymple, "Changes in Wheat Varieties and Yields," 21–30; Richard C. Sheridan, "Chemical Fertilizers in Southern Agriculture," *Agricultural History 53* (January 1979): 315–17; Glover, "Economic Analysis of Selected Cotton Production Practices," 41.

31.   Peterson, "Discovery and Development of 2,4-D," 249–57; Ebeling, *Fruited Plain,* 151; Frank O. Leuthold and Cindy Hart, "West Tennessee Farmers' Use of No-Till Planting," Tennessee Agricultural Experiment Station, *Bulletin 660* (1989), 8, 18; Philip J. Gersmehl, "No-Till Farming: The Regional Applicability of a Revolutionary Agricultural Technology," *Geographical Review 68* (January 1978): 66–78; Aaron J. Ihde, "Pest and Disease Controls," in *Technology in Western Civili-*

Agricultural developments have generated far-reaching changes in management. They have influenced farm size. Heavy investments in labor-saving machinery and livestock, coupled with increased operating costs from herbicides, insecticides, and fuel, necessitated larger-scale operations to turn a profit. The average farm size in 1945 was 130 acres, ranging from 75 acres in Mississippi and Tennessee to 367 acres in Texas; in 1992 it was 390 acres, ranging from 149 acres in Tennessee to 725 acres in Texas. In a half-century, the typical southern farm tripled in acreage. Asset values grew accordingly, averaging about $300,000 per farm in 1988. High investment and operating expenses forced some farmers to take on sizable debts. Although 60 percent of the operators in 1988 were free of debt, almost a third had incurred obligations ranging up to 40 percent of their asset holdings and 10 percent had incurred obligations greater than 40 percent of their asset holdings. Still, according to a study by the United States Department of Agriculture, three-quarters of the operators enjoyed a secure financial position.[32]

Another consequential development has been the entry of corporate enterprise into farm management. Business firms assumed a variety of functions. Many supplied operational inputs, such as seeds, fertilizers, herbicides, insecticides, and feed, to farmers with whom they contracted to produce marketable commodities. Some performed specialized services, such as financing, crop and livestock insurance, aerial application of fertilizers and chemicals, and harvesting, for those same farmers. A few purchased land and equipment and went into production on their own. Whatever their role, the firms were typically deeply involved in making and administering decisions on production and marketing. Agribusiness, as this form of corporate farming has been labeled, became most prevalent in fruit, vegetable, timber, and poultry production; less frequently, it entered rice, cotton, egg, and beef cattle production.[33]

Farmers realized benefits and suffered drawbacks from the rise of agribusiness. Perhaps the most important advantage has been a guaranteed market, often at a prescribed price, for their products. Under this arrangement, business firms assumed some of the risk traditionally borne by the producers. In providing supplies, services, and credit, the firms reduced the farmers' need for operating cash. Companies widened the market for agricultural commodities by developing

zation, ed. Melvin Kranzberg and Carroll W. Pursell, Jr. (New York: Oxford University Press, 1967), 2:376–77; Ian Manners, "The Persistent Problem of the Boll Weevil: Pest Control in Principle and Practice," *Geographical Review* 69 (January 1979): 37–38.

32. "Financial Characteristics of U.S. Farms," 10, 148–49.

33. B. R. McManus, William D. Pitt, Jr., and W. J. Free, "Tennessee Agribusiness," Tennessee Agricultural Experiment Station, *Bulletin 592* (1979), 6–7; Stephen D. Reiling and Fred H. Wiegmann, "Louisiana Agriculture: Economic Trends and Current Status, 1940–1977," Louisiana Agricultural Experiment Station, *Bulletin 718* (1979), 64; Shover, *First Majority–Last Minority*, 175–222; Gilbert C. Fite, *American Farmers: The New Minority* (Bloomington: Indiana University Press, 1981), 126–29.

greater production efficiency, new and improved consumer goods, methods of quality control, and reliable distribution systems. Moreover, they have been a valuable source of new technology and information.

Farmers won these advantages at the cost of control over management decisions. The business firms frequently dictated what to produce, how to produce it, and where to market it. Farmers may have owned the land, facilities, and equipment, but they often became no more than employees of the companies. In the process, they lost much of their traditional independence. A broader problem has been agribusiness's expanding influence over the country's food and fiber industries, which has created at least the possibility of restricted competition in the agricultural market.

Developments since 1945 have had crucial implications for land tenure. For a long while after the Civil War, tenants made up a substantial segment of the South's agricultural population. Some used tenancy as a stepping-stone to landownership; others remained renters throughout their farming careers. As recently as World War II, tenants made up over 40 percent of all farm operators, but by the middle of the 1990s, their proportion had fallen to under 10 percent.

A combination of factors contributed to the decline in farm renting. Tenancy thrives under labor-intensive agricultural systems, and, until the 1940s, cotton production was ideally suited to this form of land tenure. Large landowners normally divided their properties into small plots of thirty to forty acres to rent out to sharecroppers, who provided the labor in exchange for a portion of the cotton crop. Labor-saving machinery, however, sharply reduced the need for hand labor and created incentives to produce on larger scale. Landowners responded by consolidating their tenant plots into fields more conducive to mechanized cotton production, which they either worked themselves or rented out to other landowners who wished to expand their crop acreage. The switch to soybeans, which were less labor-intensive than cotton, had much the same result. Replacing cotton and tobacco production with livestock raising reinforced the decline in tenancy, for beef and dairy cattle required relatively less labor and more land than field crops.

If developments in agriculture created conditions that pushed tenants out of farming, developments outside created conditions that pulled them into other occupations. The attraction of high-paying urban jobs in industry, construction, and services reduced the number of young people electing to become farm tenants. Greater opportunities for a college education also contributed to a decline in those choosing to stay in agriculture. Although tenants remained part of the agricultural population, most operators by the 1990s owned at least a portion of the land they farmed.[34]

34. Wilcox, *The Farmer and the Second World War,* 307; Fulmer, *Agricultural Progress in the Cotton Belt Since 1920,* 74–76.

As farmers expanded the size of their operations and adopted scientific methods, they also became more commercialized. From its beginnings in the seventeenth century, southern agriculture had always been deeply involved in the market, but it had also included a strong commitment to providing goods for household consumption. After World War II, the balance between commercial and subsistence production shifted considerably. As late as 1940, goods for household consumption made up almost a quarter of total farm production. The subsistence portion of farms with full-time operators in the 1980s had fallen to less than 5 percent. A sizable number of small part-time farmers, most of whom derived the major part of their income from employment outside of agriculture, produced largely for household consumption. Full-time farmers typically specialized in a narrow range of market goods. In 1988, 70 percent of the commercial operators emphasized livestock products, 30 percent cash crops. Still, with the exception of those specializing in poultry and egg production, livestock farmers generated relatively smaller sales. Of an average money income of just under $50,000 in 1988, over half came from crop sales. And while the returns on investments and labor were often lower than those in other areas of economic activity, fully 80 percent of southern farms recorded a positive net income from commercial activities. For the vast majority of full-time operators, farming had assumed the trappings of a business enterprise.[35]

The wide-ranging changes in agriculture since World War II have required farmers to become more knowledgeable. Decisions on the use of scientific methods, such as improved varieties of crops and livestock, mechanized equipment, herbicides, and insecticides, rested on a body of technical information. The increasingly commercial orientation of southern agriculture necessitated a deeper understanding of markets, financial arrangements, and accounting. A variety of resources were available to farmers. Agricultural colleges and experiment stations not only developed many of the scientific innovations, but they also instructed farmers on when and how to adopt them. In addition, they furnished vital economic information on supply and demand, costs of production, and rates of return. Customarily, operating farmers have been the ones to take advantage of these services. Some of the more enterprising have even set up computer links with agricultural colleges, through which they evaluate the productivity of livestock, receive economic data, or keep financial records. Increasingly, though, aspiring farmers attended academic institutions to receive formal training in agricultural science and economics before they began their careers.

Farmers tapped other sources of information as they adjusted to postwar changes. The county agricultural extension service, working closely with the col-

35. Joe A. Martin and B. H. Luebke, "Types of Farming in Tennessee," *Tennessee Agricultural Experiment Station, Bulletin 311* (1960), 26–27; John Fraser Hart, "Nonfarm Farms," *Geographical Review* 82 (April 1992): 166–72; Skees and Swanson, "Farm Structure and Rural Well-Being in the South," 259–60; "Financial Characteristics of U.S. Farms," 4, 53, 100.

leges and experiment stations, provided a nearby repository of expert advice. Staff held demonstrations on new techniques and guided individual farmers in solving particular problems. The publications of the United States Department of Agriculture informed both farmers and specialists in academic institutions and the extension service on a variety of issues vital to agriculture. Manufacturers of equipment, fertilizers, and chemicals likewise supplied information on the uses of their products. Earlier, farmers may have disdained book farming, as they called it, but the postwar generations have taken advantage of these sources of information and advice.

The modernization of southern agriculture has had another powerful effect. Despite an enduring commercial orientation, farming has traditionally played a broader cultural role. Rural southerners saw farming as a way of life and as a social organization for perpetuating worthwhile values. Although they never precisely defined the substance of that life or those values, they emphasized the importance of household independence, family cohesion, community sharing and cooperation, and the virtue of working the land. These became their objectives and the goals they sought to pass on to future generations. The expanding size of operations, wider adoption of scientific agriculture, growing commercialization, and greater dependence on technical knowledge and information eroded farming's cultural function and changed its role in rural life. Some part-time farmers have attempted to preserve the traditional conception of rural life, but in doing so they have had to resort to nonagricultural employment to sustain their lifestyles. Full-time farmers often found the perpetuation of cultural values inconsistent with the demands of modern agriculture. Farming as a business has, for the most part, undermined farming as a way of life.[36]

Southern agriculture in the mid-1990s looked much different than it did at the end of World War II. A far smaller portion of the region's population was involved in it, and those who remained practiced a radically changed type of farming. Long-standing cash crops continued to occupy a central place in the rural economy, but other crops and livestock products had joined them and some even superseded them in importance. In the immediate postwar period, farmers still performed most of their tasks by hand or with animal-powered machinery. Fifty years later, they employed tractor-pulled or self-propelled equipment for virtually all of their field work. At the same time, they began using improved strains of crops and livestock that delivered higher yields and better quality and a wide variety of sophisticated chemicals to control weeds and insects and to fertilize plants. These adoptions significantly enhanced the productivity of labor, livestock, and land. They also required farmers in the 1990s to operate on a larger

---

36. Donald L. Winters, *Tennessee Farming, Tennessee Farmers: Antebellum Agriculture in the Upper South* (Knoxville: University of Tennessee Press, 1994), 187; Pete Daniel, "The Transformation of the Rural South, 1930 to the Present," *Agricultural History* 55 (July 1981): 231–48.

scale, to develop more effective management strategies, and to become more knowledgeable than their counterparts in the 1940s. The rural population reacted with ambivalence to these developments. For all of its obvious advantages, the postwar agricultural transformation also irrevocably altered a traditional way of life. Some southerners asked if the costs were too high.

Race Relations in the Rural South Since 1945

ORVILLE VERNON BURTON

I use the train as a symbol of the other civilization—the white civilization, and its encroachment upon the lives of blacks. The train was always something that could take you away and could also bring you to where you were. And in the little towns, it's the black people who live near the trains." Thus African American artist and poet Romare Bearden (1912–1988), born in North Carolina and reared in New York City, described the dominant motif in his paintings. Indeed, the train was also a powerful symbol for nineteenth-century America and the age of industrialization. Trains standardized time across four zones in America. Trains changed the nature of rural life as farmers shipped their crops to market from towns that grew up around the railroads. In the 1950s and 1960s, as great migrations of blacks and whites continued from the South, particularly from the rural and small-town South, to the North, trains even took on special names. So many North and South Carolinians took the train to Washington, Philadelphia, and New York that the line was nicknamed the "Chicken Bone Express"; African Americans brought their fried chicken on board when they left the South because they were not allowed to eat in the segregated dining car.[1]

At one time, rural folks could gather in a nearby town, and around the rail-

I would like to thank David Herr for research assistance made possible by a grant from the University of Illinois at Urbana-Champaign Research Board. Georganne Burton improved this essay in countless ways with primary research and her editorial skill. I would also like to thank the National Endowment for the Humanities, which offered me a fellowship in 1994–95 at the National Humanities Center, where I conducted research for this essay. Also, the Pew Foundation provided support and released time for me to write and rewrite this essay.

1. Dwayne E. Walls, *The Chickenbone Special* (New York: Harcourt Brace Jovanovich, 1970).

road depot downtown they could find friends, gossip together, listen to music, gamble. Today few passenger trains stop in small towns, not even in most county seats. Even freight trains have been replaced by trucks. The South has become a car culture.

Cars provided one of the first opportunities for equality between blacks and whites; the rules of the road applied equally to all. As opposed to buggies and wagons, which folks could clearly see who was driving, cars provide some anonymity. Cars isolate people from each other. Drivers speed down the road oblivious to their surroundings, whereas buggies used to stop and pick up a person walking.[2]

The interstate highway system has dissected the rural South, nudging away its isolation and forcing adjustments in its race relations. As interstates attract roadside businesses, the line between urban and rural has blurred. Today, driving south from New York on I-95, one sees a South very much accommodated to the nation. McDonald's, Burger King, and Hardee's are as ubiquitous as in the North. But away from the interstates one finds another South, still rural, left behind in the modernization since World War II. Political scientist David Garrow noted that "the distance in time between small rural towns and an Atlanta or a Birmingham is a difference of decades."[3]

Categorization of race relations fails to reflect its complexity; relationships among people are as complicated and contradictory as the individuals and groups involved. Nevertheless, some scholars have defined styles of race relations as either paternalistic or competitive. In the paternalistic system, race relations follow a master-servant model in which whites rationalize their dominance as benevolent; the subordinates are considered to be irresponsible but lovable "in their place." The subordinate group may accommodate to a lesser status and internalize feelings of inferiority. Because role and status are sharply defined along racial lines, friendliness is no threat, and physical segregation is not necessary. In contrast, the competitive form of race relations no longer defines role and job by race. Where African Americans are not excluded from voting and competing for jobs, physical segregation preserves the white position. Instead of the jolly, irresponsible child-race of paternalistic days, whites may consider African Americans "uppity," insolent, and aggressive. In place of the condescending benevolence and noblesse oblige of the old days, tension erupts and the races openly disrespect each other. Virulent race hatred may appear, and conflict may erupt in lynchings and riots.[4]

2. Jack Temple Kirby, *Rural Worlds Lost: The American South, 1920–1960* (Baton Rouge: Louisiana State University Press, 1987), 257. Of course, some white police officers did not treat African Americans equally at all.

3. Garrow quoted in David R. Goldfield, *Black, White, and Southern: Race Relations and Southern Culture, 1940 to the Present* (Baton Rouge: Louisiana State University Press, 1990), 271.

4. C. Vann Woodward, "The Strange Career of a Historical Controversy," in *American Coun-*

Since World War II, race relations in the South have undergone a revolution. Before the civil rights movement (starting with the school desegregation order in 1954), race relations were unabashedly oppressive. White supremacy was ingrained in the culture, and institutional racism prevailed throughout the Jim Crow South; violence and intimidation kept the system in place. During the civil rights movement, when African Americans demanded change, many whites reacted viciously, and most whites acquiesced in the violence. Nevertheless, African Americans continued their arduous and perilous quest, and finally, in this country, which values freedom and fairness, African Americans won their political rights with the passage of civil rights and voting rights legislation.

Political rights have not ended all racism, and people of all colors still harbor prejudice. Tough economic times can bring racism all too quickly out from under the surface. Nevertheless, the culture has changed. Overt racism is no longer the norm but an aberration.

When World War II ended, the South was immersed in the age of segregation, put in place in the early 1900s. The South Carolina House of Representatives passed a resolution in 1944 denouncing "indignantly and vehemently" any and all "amalgamation of the White and Negro races by a co-mingling of the races upon any basis of equality." It further resolved an affirmation of "White Supremacy as now prevailing in the South" and pledged "lives and our sacred honor to maintain it, whatever the cost, in War and Peace." Before the civil rights movement, the parameters of race relations were dictated by whites. If African Americans were quiet and did not vote, whites thought their community had "good race relations." Some truly egalitarian communities and organizations existed, the Christian-based Koinonia in rural Georgia since before World War II, for example, and the Southern Tenant Farmers' Union, organized in rural Arkansas in the 1930s, as well as Tougaloo College to a degree. Aside from these very few exceptions, almost universally race relations were firmly fixed in white supremacy and based on the second-class status of African Americans. Under this umbrella of white supremacy, the way people related to one another in the rural South was as varied as the people involved. Styles of race relations ran the gamut from white pathological racism and brutality to cordiality and cooperation. Historian Jack Kirby has found that whites were the most brutal in the areas of the lower South where they were outnumbered. He found that in the upper South whites tried to maintain "restraint and allegiance to an ethic of decency" (albeit with condescension) toward black folk. No overwhelming change occurred in this system of race relations until school desegregation and the civil rights movement. World War II, however, laid the foundation for change in race relations. African American veterans helped erode the isolation and parochial-

---

terpoint: Slavery and Racism in the North-South Dialogue (New York: Oxford University Press, 1971), 234–60, is the most compelling application of this model of race relations.

ism of their rural communities and exhibited an unwillingness to submit to segregation and degradation.[5]

Even as the white South was attempting to create and preserve a segregated society, the culture was actually integrated in shared community elements of a large number of European ethnic groups and an even larger number of African and Native American ethnic groups. Furthermore, segregation was impossible in certain rural areas where whites and blacks lived and worked side by side. Elvis Presley, for example, worshiped by youth of all colors, grew up in rural Mississippi. Before moving from Tupelo to Memphis to live in a whites-only public housing project in 1948, the Presleys lived in a black neighborhood. His home, known by all to be the house that was passed from one white tenant to another, was in the middle of an African American neighborhood. This pattern of housing, sometimes termed the "salt-and-pepper" pattern of racial housing, existed at that time in many older communities of the South.

Another rock-and-roll musician, Carl Perkins, as a child worked in the fields of Tennessee with about forty-five African Americans. A black man, John Westbrook, taught Perkins a better way to pick cotton (from the bottom up), sold him his first guitar for three dollars, and taught him the three chords he knew. Others also, white and black sharecroppers in the rural South, sang and played music alongside each other on a summer's evening when farmwork was done for the day.[6]

Farm life revolved around the rhythms of the land. Black and white farming families, including all the many children, worked hard and had little time for leisure while the sun shined. Blacks and whites also shared the idea that Sunday was a day of rest to be spent in church activities, although in segregated churches. Whether cotton, tobacco, or rice was the major cash crop, farmers of all races shared a reverence for the land and paid attention to the weather and when to plant, weed, and harvest. All farmers shared concerns about the amount of rainfall, the price of cattle, and how to deal with pest infestations. In rural communities of the American South, "taking turns" was a tradition among black and white males. While waiting in line for a turn at the cotton gin, for instance, a white and a black farmer might strike up a friendly conversation about common concerns. In rural settings the possibilities existed for closer connections and less formality, and it was not unusual in this hierarchical culture to find black and white farmers sitting on each other's porches discussing farm-related issues.

5. *Journal of the House of Representatives of the Second Session of the 85th General Assembly of the State of South Carolina, Being the Regular Session, Beginning Tuesday, January 11, 1944, Resolution Dated February 29, 1944,* 569–70; Kirby, *Rural Worlds Lost,* 247; Adam Fairclough, *Race and Democracy: The Civil Rights Struggle in Louisiana, 1915–1972* (Athens: University of Georgia Press, 1995), 73.

6. Pete Daniel, "Rhythm of the Land," *Agricultural History* 68 (Fall 1995): 10.

Ideally, the farmer and his family worked together to earn a living from the good earth, independent and undisturbed by other people. The ideal never existed, and farmers have always had to contend with bank mortgages, equipment needs, transportation networks to sell produce, and government programs that might help or hurt them. Southern landlords pursued investment strategies and public policies that perpetuated isolation and low-wage labor; tenants could never establish their independence because landlords and creditors forced them to plant a cash crop, usually cotton or tobacco. Tenants then had to purchase the basic necessities of life on credit, and lien for credit and rent came ahead of any tenant's claim, compounding the problem. In addition to this system, which limited any poor farmer, African American farmers faced an additional problem surpassing all others, racism.

Rural race relations after World War II were blatantly oppressive toward African Americans. Junius Scales, white Communist party leader for the Carolinas, Virginia, Tennessee, and northern Mississippi, remembers the terrible state of race relations in the rural South in those years. To enter a black home without any suspicion, he would disguise himself as a bill collector since a white pursuing money from African Americans was not suspect. In those early years, any meetings about improving the life of African Americans had to be secret and were very often held in church basements—white and black. Scales found that the most militant, aware, and active of rural and urban African Americans in the South in the late 1940s and early 1950s were the World War II veterans. He also noted the extraordinary leadership and ability of older black women in the community.

Local groups occasionally called upon Scales to investigate problems in race relations. One such problem in rural North Carolina illustrates the changed atmosphere from the hellish days of lynching that preceded World War II. In 1951, in Caswell County, a black sharecropper, Mark Ingram, went to a neighboring white sharecropper's home to borrow a trailer. The two farmers shared equipment and often traded labor to help each other out, a common practice among rural farm folk. The nineteen-year-old daughter of the white tenant farmer was home alone, and, fearful of the black man, she panicked and accused Ingram of rape. Scales's investigation disclosed that Ingram, a married man with ten children of his own, had never been closer than twenty-five feet to the young white woman. Scales called a journalist, African American Ted Poston of the *New York Post,* who wrote a column about this incident, and in one day the authorities in Caswell County received more phone calls than they had in the previous two and a half years. The National Association for the Advancement of Colored People (NAACP), founded in 1909, got involved, and Ingram was acquitted. The difference from a decade or two earlier was remarkable. Then the accusation of rape would have brought out a lynch mob. Very few mob lynchings occurred after World War II, but all too often during the civil rights movement whites committed murder with impunity and often without the national publicity such as that accompanying the murder of Emmet Till in 1955.[7]

Violence and the threat of violence kept white supremacy in place, and fear underlay the fabric of social interaction. In 1957 a white band director at Camden High School, South Carolina, was brutally beaten by a hooded gang because they mistakenly thought he was in favor of integration. Racists in this rural county had also burned three black churches and a black residence. The local paper decried this violence, warning that if it were to continue, it might warrant federal intervention. Often white people, though opposed to racial equality, deplored chaotic violence, and, if not that, at least the national publicity it might bring.[8]

Violent episodes encouraged African Americans to respect Jim Crow even when other alternatives to that system arose. African American Ned Cobb, raising a crop of cotton that netted six bales in Alabama in 1950, hired a poor white family to help with the chopping. These whites referred to him as "Mr. Cobb." Cobb asked them not to, fearful that other whites would hear them call him "Mister" and take retribution on him. Even among friends, the standard practice was to call the black person by a given name and the white person by "Mister" or "Missus."[9]

Something akin to respect may have developed in rural communities when men went hunting together. The poor of both races hunted as a necessity to put food on the table. Upper-class whites often hunted with black guides, but groups of whites and blacks seldom hunted together. Occasionally these armed groups would encounter each other, usually for the purpose of claiming game. It was hard to know who had killed the game because animals might run some distance after being shot. Custom decreed that no matter who killed it, the game went to the one "whose dog was first on the chase." A certain etiquette usually prevailed in fishing also. Some places on the riverbank were reserved for whites, but in most places the one who got there first had the right to the bank.[10]

Hunting, fishing, and taking turns in line fell outside the usual boss-servant relationship. Rural women did not have that opportunity to interact across racial lines except where white women "managed" black women who cleaned, cooked, and supervised children for them. Women mingled at church or at quilting bees,

7. Junius Irving Scales and Richard Nickson, *Cause at Heart: A Former Communist Remembers* (Athens: University of Georgia Press, 1987), 227–30.

8. *New South* 12 (Fall 1957): 12, reprinted from an article in the *Cheraw Chronicle*, February 1957.

9. James W. Loewen, *The Mississippi Chinese: Between Black and White* (Cambridge, Mass.: Harvard University Press, 1971), 80, 183; Theodore Rosengarten, *All God's Dangers: The Life of Nate Shaw* (New York: Knopf, 1975), 455–56.

10. Kirby, *Rural Worlds Lost*, 252; Stuart A. Marks, *Southern Hunting in Black and White: Nature, History, and Ritual in a Carolina Community* (Princeton: Princeton University Press, 1991).

but only within their racial group. Rural women tended to be more isolated than their menfolk and rarely socialized across racial lines.

If a shared way of life in rural communities smoothed over the worst race relations, a modern South with more cities and towns and fewer farms has had a significant effect. A major change in the South since World War II has been its urbanization and mechanization. As farm owners used tractors rather than farm workers, this modernization removed black and white southerners from the land. Sociologist Arthur Raper claimed that every tractor displaced at least one family. Pete Daniel has described a "vast enclosure movement" that "swept millions of rural workers from the land." In Daniel's words, "The depression caught cotton planters at just the wrong point between feudalism and modernization, and the Cotton Section of the AAA [Agricultural Adjustment Administration] did not ease the transition. One disaster after another—boll weevil, flood, drought, the AAA program, tractors, war, and picking machines—swept croppers, wage hands, and small owners from the land."[11]

The South's largest manufacturing industry, lumber and timber, provided jobs almost exclusively for blacks, but the jobs proved temporary, and when the cutting was done, workers went back to the farm labor market. When black laborers moved from the fields to the factory, they still encountered racism obstructing their way. The factory might pay more than the farm, but it was an option for only certain people. Black men and particularly women found themselves unable to obtain work where white women or men composed the majority of a mill work force or a factory floor. Textile mills remained segregated until the late 1960s; white women and children were cheaper than African American males. When they could find jobs in industry, blacks were generally relegated to the most mundane and lowest paying jobs such as janitorial duties. Wages for African Americans were so low and job opportunities so rare in the rural and small-town South that even white mill workers could afford to hire black domestics, often called "cooks," to clean their homes, prepare meals, and care for their children while both parents worked for minimum wage at the mill. Minimum wage was much better than the one to four dollars an African American received for a full day's work.

The mill villages were for whites only, and as opposed to the personalism of the agrarian setting, where everyone knew each other and blacks and whites had almost daily interaction, the enclosed isolation of these villages intensified racism. Over the decades, as white families were further removed from inter-

11.   Arthur Raper, "Machines in the Cotton Fields," *New South* 1 (September 1946): 11; Pete Daniel, "The Transformation of the Rural South, 1930 to the Present," *Agricultural History* 55 (July 1981): 246–47; Pete Daniel, *Breaking the Land: The Transformation of Cotton, Tobacco, and Rice Cultures Since 1880* (Urbana: University of Illinois Press, 1985). This book along with Kirby, *Rural Worlds Lost*, and Gilbert C. Fite, *Cotton Fields No More: Southern Agriculture, 1865–1980* (Lexington: University Press of Kentucky, 1984), provide excellent overviews of the rural South.

change with African Americans, black people became easy scapegoats as an un-known "other." Mill villages were notorious for their race hatred, and the Ku Klux Klan of the 1950s and 1960s flourished in these segregated villages.

In 1940 African Americans represented 25 percent of the South's population and 28 percent of its labor force. By 1980 the figures were respectively 18 percent and 15 percent. The out-migration of blacks from the South and the large influx of whites account for much of this change. It is also true, however, that southern blacks were denied entry into the growing southern economy. In nonmetropoli-tan areas in the lower six states of the South, white workers gained 287,000 jobs in the 1960s while blacks lost 97,000. In 1965 fewer than one in ten black male southerners was a skilled craftsman. Eighty-five percent of black women held blue-collar jobs, and more than half of those were labor and service jobs. Black southerners were at the bottom of the bottom.[12]

The United States census shows that the time between 1940 and 1990 was generally one of expansion and growth for the South (see appended table). Both urban and rural areas increased in population, but generally the urban areas ex-perienced economic expansion as well as population growth, while rural regions shifted dramatically from agricultural centers to economically isolated areas and bedroom communities for larger cities. In most states rural areas declined as a percentage of the total population, and in all the southern states the number of farmers plummeted.

The black population of many southern states remained relatively constant from 1940 to 1990 but declined as a percentage of each state's population. The proportion of African Americans in Alabama, for example, declined from al-most 35 percent to 25 percent. Georgia, representative of most southern states, gained almost 700,000 African Americans between 1940 and 1990, but their pro-portion dropped from 34 percent of the state's total population to 27 percent. Rural blacks declined numerically in all the southern states as a ratio of the black population and as a ratio of the total population. Rural workers regardless of race found themselves displaced by technological advances and the influence of agribusiness. The changes were most dramatic between 1940 and 1960. In 1940 the two states with the largest percentage of farmers in the population were Mis-sissippi, with 19 percent, and South Carolina, with 18 percent. In 1960 only 3 percent of Mississippi's population was farming, and in South Carolina just un-der 2 percent. Almost 270,000 black Mississippians farmed in 1940, a quarter of the state's black population. Three thousand black farmers remained in 1990, representing less than 1 percent of the black population. States with small black and farm populations have almost seen the end of black farming. Kentucky, in 1990, had only 922 black farmers among 57,754 farmers, who represented less

12. Numan V. Bartley, *The New South, 1945–1980* (Baton Rouge: Louisiana State University Press, 1995), 289.

than 2 percent of the state's population. Yet, in South Carolina as late as 1980, almost half of all African Americans lived in rural areas. As farming virtually disappeared as an occupation for African Americans, those who did not emigrate to cities or find industrial employment were left in abject poverty. They lived in dilapidated shacks and hoped a little garden plot would feed the family all year. They performed seasonal day labor when and if they could find it.

The changes in agriculture worked differently throughout the South. In Kentucky, North Carolina, and Virginia, blacks and whites who planted tobacco fared somewhat better than those who grew cotton. The Agricultural Adjustment Administration helped these farmers to work small plots of land, and tobacco was labor-intensive and slow to be absorbed by agribusiness. When mechanization came in the 1960s, many tobacco farmers were prosperous enough to change over, and those who could not often had little trouble moving into industrial and other employment without physical dislocation. Diversified regions also did better. Tennessee, Virginia, Kentucky, and Florida were the areas in which family farms, mostly dairy, truck gardening, fruit growing, and grain production, were most likely to survive. In less diversified Appalachian highlands, where few if any African Americans lived, farmers were among the South's most impoverished.[13]

A look at one particular rural locale shows how the modernization of agriculture has affected African Americans economically since World War II. According to historian James Cobb, the Mississippi Delta is "the most southern place on earth." In the midst of major urbanization, this area remained rural, and its poverty was somewhat comparable to that of Third World countries. In a system developed after Reconstruction, whites owned large farms, and African Americans provided the labor through sharecropping. Sharecropping was a hard way of life for black and white families, but in addition, African Americans had to suffer the usual pattern of white landlords, bankers, merchants, and salesmen all conniving to cheat them.[14]

After World War II, landlords preferred to mechanize and consolidate, receiving government subsidies to do so. Ending any pretense of paternalism, the landlords evicted workers and their families from the land. But agriculture was the only occupation available in the area; no alternative existed for the African American population. A survey in 1959 found 17,563 sharecroppers in the Delta; five years later there were 8,788 and by 1967 almost none. Getting day work was the best one could do, and that was diminishing also; by 1967 only 5 percent of cotton was picked by hand. Seasonal jobs for cotton pickers and choppers fell by more than 50 percent between 1965 and 1966. Jobs were totally dependent on

13. Ibid., 130.

14. James C. Cobb, *The Most Southern Place on Earth: The Mississippi Delta and the Roots of Regional Identity* (New York: Oxford University Press, 1992).

white landowners. When the minimum wage law went into effect in 1967 and workers were to earn at least $1.00 per hour instead of the usual $3.50 per twelve-hour day, landowners refused to hire day laborers at all. During 1967, 12,000 African Americans left the Delta.

Those African Americans remaining in the Mississippi Delta had either day work, migrant work, or no livelihood at all. Before 1964 the poor received monthly food allocations of flour and canned goods from the federal commodity program. When that program was replaced by the food stamp program, the poor were left much worse off. Many had to borrow money from white planters to purchase their food stamps. Some major landowners in the area, such as Senator James O. Eastland, charged high interest on these loans, creating a personal peonage system. In several counties, although the number of people in poverty grew fourfold, only half as many families qualified for food stamps as had received help under the commodity program. Government relief programs, originated in the New Deal and continued during and after the war, gave subsidies to landowners. Thus federal handouts went to large plantation owners, not the poor—black or white. Federal subsidies to wealthy farmers in Sunflower County, Mississippi, in 1967 amounted to $10.2 million; federal food program expenditures were less than 5 percent of that.

Because of a history of paternalism, boards set up to administer aid programs were made up of whites. Whether a particular family received commodity help or qualified for food stamps was dependent on the goodwill of the whites in charge of the local distribution. In one particular case in 1962, the local board suspended distribution of food as a warning to local African Americans not to register to vote.

Few African American families in the Mississippi Delta had proper sanitation in their homes; 80 percent of the dwellings in Tunica County had neither bathroom nor toilet facilities. If, in the paternalistic past, African American tenants or sharecroppers had some health care, by the mid-1960s they had none. With no cash in hand, some died even while sitting in the waiting rooms of hospitals. With cash to pay for care, African Americans could see a doctor, but many a white doctor would simply inquire about the illness, refusing to examine or touch a black person. Furthermore, the impoverished in the Delta were malnourished and anemic. Mortality rates for black infants in the Delta were 109 percent higher than for white infants. The infant mortality rate among black Mississippians worsened as the farm economy modernized, climbing from 4.18 deaths per 1,000 births in 1946 to 55.1 in 1965. In 1967 a group of doctors examining Delta children found them to be living under "such primitive conditions that we found it hard to believe we were examining American children of the twentieth century."[15]

15. Ibid., 263–64.

With the demise of day labor, many African Americans in Mississippi turned to migrant farm labor in the middle and late 1950s. By 1952 migrant laborers, according to Department of Labor estimates, numbered twenty-four thousand, mainly African Americans. Their number probably doubled in the early 1950s. Since white crew leaders contracted laborers to farmers and collected and distributed their pay, whites again held the power over African American labor and generally misused it.

Patterns prevalent in the Mississippi Delta were evident in areas throughout the South, and rural poverty overwhelmed both blacks and whites. For instance, the South led the United States in poor housing conditions during the 1940s. Two out of three houses fell short of minimum standards. Although conditions improved during the 1950s, in 1960 in Robeson County, North Carolina, 75 percent of homes, excluding those in the county seat of Lumberton, were unsafe to live in. As white southerners began to improve their lot, blacks remained far behind. Sanitation was also substandard, fire protection negligible, and health care nonexistent or inadequate (although medical advances did almost eliminate hookworm, pellagra, and tuberculosis from rural areas).[16]

Wealthier people refused to acknowledge the poverty afflicting many rural areas. South Carolina senator Ernest F. Hollings was a skeptic until he himself investigated and found truth in the statistics. In his book on hunger, Hollings wrote of farmers who received hefty subsidies for not growing anything. Hollings noted the irony of these government handouts. Politicians did not see the subsidies as affecting the hardworking character of the farmer. "But give the poor, little hungry child a forty-cent breakfast and you've destroyed his character. You've ruined his incentive." Negative stereotypes of African Americans dominated the rural white culture. Not given jobs, African Americans were disparaged as "lazy." Not allowed proper sanitation, they were reviled as "filthy." With inadequate nutrition and health care, some African Americans did lose energy, and some lost hope.[17]

To keep white supremacy in its place, a pattern of racial violence prevailed throughout the rural South. Even as personal attacks on African Americans became less acceptable in the culture, racial violence continued, often hidden behind an official badge. Police brutality from all-white departments was particularly vicious in rural areas where African Americans had no recourse against a vindictive sheriff, and local white juries would not convict whites of crimes

16. Ibid., 273; "Housing in the South," *New South* 3 (April 1948): 1; North Carolina Fund Report, *Profile of Community Problems: Richmond, Scotland, and Robeson Counties* (N.p.: Tri-County Community Action, 1967).

17. Ernest F. Hollings, *The Case Against Hunger* (New York: Cowles, 1970), 222, 232. When Mae Bertha Carter of Sunflower, Mississippi, sent her ten children to school, she made sure they washed themselves well and wore clean clothes. Yet the white teachers called them dirty (Constance Curry, *Silver Rights* [Chapel Hill: Algonquin Books, 1995]).

against blacks. Sheriffs were often bullies who enjoyed terrorizing African Americans and especially liked humiliating those who had some wealth, education, or self-esteem. White policemen could kill black prisoners with impunity, claiming the suspect was "fleeing." These episodes of normal police practice were actually legal lynchings.[18]

Ulrich B. Phillips has written that the central theme of southern history was that the South should remain a white man's country. Of course, the South is not and has never been exclusively white. It has been at least triracial since Native Americans began to share the land with whites and African Americans. Furthermore, in the post–World War II American South, the central theme has not been white supremacy but the civil rights movement. World War II, a war about human rights, gave impetus to events and movements already under way. As rural southern African Americans moved to cities, more than 1 million to southern cities and 2 million to the industrial North and West, they doubled the number of northern black voters in key areas between 1940 and 1948.[19]

Articulate black people had been demanding educational opportunities and civil rights ever since the overthrow of Reconstruction, and some gains were finally made during the 1930s and 1940s. On a grass-roots level, unsung African American heroes such as Amzie Moore in Mississippi, Charles Gomillion in Alabama, and Septima Clark in South Carolina developed the impetus for civil rights legislation. No matter how oppressed, rural and poor African Americans valued literacy and the ability to read the Bible, even though working in the fields for "the man" took precedence over schooling for almost all rural black children. Septima Clark and Esau Jenkins started citizenship education schools on rural Johns Island, South Carolina, in 1957 for African Americans. Clark and Jenkins had trained at Myles Horton's Highlander School in rural Tennessee, as had Rosa Parks, the heroic Montgomery seamstress. It is no surprise that the civil rights movement began because of the need for a decent education. The tide in race relations that had run against blacks since the 1890s reversed during the New Deal and World War II and was flowing faster by the 1950s, when the Supreme Court in 1954 ruled in *Brown v. The Board of Education* (Topeka) that schools could no longer be segregated.[20]

Most of the writing on this complex movement has emphasized the successful urban components such as bus boycotts and lunch counter sit-ins, but rural areas also figure in the story. In his monumental 1976 study, *Simple Justice,* Richard Kluger wrote, "If you had set out to find the place in America in 1947 where life among black folk had changed least since the end of slavery, Clarendon County is where you might have come." And yet, in this most unlikely of places, rural

18. Fairclough, *Race and Democracy,* 122.
19. Ulrich B. Phillips, "The Central Theme of Southern History," *American Historical Review* 34 (October 1928): 31.
20. See also Ann Moody, *Coming of Age in Mississippi* (New York: Dial Press, 1969).

low-country South Carolina, African Americans initiated a lawsuit *(Briggs v. El-liot)* that culminated in the end of segregated schools *(Brown v. The Board of Education)*.[21]

In 1951, the segregated Clarendon County public schools had an enrollment of 6,531 African American and 2,375 white students. Total expenditures for white students exceeded those for black students by $112,379, or 300 percent per pupil. The county's black parents brought a suit against the Summerton school district, where one school serving 600 black students had only two outdoor toilets and students had to carry drinking water in a bucket from a neighbor's home. These conditions were horrendous, but it was transportation that African American parents were demanding. White children had buses; black children had to walk—some of them many miles.

The Reverend J. A. Delaine, who pastored several rural churches, taught at Summerton and requested a school bus. Denied, he was told that whites paid more taxes and deserved better service. A persistently stubborn black farmer, Levi Pearson, bought an old bus and fixed it up to drive children to school and then, with the support of Rev. Delaine, sued the Summerton school board. His suit was thrown out because his farm was on the line that separated Summerton from a neighboring school district. In spring 1950, Delaine brought another suit, this time asking for equal school facilities in compliance with the 1896 law of the land, *Plessy v. Ferguson.* Ultimately, with the aid of the NAACP, a suit filed by forty black parents argued that segregated schools, even if facilities were equal, violated the Fourteenth Amendment. Four years later, on May 17, 1954, the United States Supreme Court handed down its decision in *Brown v. The Board of Education* (Topeka). Chief Justice Earl Warren reported the unanimous conclusion: "Separate educational facilities are inherently unequal." The *Brown* decision, which encompassed five cases from five different states, had originated in one rural school district in an effort by black parents simply to get a bus.

During the next years the full array of Jim Crow terror and repression played out in rural Clarendon County. For their heroic efforts Rev. Delaine and his wife lost their jobs and received death threats signed "KKK." Their house burned to the ground while the all-white fire department stood by and watched. When Delaine fired his gun in self-defense against some whites, he was charged with a felony and forced to flee the state. When Harry Briggs, the black mechanic for whom the case was named, stubbornly resisted white pressure to remove his name from the list of plaintiffs, he and his wife lost their jobs, and they too had to leave the county. All forty rural black unacknowledged heroes of Clarendon County, having challenged the South's racial codes, suffered. Whatever elements of white paternalism or leniency had existed quickly faded. Long-standing debts, an everyday occurrence in southern agricultural economy, were called in,

21.   Richard Kluger, *Simple Justice* (New York: Knopf, 1976), 4.

and whites refused to sell black plaintiffs seeds or supplies. Equipment usually loaned willingly to help African Americans with harvests or plowing was refused; crops rotted in the fields.

While African Americans throughout the South were condemning the degradation dumped on them by a racist system, and certain whites throughout the South moved vehemently to suppress the protests, rural blacks faced harder repression than urban blacks. African Americans living in cities possessed a degree of anonymity that rural people did not. In Summerton, for example, the nephew of the white superintendent of schools owned several farms rented by black tenants; the owner made activism synonymous with economic hardship. Thus, whereas urban communities throughout the South saw successful mass marches and boycotts, in rural Clarendon every black person who signed a petition to improve conditions lost a job, was denied the ability to trade for necessary agricultural goods, and was threatened with physical violence.

The systematic terror and repression encountered by the parents of black schoolchildren in rural Clarendon County was not at all unusual in the experience of African Americans living in the South under Jim Crow segregation. In small, rural southern communities, those who protested and attempted to organize the black community, those most aggressive in pursuit of social justice, were often forced to leave for their personal safety. The community was thus stripped of its local leaders. The NAACP in Louisiana found that building support was very difficult in rural areas. As Adam Fairclough put it, "In the farming community where old boss has had the say about everything it is hard to get the tenant to stand for the right."[22]

Like whites throughout the South, those in Clarendon argued that African Americans were happy under segregation and had been deluded into believing they were dissatisfied by "outside agitators," generally meaning the NAACP. Journalist Carl Rowan reported an exchange with Rebecca Brown of Summerton:

"The mayor just told me that you Negroes tell him you didn't mean to sign that petition, that you got tricked into this suit by the NAACP. . . . "

"He's a liar and the truth ain't in him," exclaimed the grandmotherly Negro storekeeper. She started to take off her apron as she added, "And let's go back up there. I'll tell him to his face."[23]

Although African Americans won the 1954 Supreme Court decision, Clarendon continued to maintain separate schools until 1965. Then the state allowed students to select the schools they would attend, and four black students attended the white school in fall 1965. In reaction, whites established a private academy, Clarendon Hall, and in 1969 only 281 white students were left in the

22. Fairclough, *Race and Democracy,* 47.
23. *Minneapolis Tribune,* December 8, 1953, 9.

Summerton public school system. One year later, when the schools officially desegregated, 16 white students were left. In 1991, of the 1,274 students in Summerton's public schools, only 23 were white. In an article on Summerton in 1991, the *New York Times* reported, "Whites and blacks coexist with an easy surface sociability that is far more amiable than can be found in many Northern cities." Yet in 1997 the Summerton public schools were still nearly all black (the school superintendent was white). Summerton typifies rural Black Belt schools from which white students withdrew after desegregation.[24]

In sharp contrast to Summerton is the nearby town of Manning, the county seat. Manning has integrated successfully, as have many schools throughout the South. Some whites in the Summerton school district oppose racism and want their children to attend integrated public schools. They find themselves with a dubious choice—to send their children to a segregated private academy or to an underfunded black school. Some have opted instead to send their children to the integrated public schools in Manning. (South Carolina law allows parents to send children to schools in any school district where the parents own property.) Of course, most African Americans do not have even this limited choice.

Clarendon mirrored the reaction to school desegregation throughout the South. After the *Brown* decision, outspoken white politicians did not view integration of schools as a done deal. Senator James O. Eastland of Mississippi declared, "The South will not abide by, or obey, this legislative decision by a political court." Southerners in Georgia elected Marvin Griffin as governor on his pledge, "Come hell or high water, races will not be mixed in Georgia schools." Throughout the South, schools, churches, and homes were dynamited when conflict arose over integration. Virulent white supremacists drew praise from the Ku Klux Klan and organized groups such as the Association for the Advancement of White People. Southern judges and journalists excoriated the Supreme Court for the *Brown* decision. Senators John Stennis of Mississippi, Richard Russell of Georgia, Samuel Ervin of North Carolina, and J. Strom Thurmond of South Carolina drafted the "Southern Manifesto" and commended states that resisted "forced integration." The vast majority of southern legislators signed the manifesto.

In Virginia, arguing that the state wanted to uphold the law peacefully, Governor Thomas B. Stanley's all-white commission recommended in November 1955 that local school boards have broad authority to assign pupils to appropriate schools and that tuition grants be set up so that whites in integrated schools could go to private academies. This plan's high degree of decentralization made

---

24. *New York Times*, April 21, 1991, 18L. See also Raymond Wolters, *The Burden of Brown: Thirty Years of School Desegregation* (Knoxville: University of Tennessee Press, 1984), 129–74; Jeff Miller, "What Tomorrow Can Bring," *Southern Exposure* 22 (Summer 1994): 16–23.

court-ordered integration a slow and expensive process; it allowed token integration and, to maintain the appearance of nondiscrimination, relied on complex and ostensibly nonracial criteria for school assignment. By shifting the burden of initiation to individual schoolchildren in thousands of localities, it made rapid integration virtually impossible. Senator Harry Byrd and the Defenders of State Sovereignty, however, thought the plan was too lenient; instead, Byrd sponsored Massive Resistance, which denied state authority over local school districts, provided penalties designed to harass the NAACP, and made it difficult to bring a lawsuit for school integration.

When the NAACP won a lawsuit to integrate schools in Norfolk, the local school board endorsed Massive Resistance. In a November 18, 1958, referendum, the city approved Massive Resistance and closed schools by a 60 percent vote (most blacks could not vote). In this urban area, local segregationists were able to organize and set up private schools for white children. The Norfolk ministerial association and one of the two daily papers denounced Massive Resistance but to no avail. Behind the scenes, businessmen and the Chamber of Commerce argued that Massive Resistance hurt the state economically, that industry did not want to come where a school system was in turmoil. The business lobby was a critical factor in the cities that finally decided to forgo Massive Resistance. In contrast, rural areas kept up the resistance interminably. Rural Prince Edward County, Virginia, for instance, kept its schools closed for five years. Lack of a rural middle class left power in the hands of a few white men who controlled jobs, housing, schools, police, and local government in a system akin to feudalism. According to historian Numan V. Bartley, the county elites benefited from the one-party domination of the Democratic party; "the planter, banker, merchant, and usually old-family governing class" commanded politics and public concerns.[25]

Similar strategies were at work throughout the South. North Carolina governor Luther Hodges in 1956 engineered the Pearsall Plan allowing individual school systems to determine how they would address desegregation. Under the plan the state agreed to support the local school systems even if they decided to shut down their schools rather than desegregate. In Mississippi, school districts offered a choice of schools, knowing full well they could "persuade" the African Americans to choose black schools. Persuasion worked for many, but always there were heroes willing to suffer the hatred, the insults, the spit, and the physical abuse of whites so as to gain an education and escape the life of sharecropping. When schools in Grenada, in rural Mississippi, opened in September 1966, 150 black students attended. The white students left, but when the black stu-

25. After public schools were reopened in 1964, virtually no whites attended. Today about 40 percent of the students in the public school system are white (R. C. Smith, "Prince Edward County, 1979: 'Just Say We Remember,'" *Southern Exposure* 7 [Summer 1979]: 64–71; Bartley, *New South,* 31–32).

dents tried to leave, a white mob set upon them and brutally beat the children with chains and ax handles, while white police officers and FBI agents watched without interfering to protect the children. Thirteen-year-old Richard Sigh was beaten, his leg was broken, and, in addition, his father was fired from his job. In rural Sunflower County, Mississippi, the Carter family chose the better schools, and the children had to endure "years of hell."[26]

The battle for desegregation had to be fought again and again to a wearying and frustrating degree. Cases had to be initiated in almost every local school district. Resistance was present throughout each state and in every county. In 1964, ten years after *Brown*, 98.9 percent of black children in the South were still attending all-black schools. Then, just as the North was undergoing extreme white flight that was segregating its schools, victories in court brought about a great tide of desegregation in the South. In 1966–67 15.9 percent of black children attended integrated schools. In 1969–70 the figure had risen to 30 percent. In 1963 some 60 percent of white southerners objected to integrated education. When, just seven years later, only 16 percent objected, George Gallup commented, "This finding represents one of the most dramatic shifts in the history of public opinion polling."[27]

Throughout the 1970s desegregation cases have made areas like Summerton, South Carolina, the exception. In 1988 throughout the United States, 33 percent of African American elementary and secondary schoolchildren attended schools that were at least 15 percent and no more than 50 percent African American. In 1989 in a careful study that measured integration, scholars found that the South was "the most integrated region . . . though its schools have by far the largest proportion of black students." The study warned, however, that from 1984 to 1986 there had been a "gradual movement backward." This movement backward toward segregation occurs in large cities such as Birmingham, and, as the South urbanizes, residential patterns and school systems become more segregated, as they now are in the non-South.[28]

In rural areas of the South, African Americans and whites now attend the most integrated public schools in the United States. Many rural school districts have only one school for all to attend. Because of the South's love of sports, athletic teams have helped make integrated schools more acceptable. Nevertheless, blacks and whites, while attending the same schools, are often worlds apart be-

26. John Dittmer, *Local People: The Struggle for Civil Rights in Mississippi* (Urbana: University of Illinois Press, 1994), 404–5; Curry, *Silver Rights*, xv.

27. Goldfield, *Black, White, and Southern*, 263.

28. U.S. Department of Education, "1988 Elementary and Secondary School Civil Rights Survey, State and National Summaries," March 1991; Gary Orfield, Franklin Monfort, and Melissa Aaron, "Status of School Desegregation, 1868–1986: A Report of the Council of Urban Boards of Education and the National School Desegregation Research Project," University of Chicago, March 1989, 5, 9.

cause of economics or housing patterns. Furthermore, educational practices that separate students by "ability" can result in classroom segregation. Students of both races attend one school without much overt racism but also without much real communication. Exceptions are becoming less remarkable as friendships develop, and interracial dating is no longer out of the ordinary.

The early aims of the civil rights movement were to achieve immediate and visible improvements in the daily lives of blacks and to achieve psychological liberation, freedom from fear and from the habit of submission. Activists were African American and tended to be urban rather than rural. White opponents varied in the degree of antagonism, but practically every white southerner resisted the movement. Some antagonists resorted to murder and arson, but white sheriffs arrested few perpetrators, some of whom bragged about their exploits. Gunnar Myrdal, the Swedish sociologist best known for his study of U.S. racial problems, concluded that officers of the law served "as agents of the planters and other white employers." White juries let the murderers and arsonists off, and the majority of white citizens acquiesced by their silence.[29]

The march from Selma to Montgomery spurred a change in the movement. When the unmitigated violence of frenzied police against innocent men, women, and children was portrayed on television, many whites felt they could no longer ignore the plight of African Americans. The violence on the Edmund Pettis Bridge was a catalyst for the 1965 Voting Rights Act, and when the march to Montgomery resumed, the world saw via television an integrated civil rights group walking through rural Alabama.

Civil rights laws were passed in 1957, 1960, and 1964. The Civil Rights Act of 1964 forbids discrimination because of race, color, religion, ethnicity, and, in employment, discrimination based on gender. Yet civil rights and the end of legal segregation did not automatically bring an increase in the African American vote. Despite formidable efforts of local black leaders, civil rights organizations, and voting education projects, Alabama still had less than one-fifth of eligible blacks registered to vote in 1965. In Mississippi, where Bob Moses valiantly struggled in the 1960s, only 6.4 percent of blacks were registered to vote in 1965. The white South continued to use literacy and property tests, poll taxes, and actual disfranchisement to keep African Americans from voting. White intransigence enabled reformers to convince Congress of the need for voting rights legislation. Between January 1, 1955, and January 1, 1959, the Southern Regional Council counted 225 separate acts of racial violence, and after passage of civil rights legislation in 1957 and 1960, southern white violence toward blacks escalated. Moreover, the violence of the 1964 Mississippi Freedom Summer demonstrated the need for federal intervention to protect civil rights workers and pro-

29. Gunnar Myrdal, *An American Dilemma: The Negro Problem and Modern Democracy* (New York: Harper and Brothers, 1944), 536.

testers. One study of the 1964 Mississippi Freedom Summer chronicled six deaths, thirty-five shootings, sixty-five bombings, and eighty beatings. No wonder only twelve hundred blacks registered. Chief Justice Earl Warren pronounced the Civil Rights Acts of 1957, 1960, and 1964 as failures in ameliorating the problem of voting discrimination. In 1965 the goal was straightforward: the right to vote.

With the passage of the Voting Rights Act in 1965, the first nine counties chosen to receive federal registrars quadrupled black registration within one week, from 1,764 to 6,998. Nevertheless, many rural African Americans knew better than to try to exercise their right to vote. Because Mississippi was the state where white terrorism was most virulent, James Meredith (the African American who integrated the University of Mississippi in 1962) decided to undertake a "March on Fear" through the rural part of the state. Meredith set out on June 5, 1966, and planned to walk 220 miles down highway 51 from Memphis to Jackson to encourage rural blacks to overcome fear and to exercise their right to vote, granted by the 1965 Voting Rights Act. The next day a white man stepped out of the underbrush and fired three shotgun blasts at Meredith, severely wounding him. Publicized on TV, the event again focused the nation's attention on the front lines of the civil rights movement. When the march resumed, more than fifteen hundred people joined in. Whenever the march encountered hostility and assault from local whites, the local police force entered the fray with a vengeance; they tear-gassed, clubbed, and arrested the marchers—men, women, and children— for disturbing the peace.

Among various organizations working on civil rights were the NAACP, the Congress for Racial Equality (CORE), the Southern Christian Leadership Conference (SCLC), the Urban League, and the Student Nonviolent Coordinating Committee (SNCC). SNCC was the most active in rural areas. SNCC increasingly identified with the southern proletariat, symbolized by members' wearing blue bib overalls. At its peak in 1963 and 1964, SNCC had about three hundred field and staff workers. One of the SNCC voter project proposals stated that the group would engage in a battle of minds to overcome the psychic enslavement of African Americans; they would oppose every "apparent procedure, purging or inflating of voting lists, economic warfare, police brutality, etc., all attempts to nullify the right to vote among Negroes." With dedicated workers such as rural southerner Fannie Lou Hamer, SNCC captured the consciences of black and white student activists, northern and southern, who wanted to help African Americans in the rural South liberate themselves. These students set up cooperatives, established health clinics, taught rural blacks to read, write, and think about freedom, and registered many voters.

SNCC's early focus was biracial, integrationist, nonviolent, and nonrevolutionary. The group included middle-class integrationists working for full citizenship in American society. Working in Mississippi and confronting the brutality of the Mississippi police, particularly in rural areas, hardened SNCC. With the election of college-educated New Yorker Stokely Carmichael as its chair, SNCC became separatist and nationalist and moved into a stance of alienation from American society: "We been saying freedom for six years and ain't got nothing. What we're gonna start saying is Black Power." Martin Luther King, Jr., expressed regret at the term: "We must never seek power exclusively for the Negro, but the sharing of power with white people."[30]

Desegregation underlay the objectives of the civil rights movement, but activists also expected economic and institutional improvements through better education, better jobs, and better housing. Recalcitrant government action and persistent white resistance marked the dynamic transition of the civil rights movement from desegregation to black power. Calling on audiences to resist their white oppressors and seize power, Carmichael became more alienated and subsequently withdrew from Mississippi and moved to rural Lowndes County, Alabama, where not a single black voter was registered although they were a majority of the population. There he set up an all-black party whose symbol was the black panther.[31]

Joyce Ladner, in her interviews with black activists in the South in 1966–67, found that black power was a concept that appealed to the young, urban, and militant, especially those from the North. It did not appeal to the rural activists who had strong ties to the local church and community in the South. Tempered by a powerful Christian conviction, rural blacks did not feel the rage that overwhelmed African Americans from urban ghettos. Many rural African Americans felt they were better off than they had been five years before and expected their situation to continue to improve.

The civil rights movement has moved from the streets to the courtrooms, where African American plaintiffs now must sue to have their rights enforced. The attorneys for the plaintiffs, black and white, have been a dedicated lot, working for low wages in organizations such as the NAACP and the American Civil Liberties Union (ACLU). Often rural counties bring the suits. A complex set of litigation involved rural Edgefield County, South Carolina, home of U.S. senator J. Strom Thurmond, who had bitterly opposed the original Voting Rights Act in 1965 and who fought extensions in 1970, 1975, and 1982. In Edgefield in 1969, black activist Thomas McCain began efforts to open local governing bodies to African Americans. After fifteen years of complex legal maneuvering (including the Supreme Court's overruling of a South Carolina panel and

30. Goldfield, *Black, White and Southern*, 224; Harvard Sitkoff, *The Struggle for Black Equality, 1954–1992* (New York: Hill and Wang, 1993), 199.

31. According to Goldfield, *Black, White, and Southern*, 246, in Lowndes County, where now 80 percent of registered voters are black, "two decades of black rule" has "not changed the fact that it was among the nation's ten poorest counties, or that more than 45 percent of its residents still lived below the poverty line, or that it continued to have one of the nation's highest infant-mortality rates."

various objections from the Department of Justice to at-large elections), *McCain v. Lybrand* ultimately resulted in the end of at-large elections for the Edgefield County Council and the institution of single-member districts. Under this new plan, three African Americans were sworn in on January 1, 1985, as county council members, giving them majority control. The ceremony took place in the same courthouse that had been seized at gunpoint by the "Redeemers" of 1876 to control the ballot count and prevent African Americans from voting. The newly inaugurated county council in 1985 replaced the incumbent county administrator and appointed Thomas McCain, the African American educator who had led the court battles responsible for the victory. After that, Edgefield County could never go completely back; when whites recaptured the majority on the county council, the new council elected an African American to chair the county council and did not replace the popular McCain as county administrator. As in Edgefield, where the Voting Rights Act has been enforced, the 1965 act has made a real difference throughout the rural South. Specifically, it has reduced election-related violence, increased responsiveness and the provision of services to minorities, made the political resources of the African American community more available to society as a whole, made it possible for southern solons to support civil rights, made racial politics unfashionable, and opened opportunities for minorities to pursue careers in politics.[32]

As successful as the Voting Rights Act has been in allowing people to register and vote and as successful as court cases have been in ameliorating vote dilution, the Voting Rights Act does not and cannot directly confront problems of economic racism in society. If American society was ready to confront the evils of racism, it remained unwilling to confront the evils of poverty. King in 1967 wrote, "With the Voting Rights Act one phase of development in the civil rights revolution came to an end. A new phase opened. . . . White America was ready to demand that the Negro should be spared the lash of brutality and coarse degradation, but it had never been truly committed to helping him out of poverty. . . . Jobs are harder and costlier to create than voting rolls." Some even suggest that King was assassinated because he had moved from issues of race to those of class.[33]

The civil rights movement was a process, and this process moved slowly in rural areas. One particular rural small town, Plains, in Sumter County, Georgia,

32. *McCain v. Lybrand* 465 U.S. 236 (1984); Vernon Burton, "Race and Reconstruction: Edgefield County, South Carolina," *Journal of Social History* 12 (Fall 1978): 31–56; Orville Vernon Burton et al., "South Carolina," in *The Quiet Revolution: The Impact of the Voting Rights Act in the South, 1965–1990,* ed. Chandler Davidson and Bernard Grofman (Princeton: Princeton University Press, 1994), 191–232, 420–32; *Columbia State,* October 18, 1987, 5B; Margaret Edds, *Free at Last: What Really Happened When Civil Rights Came to Southern Politics* (Bethesda, Md.: Adler and Adler, 1987), 50.

33. Martin Luther King, Jr., *Where Do We Go from Here: Chaos or Community?* (New York: Bantam, 1967), 4, 6.

caught the attention of the nation when its Sunday school teacher and Baptist deacon, James Earl Carter, was elected president in 1976. Plains shows some of the patterns of race relations prevalent in certain parts of the small-town South. In occupational patterns race made a difference. From the 1930s until the 1970s, the number of farms in Plains had decreased to 404, only 14 percent of the number in 1910. Most of the farms were worked by their owners, thirty-three of whom were African American. One-quarter of farm owners earned money off the farm to support their farming. Of the forty-four farm tenants in the county, only three were African American. Most blacks who still worked in agriculture were day laborers. Other African Americans worked as domestics for the white population. On the farm, cotton took a back seat to peanuts, chickens, beef, and dairy cattle. The Carter family owned a farm and a peanut processing plant, which employed African American workers.[34]

Residential patterns in Plains in the early 1970s showed whites living on one side of the railroad tracks and blacks on the other. Whites lived in decent housing with plumbing, blacks in poorer homes, and only about one-third had indoor plumbing. When residences were close by, even just across the tracks, children played together across racial lines. Children had to be taught racism and usually learned the lesson by adolescence; then the two groups separated themselves. Interracial sex was a strong taboo, and even today many rural blacks and whites do not approve of interracial dating and marriage, which nevertheless do occur and usually without incident.[35]

Most communities had some egalitarians as well as some avid racists among the white population. One moderate in Americus, Georgia, was attorney Warren Fortson. Appalled by the total disrepair of black schools in the county, Fortson called for the formation of a biracial committee to address the situation. For this, he was branded a radical and literally run out of town. In the 1950s Jimmy Carter, who, as a member of the local school board, accepted segregation, nevertheless refused to join the White Citizens' Council. His business suffered mightily but survived. In 1964 Carter argued that his Plains Baptist Church should accept black members, but his argument did not prevail. After Carter's election as governor, this white plantation owner from rural Georgia hung a portrait of another Georgian, Martin Luther King, Jr., in the state capitol.

Rural Sumter County fomented its share of activity during the civil rights movement. Ku Klux Klan violence threatened Koinonia, which also had to argue

34. Mark Pinsky, "Finances: Double Dealing in Plains, Georgia," *Southern Exposure* 7 (Summer 1979): 98–102; William J. Cooper, Jr., and Thomas E. Terrill, *The American South: A History* (New York: McGraw-Hill, 1991), 740–42.

35. An excellent example of learning about racial etiquette is Harry Crews, *A Childhood: The Biography of a Place* (New York: Harper & Row, 1978), 56–59. Interracial marriages were illegal in the South; see Joel Williamson, *New People: Miscegenation and Mulattoes in the United States* (New York: Free Press, 1980), and Kirby, *Rural Worlds Lost*, 248–52.

against injunctions designed to shut down that interracial Christian community. Local authorities arrested scores of African Americans and SNCC workers for registering voters, charging them with insurrection, at that time a capital offense in Georgia. The local prosecutor claimed that he did not actually seek the death penalty but charged them with insurrection to keep them in jail without bail.

Nevertheless, African Americans voted and also challenged the dilution of their votes by local whites. In 1967, two years after county officials were enjoined for enforcing segregation, the U.S. Fifth Circuit Court of Appeals overturned Sumter County's election results as "gross, spectacular, completely indefensible state-imposed, state-enforced racial discrimination." By 1976 private segregated academies were in decline, and white enrollment was increasing at the black-majority county high school. In towns like Plains, with only one public high school, athletics often brought a community together. Both black and white parents cheered as their athletes competed in two state championship football teams. After the high school years many southerners, black and white (Jimmy Carter also), joined the military. The military was integrated; it was a patriotic duty, an escape from the rural South, and it was a job. For rural African Americans a military paycheck regularly sent home to mothers or wives might be the only cash they saw. In an agrarian staple-crop society, many families received money only once a year, when the crop was sold, and often the money was owed before it was received, and farmers were lucky to be left with enough food for the year. Military pay, pensions, and veterans' benefits have kept many a rural family out of destitution.

Many of these patterns from the 1970s persist today. Present-day rural race relations are complicated in many ways. One is the difficulty in defining what is rural. Can a rural area include small towns located outside large cities? How rural is the countryside that houses a gigantic industrial plant? Urban-rural difference is a continuum rather than a dichotomy, and along this continuum race relations vary greatly. Another complication is the confusion of a system in flux. The old patterns of Jim Crow segregation are gone, and race relations are changing and unpredictable, often dependent on place. Patterns in "rural" northern Virginia suburbs (not far from Washington, D.C.) differ markedly from those in the Mississippi Delta.

In response to this new unpredictability and unease, racist organizations have found homes in both North and South. The Alabama-based Klanwatch estimates that there are 5,500 members of the Klan nationwide, half of the membership in the early 1980s and down from 42,000 in 1965. But at the same time, white supremacist groups and some rogue militia movements are growing, and some of these are prevalent in rural communities throughout America. Klanwatch estimates that since 1990 the number of white supremacists in these groups has increased from 22,000 to 25,000.[36]

36. Tony Horwitz, "A Death for Dixie," New Yorker, March 18, 1996, 69.

The relative strength of white racist power in rural southern areas correlates with the popularity of political figures and whether they favor racist agendas. The Republican party's victories in the South owed much to its voiced opposition to affirmative action, busing, and welfare. Although numerically more whites are on welfare rolls, "welfare dependents" is a code word for blacks. Some white southerners attune themselves to the North for clues on what racist agendas are within acceptable limits. Ronald Reagan opened his presidential campaign in 1980 with a political speech at the county fair in Neshoba County, Mississippi, where three civil rights activists had been murdered in 1964. He spoke of states' rights, a euphemism for opposition to racial justice. During the Carter administration, African Americans in Sumter County, Alabama, developed a successful organization to apply for land and home ownership under a federal minority program. Later the Reagan administration challenged whether blacks were a minority in this county since the county was predominantly populated by African Americans. With the aid of civil rights attorneys, African American plaintiffs challenged the ruling; in return, the Reagan administration simply did away with the program.[37]

Today in Sumter County more than a third of all residents are below the poverty level, and all but 7 percent of these are African Americans. In 1986 more than one out of every five persons were on welfare. Half of the county's revenues come from a toxic waste dump. Environmental racism plays a part today as the more rural and poor, that is, black, areas receive the landfills and toxic waste generated by affluent urbanites. Explained an Alabama state district attorney, "The strategy is to find predominantly black, economically distressed areas and make their economies dependent on hazardous waste to the extent that the people who live there become hazardous waste junkies."[38]

People are willing to risk living with toxic waste because, despite the monumental changes resulting from the civil rights movement, jobs for African Americans have not been forthcoming. Many southerners, and most particularly black southerners, have been left out of the new prosperity of the Sunbelt, and pockets of severe poverty persist. Within these pockets, which tend to be rural, is a population without adequate housing, education, health care, and jobs. According to the Children's Defense Fund, about two hundred thousand African American children in Mississippi lived in poverty in 1990.[39]

As farm jobs have disappeared, seasonal employment is taken by migrant workers. Although Texas has always had a large Mexican American population and Mississippi has had Chinese workers, it has been a recent phenomenon that thousands of immigrants from Latin America have settled in the South, many to

37. John B. Boles, *The South Through Time: A History of an American Region* (Englewood Cliffs: Prentice Hall, 1995), 513; *Panola Land Buying Association Housing Development Corp. v. Vance Clark et al.,* CA no. CV-83-G-1216W, Sumter County, Alabama.

38. Goldfield, *Black, White, and Southern,* 248.

39. Dittmer, *Local People,* 427.

perform agricultural labor for agribusinesses. In Florida and Louisiana, Haitians and Jamaicans cut sugarcane for notoriously abusive corporations. Mexican migrant laborers pick tobacco, tomatoes, strawberries, peaches, and vegetables as they travel through the South. They often are exploited, underpaid, and put in substandard housing. They seldom have schools for their children or access to doctors or health facilities. In rural South Carolina, a major employer of African American workers, Greenwood Packing Plant, recently dismissed many longtime African American employees when they were near retirement age and replaced them with contract laborers from Latin America. In 1997, the Justice Department raided the packing plant and discovered that many of the migrant workers were illegal aliens. The assessed fine was inconsequential compared with the savings in wages and unpaid retirement benefits. The exploitative treatment of these nonblack immigrants and migrant workers, as well as the older African American employees, again raises questions about race and class disparity.[40]

Problems facing the poor in the United States today fuel racial stereotypes and prejudice. Yet family breakdown and the growing gap in education and health point to a convergence of race and class. Poverty does not claim all blacks; many are moving into the middle class. This does not minimize the seriousness of the problems of those who remain behind in rural areas. This division of blacks into haves and have-nots is a significant difference from the time before the civil rights movement, and one that is separating leadership and role models from a group trapped in poverty.

In rural areas, as elsewhere, underlying problems in race relations can erupt into violence. Todd County, Kentucky, with a population of 10,900, is one such rural community. In Todd County the town of Guthrie has a population of 1,600, one-third of whom are African American. The mayor and all members of the city council and the school board are white. Any polite and friendly race relations became strained for this community in 1987, after the Southeast Region NAACP passed a resolution condemning the flying of Confederate flags over state capitols. In Guthrie lived an African American teenager, Freddie Morrow, whose mother had sent him there to live with his aunt to escape gang activity in Chicago. Also in town lived a white teenager, Michael Westerman, whose mother described him as "a country boy and proud of it." In his pickup truck, Westerman displayed the Confederate flag, the symbol of his high school sports team, the Rebels. One night as Westerman and his wife were out driving around, Morrow was also out driving with some African American friends. Morrow shot Westerman while both were in their cars. Since the trial and conviction of Morrow, many black teenagers want to escape Todd County as soon as possible; they

---

40. Loewen, *Mississippi Chinese,* has argued that whites in the South could be tolerant with small groups such as the Chinese.

avoid going to town after dark and look forward to the day they can join the army.[41]

In Todd County and other areas throughout the South, fights and harsh words have erupted as aggrieved whites feel the civil rights movement has gone far enough. Since 1993 a host of African American churches in the South, mostly in rural areas, have been targets of arson. In those cases in which the police have made arrests, they found that racial hatred was a factor. A person living near one of the burned churches shared her feelings with a newspaper reporter: "I'm white, and it doesn't matter what race you are. It's scary to think I could have people next door to me who hate that much." The majority of whites deplore such violence, no longer quietly acquiescing. Both blacks and whites opposed a store in Laurens, South Carolina, whose proprietor sold KKK paraphernalia; one white man drove his van through the front of the store.[42]

The politics of race relations are also complicated and in flux. Some whites who would never deny African Americans the right to vote are willing to deny single-member districts that provide an opportunity to elect black representatives. White politicians often lament that they are perfectly able to represent African Americans in the legislature, yet they fail to grasp that an African American would be equally capable of representing all the people. Whites willing to allow African Americans the choice of candidates in an urban precinct have been totally opposed to the same principle in rural areas, where white legislators refuse to let go of their local fiefdoms. There is a renewed effort on the parts of both northern and southern whites to do away with affirmative action and undermine the Voting Rights Act. In the last few years, the courts have generally found for white defendants against black plaintiffs in voting rights cases in the rural South.

My hometown of Ninety Six, South Carolina, offers one example of changes wrought in the South since the civil rights movement. Ninety Six was the home of pre–Civil War avid slavery supporter Preston Brooks, who caned the abolitionist senator Charles Sumner like a craven dog on the Senate floor. As a boy I was taught about Brooks, and I inspected his monument in the town square. I was not taught about another native, the great black educator and theologian Benjamin E. Mays. Now that times have changed, this community is very proud of Mays as one of its native sons, and out in the country at Mays's Crossroads is an impressive monument to Mays, the mentor of Martin Luther King, Jr., and "godfather of the Civil Rights Movement."

Another symbol of change in this rural community is what used to be the home of Joe Wells, one of the last people to grow cotton in the area. Mr. Joe's cotton fields had surrounded a beautiful nineteenth-century plantation home,

41. Horwitz, "Death for Dixie," 76.
42. *Atlanta Journal/Atlanta Constitution*, March 3, 1996, H8.

and for a quarter-mile on either side of a crescent drive grew evenly spaced pecan trees. The cotton fields and home are now gone, but the pecan trees remain. Now, however, the magnificent tree-lined drive frames a huge Fuji film plant. That plant, sitting out in the country, has replaced the textile mills as the largest employer and draws from a fifty-mile radius black and white employees who drive to work. Unemployment is virtually nil in the area.

When I left Ninety Six to go to college, farmers, black and white, were still struggling to keep the farm, and it was not unusual to see an African American farmer in his mule-drawn wagon. Most farmers had other jobs as well, or their wives did. Now hardly anyone farms, and the land is planted in pine trees. When I went off to college in 1965, no African Americans attended the predominantly white schools. Now the schools are fully integrated. Then the school board and the city council were all white and elected at large. Now community leaders have cooperated in changing to a district system so that black voters would have an opportunity to elect candidates of their choice; they elected to the city council Charles Harts, an African American retired engineer who had returned home to Ninety Six from Buffalo, New York. In 1995, although only 20 percent of the town of about two thousand is black, whites supported Harts, and Ninety Six, in the midst of rural South Carolina up-country, today has a black mayor. Harts recounted how fifty years ago no African American would have felt comfortable venturing into the all-white mill village, but he knew that he needed their votes to win in the three-man mayoral contest. Harts explained, "I felt I could relate to them by being a country boy who grew up in a poor, struggling family." Harts won with a majority of all votes cast. According to this Korean War veteran, "When I left here years ago, it was probably beyond anyone's imagination that Charlie Harts, the little country boy, would come back to be mayor."[43]

Today many southern whites are more willing to confront racism than are northern whites. In the rural South, where most people attend church on Sundays and where those churches are still very much segregated, many organize joint black-white church activities yearly or semiannually. The Southern Baptist denomination, largest in the region, formally apologized for slavery. Rural church communities are openly calling for racial moderation and reconciliation; this is very different from northern or urban communities where white people prefer to deny or ignore racism.

The history of the South, including tragedy and triumph, belongs to both blacks and whites. In any given rural southern community, both black and white people share values. The majority of both hold a Christian faith, an evangelical style of worship, and a belief in being polite to other people. Whites and African Americans share family values. Both races tend to spend more time playing with their children than is true elsewhere in the country. The two races enjoy similar

43. *Greenville News* (South Carolina), January 7, 1996, B-1, 4.

music, and the integrated band Hootie and the Blowfish was offered the Order of the Palmetto, South Carolina's highest honor (the band turned down the honor as being too political). The two races eat the same foods, enjoying collards, okra, and grits. A recognition of these shared values and traditions has brought about a regional pride on the part of both whites and blacks.[44]

For the most part, this regional pride centers on the prosperous cities of the Sunbelt. The economic future of the South is in its cities and in technology and computers rather than manufacturing. What does this portend for the rural areas, where education lags in all areas and schools cannot even use electronic mail or the Internet because of the long-distance telephone costs? Some people, however, are rejecting the urban rat race and finding a higher quality of life in rural areas, where one can find human personality and interaction between races. Significantly, the great migration of African Americans has reversed, and more black people are moving to the South than are moving away.

As the old train tracks are being pulled up throughout the South, the depots still remain. Rural communities value these reminders of days gone by, but now they use them as community centers or libraries. And unlike those bygone days, these centers are now for all the people.

---

44. The South also has a significant Jewish population and a growing Muslim population, but these groups tend to live in urban areas.

Southern Rural Population Change, 1940–1990

STATE	TP	BP	% B of TP	RTP	% RTP	RBP	% RBP	% BRP	TF[1]	% FTP	BF	% BFTP	% BFTF	% BFBP
Alabama														
1940[2]	2,832,961	983,290	34.7	1,977,020	69.8	667,322	68.0	33.6	356,581	12.6	153,596	5.4	43.1	15.60
1950	3,061,743	978,545	32.0	1,833,534	56.2	525,789	54.0	28.7	160,780	5.3	49,639	1.6	30.9	5.07
1960	3,266,740	983,131	30.5	1,475,019	45.2	427,221	43.5	29.0	58,144	1.8	16,105	0.5	27.7	1.63
1970	3,444,165	903,000	26.2	1,426,680	41.4	340,115	30.3	21.2	46,299	1.3	12,524	0.4	27.1	1.39
1980	3,893,888	996,283	25.6	1,556,175	40.0	302,073	30.3	19.4	29,601	0.8	6,038	0.4	20.4	0.61
1990	4,040,587	1,020,705	25.3	1,601,038	39.6	284,795	28.0	17.8	40,246	1.0	3,754	0.1	9.3	0.37
Arkansas														
1940	1,949,387	482,578	24.8	1,517,477	77.8	377,735	78.3	25.0	301,535	15.5	96,577	5.0	32.0	20.00
1950	1,909,511	426,639	22.3	1,278,920	67.0	207,398	48.6	22.0	143,621	7.5	35,188	1.8	24.5	8.24
1960	1,786,272	390,569	21.9	1,020,969	57.2	216,842	55.5	21.2	48,174	2.6	5,881	0.3	12.2	1.51
1970	1,923,295	352,539	18.3	962,430	50.0	157,693	44.7	16.4	54,588	2.8	8,839	0.5	16.2	2.51
1980	2,286,435	373,025	16.3	1,106,879	48.4	127,633	34.2	11.5	50,455	2.2	4,046	0.2	8.0	1.08
1990	2,350,725	373,912	15.9	1,092,704	46.5	106,689	28.5	9.8	45,177	1.9	1,801	0.08	4.0	0.48
Florida														
1940	1,897,414	514,198	27.1	851,623	44.9	227,151	44.2	27.0	129,293	6.8	58,621	3.1	45.3	11.40
1950	2,771,305	603,101	22.0	957,415	34.5	207,398	34.0	22.6	40,042	1.4	7,118	0.2	18.0	1.18
1960	4,951,960	887,679	17.9	1,290,177	26.1	210,427	23.7	16.3	20,776	0.4	2,829	0.1	13.6	0.32
1970	6,789,443	1,041,966	15.3	1,244,892	18.3	182,350	17.5	14.6	110,994	1.6	43,272	0.6	39.0	4.15
1980	9,746,324	1,343,134	13.8	1,533,939	15.7	164,484	12.2	10.7	90,522	0.9	32,104	0.3	35.5	2.40
1990	12,937,926	1,759,534	13.6	1,970,598	15.2	176,641	10.0	9.0	153,286	1.2	19,973	0.2	13.0	1.14
Georgia														
1940	3,123,723	1,084,927	34.7	2,049,915	65.6	705,171	65.0	34.4	389,083	12.5	171,166	5.5	44.0	16.00
1950	3,444,578	1,062,762	31.0	1,885,131	54.7	571,916	53.8	30.3	157,617	4.6	4,560	1.4	29.7	0.42
1960	3,943,116	1,125,893	28.6	1,762,880	44.7	479,075	42.6	27.2	56,806	1.4	11,608	0.3	20.4	1.03
1970	4,589,575	1,184,062	25.8	1,821,501	39.7	402,106	34.0	22.1	75,521	1.6	25,067	0.5	33.2	2.11
1980	5,463,105	1,464,435	26.8	2,054,024	37.6	389,583	26.6	19.0	48,659	0.9	14,653	0.3	30.1	1.00
1990	6,478,216	1,759,534	27.2	2,380,877	36.8	395,104	22.5	16.6	68,174	1.0	7,718	0.1	11.3	0.44
Kentucky														
1940	2,845,627	214,031	7.5	1,996,300	70.2	97,259	45.4	4.9	309,597	10.9	15,397	0.5	5.0	7.20
1950	2,944,806	201,921	6.9	975,056	33.1	74,629	37.0	7.7	172,201	5.8	4,560	0.2	2.6	2.30
1960	3,038,156	218,073	7.2	1,684,941	55.5	218,073	29.4	3.8	92,568	3.0	2,282	0.1	2.5	1.05
1970	3,218,706	230,363	7.2	1,534,653	47.7	45,567	20.6	3.1	73,607	2.3	3,652	0.1	5.0	1.59
1980	3,660,777	259,289	7.1	1,798,594	49.1	38,453	14.8	2.1	58,202	1.6	1,663	0.04	2.9	0.64
1990	3,685,296	262,907	7.1	1,774,971	48.2	33,046	12.6	1.9	57,754	1.6	922	0.02	1.6	0.35

	TP	BP	% B of TP	RTP	% RTP	RBP	% RBP	% BRP	TF	% FTP	BF	% BFTP	% BFTF	% BFBP
Louisiana														
1940	2,363,880	849,303	36.0	1,383,441	58.5	535,208	63.0	39.0	256,128	11.0	130,283	5.5	51.0	15.30
1950	2,683,516	882,428	33.0	1,211,820	45.2	434,965	49.3	36.0	47,887	1.8	33,895	1.1	60.3	3.84
1960	3,257,022	1,045,307	32.1	1,196,416	36.7	400,293	38.3	33.5	32,130	1.0	8,968	0.3	28.0	0.86
1970	3,641,306	1,085,227	29.8	1,219,131	33.5	348,629	32.1	28.6	47,999	1.3	17,759	0.5	37.0	1.63
1980	4,205,900	1,238,472	29.4	1,318,591	31.4	299,545	24.2	22.7	25,825	0.6	9,474	0.2	36.7	0.76
1990	4,219,973	1,299,281	30.8	1,348,214	32.0	282,572	21.7	21.0	40,295	1.0	5,301	0.1	13.2	0.41
Mississippi														
1940	2,183,796	1,074,578	49.2	1,750,914	80.2	896,550	83.4	51.2	422,247	19.3	269,596	12.3	64.0	25.10
1950	2,178,914	986,494	45.2	1,571,752	72.1	754,257	76.5	48.0	206,072	9.5	110,629	5.1	53.7	11.21
1960	2,178,141	920,595	42.3	1,357,336	62.3	625,643	68.0	46.1	67,554	3.1	28,642	1.3	42.4	3.11
1970	2,216,912	815,626	36.8	1,230,270	55.5	484,178	59.4	39.4	53,714	2.4	24,552	1.1	45.7	3.01
1980	2,520,638	887,111	35.2	1,327,833	52.7	468,853	53.0	35.3	24,525	1.0	13,577	0.5	55.4	1.53
1990	2,573,216	915,057	35.6	1,362,487	53.0	455,205	50.0	33.4	34,627	1.3	3,242	0.1	9.4	0.35
North Carolina														
1940	3,571,622	981,298	27.5	2,597,448	72.7	681,935	69.4	26.3	409,050	11.5	142,821	4.0	35.0	14.60
1950	4,061,929	1,047,353	25.8	2,693,828	66.3	685,668	65.5	25.5	226,136	5.6	64,038	1.6	28.3	6.11
1960	4,556,155	1,156,870	25.4	2,754,234	60.5	699,703	60.5	25.4	116,658	2.6	26,262	0.5	22.5	2.27
1970	5,082,059	1,125,885	22.2	2,771,678	54.5	579,806	51.5	21.0	103,805	2.0	30,052	0.6	29.0	2.67
1980	5,881,766	1,319,054	22.4	3,058,914	52.0	568,717	43.1	18.6	63,859	0.3	18,363	0.3	29.0	1.39
1990	6,628,637	1,456,323	22.0	3,290,859	50.0	539,560	37.0	16.4	83,835	1.3	4,861	0.1	5.8	0.33

[1] Figures for farmers use the census category for agriculture, forestry, and fishery.

[2] Figures for blacks between 1940 and 1960 use the census category for nonwhite and contain other minorities.

KEY
TP: total population
BP: black population
% B of TP: percent blacks of total population
RTP: rural total population
% RTP: percent of total population who are rural

RBP: rural black population
% RBP: percent of black population who are rural
% BRP: Percent of rural population who are black
TF: total farmer population
% FTP: percent of total population who are farmers

BF: total black farmers
% BFTP: percent of total population who are black farmers
% BFTF: percent of total farmers who are black
% BFBP: percent of black population who are farmers

(continued)

Southern Rural Population Change, 1940–1990 (*continued*)

STATE	TP	BP	% B of TP	RTP	% RTP	RBP	% RBP	% BRP	TF[1]	% FTP	BF	% BFTP	% BFTF	% BFBP
South Carolina														
1940	1,899,804	814,164	42.9	1,433,693	75.5	643,737	79.1	45.0	261,802	18.3	159,970	8.4	61.1	19.65
1950	2,117,027	822,077	38.8	1,339,106	63.3	586,602	71.4	43.8	105,510	5.0	53,288	2.5	50.5	6.50
1960	2,382,594	831,572	34.9	1,401,208	58.8	550,683	66.2	39.3	42,310	1.8	18,555	0.8	21.1	2.23
1970	2,590,516	788,455	30.4	1,339,791	51.7	461,780	58.6	34.5	39,778	1.5	19,140	0.7	48.1	2.43
1980	3,121,820	947,969	30.4	1,432,567	45.9	464,982	49.0	32.5	19,527	0.6	11,666	0.4	59.7	1.23
1990	3,486,703	1,039,884	29.8	1,581,325	45.4	475,923	45.8	30.1	33,595	1.0	3,390	0.1	10.0	0.33
Tennessee														
1940	2,915,841	508,736	17.4	1,888,635	64.8	226,402	44.5	12.0	313,029	10.7	53,467	1.8	17.1	10.51
1950	3,291,718	530,603	16.1	1,839,116	55.9	190,318	35.9	10.3	176,070	5.0	23,104	0.7	13.1	4.40
1960	3,567,089	589,336	16.5	1,702,261	47.7	166,179	28.2	9.8	86,114	2.4	9,584	0.3	11.1	1.63
1970	3,923,687	620,636	15.8	1,605,229	40.9	123,607	20.0	7.7	62,114	1.6	8,097	0.2	13.0	1.30
1980	4,591,120	724,808	15.8	1,817,547	39.6	101,745	14.0	5.6	44,944	1.0	3,464	0.1	7.7	0.48
1990	4,877,185	778,035	16.0	1,907,237	39.1	86,815	11.2	4.6	48,712	1.0	2,739	0.1	5.6	0.35
Texas														
1940	6,414,824	924,391	14.4	3,503,435	54.6	504,281	54.6	14.4	639,114	10.0	109,984	1.7	17.2	11.90
1950	7,711,194	977,458	12.7	2,873,134	37.3	365,134	37.4	12.7	252,261	3.3	27,747	0.3	11.0	2.83
1960	9,579,677	1,204,846	12.6	2,392,207	25.0	299,757	24.9	12.5	139,420	1.5	7,094	0.1	5.1	0.59
1970	11,196,730	1,396,605	12.5	2,274,519	20.3	229,603	16.4	10.1	194,635	1.7	16,599	0.1	8.5	1.19
1980	14,229,191	1,704,741	12.0	2,896,174	20.4	201,119	11.8	6.9	156,414	1.1	8,304	0.1	5.3	0.49
1990	16,986,510	2,021,632	11.9	3,351,993	19.7	195,472	9.7	5.8	196,624	1.2	6,978	0.04	3.5	0.35
Virginia														
1940	2,677,773	661,449	24.7	1,733,098	64.7	420,574	63.6	24.3	229,563	8.6	69,092	2.6	30.0	10.44
1950	3,318,680	734,211	22.1	1,758,565	53.0	398,548	54.3	22.7	101,986	3.1	23,056	0.7	22.6	3.14
1960	3,966,949	824,506	20.8	1,762,036	44.4	386,799	47.0	22.0	56,767	1.4	10,581	0.3	18.6	1.28
1970	4,648,494	860,302	18.5	1,709,577	36.8	343,293	40.0	20.1	57,262	1.2	13,239	0.3	23.1	1.54
1980	5,346,878	1,000,665	18.7	1,817,395	34.0	307,586	30.7	16.9	43,707	0.8	7,664	0.1	17.5	0.77
1990	6,187,358	1,162,994	18.8	1,893,915	30.6	286,287	24.6	15.1	57,931	0.9	3,452	0.1	6.0	0.30

No Easy Time:
Rural Southern Women, 1940–1990

SALLY McMILLEN

I don't want no city life, because I don't like it," eighty-three-year-old Annie Perry stated in 1975. "Oh, I'd be like a bird in a cage. Catch a bird and put it in a cage—Livin' in town—that'd be like a bird in a cage." Bound to her Appalachian environment and way of living but cherishing her difficult life, Perry, like other rural southern women, reflected hardiness, pragmatism, and an ability to deal with an arduous, often impoverished, existence.[1]

Rural women have been central to the South's history since the first Europeans set foot on southern soil in the early seventeenth century. The region quickly developed an agrarian, cash-crop economy. The growing of tobacco and, later, rice, indigo, cotton, and sugarcane shaped southern settlement, the region's economy, and its very life and character. Women, whether as indentured servants, slaves, farmworkers, wives, or landowners, played a significant role in this agrarian economy. As historian Barbara Ellen Smith noted, "The history of women's survival in the South is bound up with the history of agriculture, which remained the foundation of the region's economy until well into the present century." As the South has become more industrialized in recent decades, rural women as paid employees have become crucial to the region's economic development and to their family's survival.[2]

Yet rural southern women's vital role, especially in the latter part of the twentieth century, has not benefited from much historical attention. Thanks to re-

---

1. "Annie Perry," *Foxfire* 9 (1975): 149–62.
2. Barbara Ellen Smith, "Women in the South: Economic Survival," introduction to *Picking Up the Pieces: Women in and out of Work in the Rural South*, ed. Helen M. Lewis et al. (New Market, Tenn.: Highlander Research and Education Center, 1986), 4.

search on slave and plantation life, historians know a good deal about colonial, antebellum, and Civil War women in the South. Only a few studies on modern rural southern women have been published. Gaining an accurate understanding of these women is a challenge, in part because rural southern females are an extraordinarily varied lot. They include poor Appalachian women, Hispanic laborers in the Southwest; black and white farm women; rural, nonfarm residents; low-paid industrial workers; ranch wives and owners; and middle-class and wealthy landholders. Generalizing about them is difficult. Some engage in full-time or part-time farming; many are employed full-time outside the home. Others devote their lives to home and family and spend their free time in volunteer and church activities. Rural southern women's experiences extend well beyond farm life, especially in recent decades as the number of farms has declined and more women have entered the paid work force.[3]

Scholarly interest in rural southern women's lives has waxed and waned. Rural southerners fascinated writers and scholars during the Great Depression and New Deal. Scores of Fisk University students and Works Progress Administration (WPA) employees traveled throughout the region in the 1930s interviewing former slaves, ultimately creating extensive oral documentation of African Americans. James Agee and Walker Evans *(Let Us Now Praise Famous Men)*, Margaret Hagood *(Mothers of the South)*, and Ruth Allen *(The Labor of Women in the Production of Cotton)* studied southern rural families firsthand and offered important insights into women's lives. Throughout most of this century, Farm Extension and Home Demonstration programs under the United States Department of Agriculture (USDA) have shown great interest in rural women. Concern heightened in the 1960s with Lyndon Johnson's War on Poverty, when various scholars and experts examined numerous problems such as female education, health care, and employment.

A single essay cannot do justice to the richness and variety of these women's experiences over the past half-century. I will address here only a few critical issues: black and white women's struggles and the changes that have had the greatest impact on southern females. Much will have to remain for lengthier studies.[4]

A characteristic critical to an understanding of the South and its women is the region's dual identity. Amid modernization, the region has areas and populations that still seem unaffected by the outside world. Beyond high-rise office buildings, excellent academic institutions, and vast urban medical complexes sit thousands of mobile homes and cabins strung across rolling farmland and

3. Wava G. Haney, "Women," in *Rural Society in the United States: Issues for the 1980s,* ed. Don A. Dillman and Daryl J. Hobbs (Boulder, Colo.: Westview Press, 1982), 124–35; John W. Florin, "Varieties of Southern Women," *Southern Exposure* 4 (Winter 1977): 95–97.

4. Rural southern women include a wide variety of cultures and ethnic backgrounds. In this essay, I have chosen to focus on black and white women. To treat all southern women equally would make it impossible to stay within the confines of these pages.

shacks tucked away in mountain "hollers" where the region's most economically and educationally disadvantaged reside. Today, one can leave an interstate highway and soon be driving down a rural county road. Gone is most evidence of modernity; except for the asphalt road and overhead wires, one has returned to a space and time from decades past. A totally different life emerges from the image heralded by enthusiastic Sunbelt promoters.

Excited by the New South, its high-tech industries, and showcase cities like Atlanta and Houston, one can overlook the region's large rural population. The ever-changing South has major areas that evidence little or no growth; they fail to attract new industries, and they contain unskilled and poorly educated residents who see little hope that their lives will improve. The three areas of the South considered the most rural and impoverished today are the Mississippi Delta, the Black Belt of the Deep South, and Appalachia. Black and white women in these areas have faced decades of social and economic neglect, poor health, oppression, poverty, and limited job opportunities. Many families remain tied to a small parcel of land, some barely subsisting.

A few generalizations about modern, rural, southern women hold true despite their diversity. They tend to be poorer, less educated, and less healthy than women in other regions. Even today, many marry at a younger age and live in a more traditional family structure where they often are submissive to their husbands. Frequently, their lives are more difficult than those of urban women or rural women in other regions of the country. While the South has been modernizing and industrializing at a rapid pace, poverty remains disproportionately a rural, southern phenomenon; more than a fifth of rural southerners are poor. Many of those destitute are women and children; a high percentage of them are African American. In studying black women, Vera Foster noted that they usually have less of everything—less education, fewer job opportunities and health services, poorer housing and nutrition, and lower incomes. "The only thing they have more of is poverty," she states. Outsiders may find this poverty surprising, but, those who have never known otherwise rarely question such a life. Billie Parks Douglas of Kannapolis, North Carolina, commented that, as a child, she and her siblings slept three to a bed and often went to sleep hungry. She never realized that her happy family was poor until she learned about poverty on television. In her limited experience, her life was no different from that of her kin and neighbors.[5]

5. Vera C. Foster, "Mainstreaming Rural Black Women," in *Diversity in the Non-Farm Rural Population,* ed. Paul L. Wall (Tuskegee: Carver Research Foundation, Tuskegee Institute, 1981), 132–40; Victoria Byerly, *Hard Times Cotton Mill Girls: Personal Histories of Womanhood and Poverty in the South* (Ithaca, N.Y.: ILR Press, 1986), 96. For background on female poverty, see Southeast Women's Employment Coalition, *Women of the Rural South: Economic Status and Prospects* (Lexington, Ken.: SWEC, n.d.), 9–10; Thomas A. Lyson, *Two Sides to the Sunbelt: The Growing Divergence Between the Rural and Urban South* (New York: Praeger, 1989).

On the eve of World War II, poverty was widespread in the South. Although the Great Depression that began in 1929 is regarded as a significant historical event, in the minds of destitute southerners, this period seemed little different from what preceded it. As some noted, the Depression merely gave their poverty a name. In her history of African American women, Jacqueline Jones wrote that even in the 1940s and early 1950s, rural black women "lived in a world that their slave grandmothers would have recognized in its broad outlines." The same could be said of many white women. Outsiders, however, found such conditions startling. Ruth Holland, a British novelist who visited rural Arkansas in 1935, commented, "I have traveled over most of Europe and part of Africa, but I have never seen such terrible sights as I saw yesterday among the sharecroppers of Arkansas." The following year, Secretary of Agriculture Henry A. Wallace noted that the poverty in southern cotton states was far worse than any he had seen in Europe.[6]

On the eve of the nation's entry into World War II, a majority of rural southern families lived in conditions that some characterized as "deplorable." Margaret Hagood's study describes hardened piedmont farm women who bore numerous children, worked from sunup to sundown in field and home to ensure family survival, suffered poor health, often were illiterate, and saw little hope that their lives would improve. Year after year, southern tenant farmers and sharecroppers faced mounting debts. Destitute black and white farm families often moved from one shack to another, precluding any sense of permanence. One observer estimated that as many as 65 percent of South Carolina farm homes in 1942 were without running water. Dwellings might lack an interior ceiling, screens for doors, and glass panes for windows; gaping cracks were evident between the floorboards. Kitchens often had no sink; most southern farms in 1940 did not have electricity or phone service. Family members slept in the kitchen during wintertime because the wood stove offered the sole source of warmth. An outhouse might be situated near the front door or next to an uncovered well.[7]

Yet a few changes were evident. Historian Ruth Allen's examination of Texas women noted, for example, that by the late 1930s, cotton farm families began to feel the influence of the automobile, better roads, and the radio, and they welcomed more contact with the outside world. Public Works Administration (PWA) and WPA road-building projects throughout the South ended the isola-

---

6. Jacqueline Jones, *Labor of Love, Labor of Sorrow: Black Women, Work, and the Family from Slavery to the Present* (New York: Basic Books, 1985), 261; Ruth Holland, *The Forgotten Minority: America's Tenant Farmers and Migrant Workers* (New York: Crowell-Collier Press, 1970), 110.

7. Margaret Jarman Hagood, *Mothers of the South: Portraiture of the White Tenant Farm Woman* (1939; rpr. New York: Norton, 1977). These comments are from Home Demonstration Agent Annual Reports, 1940–45, Agricultural Extension Service Collection, Manuscript Department, Strom Thurmond Center Research Library, Clemson University, Clemson, S.C. (hereafter cited as Clemson).

tion of many communities. To those who had little, these improvements were significant.[8]

World War II had an enormous impact on the South. Many men served in the military or worked in defense plants during the war. Farm owners began to enjoy greater income as prices for food and animal feed rose to new highs. The war significantly affected the region's women as well. Many southern white women took relatively well-paying jobs in defense plants. Those who remained on the farm made a substantial contribution to the war effort. With fathers, husbands, and brothers often absent from home, women took charge of farm operations. Like their ancestors during the Civil War, southern women took over plowing, planting, harvesting, and marketing produce. They made critical decisions about what and when to plant and how to sell what they raised. Women devoted more time to canning and preserving what they grew to ensure that their families were well fed. Some southern women did double duty, working in a factory during the day and, with the help of young children, performing farm duties early in the morning and late into the evening.

Widespread concern about the nation's ability to produce enough food focused attention on the agrarian South. The shortage of male farmers was cause for worry and generated demands on rural women. Adequate output was crucial to the war effort and the country's future. Newspaper writers and war propagandists argued that the nation could not fight without enough food or fill the ranks of its armed forces without healthy men and women. Farm women had to produce more food for the home front, for America's allies, and for the millions of soldiers overseas. Farm women did their part by embracing a wartime motto, "The Home Is the First Line of Defense."

Work that farm women always had performed now held patriotic significance. Articles in farm journals encouraged women to prepare meatless meals, one-pot dishes for hardworking farm families, and sugarless desserts and jams. Advertisements promoted the theme "Food Is as Vital as Bullets." Local contests encouraged the canning and preserving of food. Writers urged mothers to use less cloth for sewing and ensure that family members ate healthy meals. Using patriotic themes, the press outlined the hazards that farm women might encounter each day, including inclement weather, farm and home accidents, and insects. A woman's work on the farm was as important—perhaps even as dangerous— as a soldier's on the front or a laborer's in a defense factory.[9]

One organization that played a major role in many black and white farm women's lives was the Home Demonstration Club, established in thousands of

---

8. Ruth Alice Allen, *The Labor of Women in the Production of Cotton* (New York: Arno Press, 1975).

9. For information on women's wartime issues, see the *Progressive Farmer,* 1941–45; Mary Elizabeth Johnson, ed., and Mary Jean Hardin, narr., *Times Down Home: 75 Years with the Progressive Farmer* (Birmingham, Ala.: Oxmoor House, 1978).

rural communities across the nation. These clubs (and some continue to be active) grew out of agricultural extension programs that sought to improve the lives of farmers and instruct them on improved farming techniques. Progressive reformers saw Home Demonstration projects as enhancing rural life by teaching farm women how to improve their homes and family and clothing. In the early twentieth century, Home Demonstration agents began to offer courses and develop creative projects to help farmers improve agricultural methods, and these soon expanded to meet women's needs. In 1914, Congress passed the Smith-Lever Act placing extension programs under the USDA, with experts funded by federal, state, and county governments. In southern states, the ideal was to have at least one white and one black female Home Demonstration agent in each county to serve their respective club members, though many counties refused to fund a black agent. These female representatives, who held degrees in home economics, organized Home Demonstration Clubs for women and Tomato (later 4-H) Clubs for girls. The extension program filled an obvious need in the rural South. For example, in 1952, nearly two-thirds of all the nation's Home Demonstration agents were southern.[10]

During World War II, these agents played an important role in rural women's lives by working tirelessly to encourage farm women to be self-sufficient, increase home production, and salvage and reuse materials. Broadening rural women's limited existence was another goal. Some clubs established reading programs; others studied works of art by the masters. County agents disseminated information on scores of topics, including gardening, home management and improvement, nutrition, food preservation, diet, clothing care, sewing, poultry production, family budgeting, and health issues.[11]

Home Demonstration agents promoted "Food for Victory" programs to increase farm production and urged every woman to join the "field artillery" as a "tractorette." Especially alarming to Negro agents was the fact that more than 40 percent of all black men in some states were physically unfit for military service. They blamed this condition, in part, on years of poor diet and unhealthy living conditions. Agents taught black farm wives how to serve nutritious meals using homegrown produce. They encouraged the planting of crops that the na-

10. Schools like Peabody College in Nashville offered special courses to instruct Home Demonstration agents. See Mary S. Hoffschwelle, "The Science of Domesticity: Home Economics at George Peabody College for Teachers, 1914–1939," *Journal of Southern History* 57 (November 1991): 658–80, and "Rebuilding the Rural Southern Community: Reformers, Schools and Homes in Tennessee, 1914–29" (Ph.D. dissertation, Vanderbilt University, 1993), 165–244. Approximately one-third of all female agents in North and South Carolina were black (author's survey of Home Demonstration agents reports, 1940–50, Clemson).

11. See Home Demonstration and Subject Specialist Annual Reports, 1940–55, Clemson. For another state's Home Demonstration activities, see Danny Blair Moore, " 'Window to the World': Educating Rural Women in Mississippi, 1911–1965" (Ph.D. dissertation, Mississippi State University, 1991).

tion could not import during the war. For instance, southern families living near fresh water could do their duty by growing rice. Other farm families were encouraged to plant more peanuts and incorporate that nutritious food in their diet. Agents urged rural southern women to grow enough food to meet 75 percent of their family's needs, thereby minimizing market purchases. Indeed, as a practical matter, gas rationing left most rural women with little choice but to plant crops and a garden, and raise meat for family consumption.

Southern women's patriotic endeavors extended beyond the kitchen. One South Carolina woman tore up her great-grandmother's handmade wool comforter to make nine sateen quilts to send to soldiers overseas. Black and white women and 4-H Club girls enrolled in Red Cross first aid classes to acquire basic nursing skills. They made bandages and wrote letters to soldiers overseas. Home Demonstration agents in Virginia showed women how to cut up a man's shirt and refashion it into children's clothing, how to use feed bags to make underwear and household linens, and how to fix and repair furniture and electric cords. Women exchanged labor with neighbors and participated in home canning contests.

The Agricultural Extension Service introduced several special projects to enhance rural families' lives. Home Demonstration agents began a cotton mattress program in the 1930s that extended into the early war years. Volunteer club members, with the assistance of mill owners, made hundreds of thousands of cotton mattresses for black and white southern families who had never slept on anything but straw or pine needles. Their goal was to put a decent mattress in every home, as well as make use of the region's surplus cotton. Individuals who qualified for a new mattress often commented that it was the first comfortable bed they had ever owned. One South Carolina woman was so thrilled with her soft mattress that she insisted that not even a visiting preacher could use it. She scrubbed her entire cabin before she brought her new mattress inside.[12]

A significant demographic change during World War II was the migration of southerners from the farm. Young women were part of this shift as they flocked to southern cities as well as to the Northeast and Midwest, where they found jobs in defense plants and factories now short of male workers. Southern parents worried about daughters who had never been exposed to urban life. Magazine articles advised young women to live only at the local Young Women's Christian Association (YWCA), join a church, read their Bible, keep a photograph of their parents beside their bed, and shun unwanted male advances. New military installations, airports, and defense industries located in the South also offered white men and women relatively well-paid, off-farm employment. Blacks and illiterate whites generally were excluded from all but the most menial of these jobs, though the influx of white employees and their families to southern mili-

---

12. Home Extension Annual Reports, 1939–42, Clemson; Moore, " 'Window to the World.' "

tary bases and factories increased demand for black female domestic workers to do their housecleaning and laundry.

For the first time in memory, rural families began to enjoy more disposable income, though wartime restrictions meant that few luxuries were available to purchase. By 1942, farm prices had risen significantly. Soldiers and men and women working in defense industries added to family income by sending a portion of their paychecks home. Southerners began to pay off debts, a growing number began to purchase land and, with the aid of federal loans, buy or build modest homes. Others saved their earnings and, after World War II, paid for an electrical hookup, a kitchen sink, appliances, or a new car. Overall, southern farm families found that their economic status improved during World War II, notwithstanding the necessary sacrifices.

The war brought unanticipated changes as well. The building of highways and roads into rural areas to serve military bases and defense plants ended some families' isolation. Observers noted that southerners appeared healthier by the end of the war, perhaps because they consumed more nutritious, homegrown foods than during the Depression. Worried about the nation's health, Home Demonstration agents offered southern mothers courses in prenatal and infant care—vital information on subjects about which many knew very little. Scrap collection programs undertaken by female 4-H Club and Home Demonstration Club members produced unforeseen benefits. Women by the hundreds periodically cleaned rural farmyards and roadsides and hauled recyclable materials to distribution centers. For instance, in Charleston County, South Carolina, workers collected some twenty-five tons of trash. Not only were the materials recycled for the war, but African American agents, who had been insisting for years that black families clean up their littered homesites, now saw tidier yards and a healthier, cleaner home environment.

In contrast to the cataclysmic events of the global conflict, social life on the rural home front during World War II was quiet. Families who owned battery-operated or electric radios gathered in their living rooms to listen to serials, news, and comedies. "That radio made you a citizen of the world," Fredda Davis, a North Carolinian, proudly recalled. During the war and after, southerners' favorite radio programs included *Amos 'n' Andy, Abbott and Costello, The Grand Ole Opry,* and *Dragnet.* Many women recalled hearing President Franklin D. Roosevelt's fireside chats, news reports by Lowell Thomas, and informative programs sponsored by the Agricultural Extension Service. Families played more games such as dominoes and Parcheesi and did crossword puzzles. Annual county and state fairs still were held, and farm wives and daughters spent weeks preparing canned goods, fattening up a hog or calf, or sewing an entire wardrobe from scrap material for the fair's "fashion revue." The church remained an important outlet for rural southerners; families enjoyed church socials, Bible class, Sunday school, and weekly church service. With grown children often working elsewhere and husbands away, farm women turned to neighbors and kin to counter their loneliness. Women gathered for quilting bees, picnics, and covered-dish suppers with friends and neighbors and shared gossip and family stories. They played baseball and basketball and held community sing-alongs. Many rural women, however, were overwhelmed by the demands of farmwork and had little free time on their hands.[13]

Following World War II, the nation's attention turned to an altered, more global, and less secure world. These concerns were evident even in the rural South. Change was inevitable as farming became mechanized and more industries moved south. Home Demonstration agents urged women to fight postwar inflation and supplement family income by participating in cooperative food markets and do more sewing and home decorating. Growing numbers of black and white farm women began to seek off-farm employment and learn how to juggle a paid job, family, and farm chores. Since many southerners now enjoyed more disposable income, agents taught women how to balance the family budget and purchase new appliances. Reflecting the South's shifting population, more urban and suburban women joined Home Demonstration Clubs. Sensitive to postwar issues, farm journals featured those mothers who created "democratic farm families" whose members enjoyed working and socializing together. Magazines brought Cold War concerns into farm homes by encouraging women to sew United Nations flags and advising them on how to protect their families against a nuclear attack.

Rural women who did not work outside the home found other means to supplement family income. Some turned to producing and selling homemade goods: fashioning Christmas wreaths, making aprons, canning jellies, baking favorite cakes and breads, growing fruits and vegetables, and sewing homemade quilts. Community and roadside markets became increasingly popular because of improved roads and more car travel, and southern women learned how to organize and run such cooperative ventures. They discovered that they could earn several hundred dollars a year—a few made as much as $2,000 annually—by selling items in local markets. Such contributions to family income often enabled children to attend college or take music lessons or made possible the purchase of a new car or appliance such as a freezer or water heater.

In the agrarian South, the family unit and the labor of each individual were central to farm production. Rural families engaged in farming tended to be more interdependent than their urban counterparts, in part because there was less differentiation between the workplace and the household. Rural families usually were larger, and marriage was a strong tradition. Rural southern women were more likely to marry and bear their first child at a younger age, give birth to more

13. Lorrie Constantinos and Kemp Ward, eds., *Living History: Were Those Really the Good Old Days?* (Raleigh: North Carolina Association of Electric Cooperatives, 1986), 33.

children, and be single parents than their urban counterparts or rural females elsewhere. A repeated theme in autobiographical and oral accounts is how young many rural women were when they married and bore their first child. Girls might begin bearing children when only fourteen or fifteen and eventually have eight or even a dozen children, spending thirty-five to forty years in bearing and rearing their offspring.[14]

That farm women worked alongside their husbands picking or chopping cotton and slaughtering pigs did not, however, enhance their power within the family. In fact, sociologists have found that in rural southern households, just the opposite was true even though many women preferred field to house work. A crop that needed harvesting had priority over domestic chores. Fathers or husbands directed farmwork, usually determined the division of family labor, sold the crops, and pocketed farm income. Such authority over economic production was also displayed in the home, where men often disciplined children and made most family decisions. Farm women and men may have been called interdependent, but usually they were not equal.[15]

Farm couples rarely considered it necessary to limit family size as long as children were an economic asset. Oral accounts reveal that many women came from large families. In recent years, however, the economic value of children has declined, in part because of the expense of raising children, stricter child labor and school attendance laws, the declining number of farms, and rural families' growing dependence on two adult incomes earned outside the home. Birth rates in the South have fallen as women's paid employment opportunities have risen. Women who wish to control their fertility now have better birth control information and more assured methods than in the past. Overall birth rates in the South, as in the rest of the nation, have declined throughout this century, and states such as Utah and New Mexico now have higher birth rates than southern states. But fertility remains high in certain areas of the region, including the Cajun sections of Louisiana and Mississippi, the Mississippi Delta, and eastern Kentucky.[16]

Though more rural women today have access to health clinics and medical professionals than they did a half-century ago, many southern women, especially poor teenagers, still have limited knowledge about birth control and do not know why or how they became pregnant. Aliene Walser from Thomasville,

14.   Susan Bentley and Carolyn Sachs, *Farm Women in the United States: An Updated Literature Review and Annotated Bibliography* (University Park: Pennsylvania State University, 1984), 9.

15.   Carolyn E. Sachs, *The Invisible Farmers: Women in Agricultural Production* (Totowa, N.J.: Rowan & Allanheld, 1983), 73; Jacqueline Jones, " 'Tore Up and a Movin': Perspectives on the Work of Black and Poor White Women in the Rural South, 1865–1940," in *Women and Farming: Changing Roles, Changing Structures,* ed. Wava G. Haney and Jane B. Knowles (Boulder, Colo.: Westview Press, 1988), 15–34, Hagood, *Mothers of the South,* 14, 89–91.

16.   Linda Jean Frankel, "Women, Paternalism, and Protest in a Southern Textile Community: Henderson, North Carolina, 1900–1960" (Ph.D. dissertation, Harvard University, 1986), 98.

North Carolina, who married at fourteen, bore her first child the following year and recalled that, at the time, she had no idea how to prevent conception. Country singer Loretta Lynn married at thirteen, had her first child the next year, and later commented that for several years she did not know how she became pregnant. Mothers mentioned having no knowledge of birth control, though they would have welcomed it had they known. What little information young women acquired concerning sexuality and childbirth often came from a friend or neighbor. In 1940, a frustrated childbirth expert called prenatal and maternal education in South Carolina "deplorable," declaring that her state's largest crop was its children. Birth control was, and still is, a topic that some rural women are reluctant to discuss publicly, perhaps because of religious beliefs or embarrassment. Experts who sought to expand knowledge of maternal issues found that women often avoided classes that discussed such information. Many rural females, both today and in the past, shy away from abortion on principle, but a desperate woman who becomes pregnant might perform a risky home abortion using sticks, knitting needles, quinine, or birth control pills rather than seeking professional medical help.[17]

As already mentioned, rural southern women married when relatively young. By the age of twenty-one, or even eighteen, an unmarried woman felt "like an old maid." Girls often saw little reason to further their education, and if a paid job was unavailable, the best way to achieve independence seemed to be marriage, much as their mothers had done. In oral interviews, some women justified their decision to marry early as a need to distance themselves from an abusive father, others regarded themselves as an economic burden to their family, and many wanted to strike out on their own. Marriage seemed the logical—and often the only—choice. Yet marriage often brought little independence. Aliene Walser married a boy who was only three years her senior, and the couple lived with his parents for years, long after they had children and finally could afford their own house.

Some rural southern women endured more difficulties becoming mothers than women in other regions of the country. Southern states had (and still have) startlingly high infant and maternal mortality rates, higher than those of most Western and industrialized nations. In part, these statistics reflect the fact that many women in the rural South lived in poverty, consumed a poor diet, and lacked adequate pre- and postnatal care. Even today, at least ten southern states annually report higher infant death rates than other states. Here, women give birth to more underweight or premature babies, and they are more at risk during childbirth than women in other areas of the country. For African American

17. Byerly, *Hard Times Cotton Mill Girls,* 79–80; Loretta Lynn with George Vecsey, *Loretta Lynn: Coal Miner's Daughter* (Chicago: Henry Regnery, 1976), 52; Alisa Rubin, "Throwing Babies," *New Republic* 207 (October 1992): 19–21; Marian B. Paul, "Negro Report," in Home Demonstration Agent Annual Reports, 1940, Clemson.

women and their babies, the risks are significantly higher. The infant mortality rate among rural black women in the South is double the national average. These women also are more likely to die in childbirth, and black infants are more likely to be sick because they are born into poverty.[18]

A major change in childbirth practices in the rural South during the last half-century concerned the choice of birth attendant. Rural southern women were long dependent on midwives. As recently as the late 1960s, many rural southern women, especially black women, bore their infants at home and relied on granny midwives (as whites called them) to deliver their babies. In 1930, 80 percent of the nation's midwives practiced in the South, where they delivered a quarter of all white babies and half of all black infants.[19]

More than tradition fostered southern mothers' dependence on midwives. Some women preferred a female attendant. Also, under Jim Crow laws that had existed since the late nineteenth century most health centers and hospitals in the South would not admit black women, and there were few black nurses, doctors, or hospitals to assist them. Cost was another factor. In the past, a poor mother might be able to pay a midwife nothing more than eggs or a chicken. Some midwives reported that truly destitute women never paid anything for their services, even though a midwife delivery cost as little as two to five dollars in the 1930s. Impoverished women also had no means to get to a health center; an assistant close at hand was essential. Midwives often performed additional services such as maternal and infant health care before and after delivery. Some remained with the new mother for several days after the birth to cook family meals and ensure that the mother was healthy and ate a nutritious diet. Experienced midwives often had an excellent reputation. One Florida midwife, Gladys Milton, covered six counties in her fourteen-year career, delivered seven hundred black and white babies, and claimed never to have lost a single newborn.[20]

After World War II, the number of lay midwives began to decline, and by the 1970s most had disappeared. For example, in 1917, North Carolina had some nine thousand midwives; by 1970, only fifty registered midwives remained in the state and, a decade later, only ten. One reason for the change was the civil rights movement and the end of Jim Crow laws, which, by the 1960s, led hospitals to integrate their health services. Black patients were now welcome, and more rural women, if they could afford it, took advantage of what was regarded as the modern, and therefore preferable, approach to childbearing. In addition, health pro-

18.   Carole H. Hill, *Community Health Systems in the Rural American South: Linking People and Policy* (Boulder, Colo.: Westview Press, 1988), 17, 88–89; Sandy Smith, "Baby Boycott," *Southern Exposure* 18 (Summer 1990): 28–31.

19.   Susan Smith, "White Nurses, Black Midwives, and Public Health in Mississippi, 1920–1950," *Nursing History Review* 2 (1994): 29–49.

20.   Pegge L. Bell, " 'Making Do' with the Midwife; Arkansas's Mamie O. Hale in the 1940s," *Nursing History Review* 1 (1993): 155–69.

fessionals and doctors began to insist that all obstetrical cases be in the hands of trained professionals. They investigated the causes for the region's high infant and maternal mortality and held lay midwives responsible. Perhaps dealing with far more complex causes such as widespread poverty, poor diet, and unsanitary conditions was too overwhelming; midwives proved an easier target.[21]

Southern states embarked on efforts to get rid of unskilled midwives and upgrade and certify those who remained. Health departments created training courses to improve women's skills and ensure sanitary procedures and the registering of each birth. For instance, Arkansas created a successful program by hiring a black nurse-midwife to conduct educational programs and certify the state's midwives. Eventually these efforts led to more competent midwives and a decline in infant mortality in that state.[22]

Some rural women today, especially those in the Black Belt and Appalachia, have no doctor or clinic within miles of their home. The uninsured must rush to an emergency room or clinic to deliver their babies. Appalachian women often receive little prenatal and postnatal care. They experience pregnancy with limited knowledge about proper diet and exercise and little preparation in caring for a newborn. Many are suspicious of federally sponsored classes on prenatal and postnatal care. Today, more rural women deliver their babies in an institutional setting, though the number of doctors serving rural communities is too few to meet demand. County health programs have tried to institute home visitation programs for pregnant women and nursing mothers, but these programs exist in isolation and cease when funding ends. One researcher estimates that several hundred lay women currently practice midwifery in the South but work underground to avoid prosecution.[23]

Diseases such as malaria and pellagra were endemic to the rural South earlier in this century but have now been eliminated. Malaria was worrisome until the 1950s, when DDT spraying killed carrier mosquitoes and the draining of swampy areas eliminated their breeding grounds. A diet rich in niacin eliminated pellagra. Home Demonstration agents encouraged mothers to pursue the surest

---

21. Sandy Smith, "Grannies and Granolas," *Southern Exposure* 18 (Summer 1990): 32–36; Ruth C. Schaffer, "The Health and Social Functions of Black Midwives on the Texas Brazos Bottom, 1920–1985," *Rural Sociology* 56 (Spring 1991): 89–105.

22. For a more detailed description of this statewide effort, see Holly F. Mathews, "Killing the Medical Self-Help Tradition Among African-Americans: The Case of Lay Midwifery in North Carolina, 1912–1983," in *African Americans in the South: Issues of Race, Class, and Gender,* ed. Hans A. Baer and Yvonne Jones (Athens: University of Georgia Press, 1992), 60–78; Bell, " 'Making Do,' " 166; Smith, "Grannies and Granolas," 33.

23. John Friedl, "Health Care: The City Versus the Migrant," in *Appalachia and America: Autonomy and Regional Dependence,* ed. Allen Batteau (Lexington: University Press of Kentucky, 1983), 189–209; Carrie Lee Gerringer, Oral Interview, 1977, Southern Oral History Program Collection, Southern Historical Collection, Wilson Library, University of North Carolina at Chapel Hill (hereafter cited as SHC), for comments on childbearing and doctoring her children.

path to good health for their family: preventive medicine. They provided guidelines for a healthy diet, clean bodies and clothing, and tidy homes. They urged better sanitary measures by covering wells and moving outhouses far from the house and water supply. Screens were essential to keep out bugs. Agents urged mothers to have their infants receive DPT shots and a tuberculin test in a county clinic.

Professional medical care and preventive medicine were not the only routes to good health. Rural women who had no doctor nearby or could not afford one often relied on their own skills. Many females, especially African American, Native American, and Appalachian women, also swore by herbal and folk remedies passed down through the generations. Female folk healers occupied an important position in rural communities. Elderly women in particular, who used and prescribed herbal cures, had extensive knowledge of native plants and over-the-counter preparations such as spirits of turpentine, camphor, oil of cloves, and asafoetida for health problems. Mothers often doctored their own children with home remedies, turning to a physician only if their children were really sick. Loretta Lynn's mother, who was half Cherokee, was the family healer, and she used herbal teas and medicines for her children's health problems. Catherine Waiters of Mars Bluff, South Carolina, employed home remedies on her twelve children, including snakeroot in whiskey for fever and sassafras root for measles.[24]

Rural mothers faced problems as their children matured. Poor southern mothers with paid jobs had no choice but to return to work as quickly as possible after delivery. Finding care for a newborn or young child was (and is) difficult for those who worked outside the home or lived in an isolated area. It was not unusual for mothers to leave infants and young children in the care of an older child or even leave them home alone. In the 1940s and 1950s, Negro Home Demonstration agents took a mother's daily absence from home as the norm and assumed that a brother or sister would care for younger siblings. Agents could do little more than teach mothers how to childproof a home and eliminate fire hazards. Civil rights activist Anne Moody, raised near Centreville, Mississippi, experienced just such care when little. Her eight-year-old uncle watched over her and her younger brother while her parents worked in the cotton fields. The boy had little desire to baby-sit and, at one point, abandoned the youngsters in the woods. Another time, because of his negligence the family cabin almost burned to the ground. Some mothers hauled their children to work with them by bringing them to the field or placing them in a convenient spot in the barn while they completed farm chores. A Missouri woman who drove a combine on the family farm let her babies sleep on the cabin floor. Mothers with no husband or relative

24. Gretchen Maclachlan, *The Other Twenty Percent: A Statistical Analysis of Poverty in the South* (Atlanta: Southern Regional Council, 1974), 40; Lynn, *Loretta Lynn*, 17–19; Amelia Wallace Vernon, *African Americans at Mars Bluff, South Carolina* (Baton Rouge: Louisiana State University Press, 1994), 56.

nearby might leave their children totally alone. Emma McCloud had to labor in the fields to feed her three children. In thinking back on her makeshift child care, she regretted that she had no choice but to leave her youngsters to fend for themselves. "I have shed enough tears to do a washing," McCloud recalled.[25]

In recent years, more rural mothers sent their infants to day care though facilities were, and are, inadequate. Welfare payments and food stamps enabled more women to stay at home with their children, but most of these families survived at or below the poverty level. In the rural South when family members lived nearby, a grandmother or aunt watched the youngsters and played a significant role in their upbringing. Eula McGill, an Alabama union leader, actually gave her son to her parents to raise. She loved him but felt that her higher duty was to assist fellow textile workers. Older African American women accepted it as a given that they would help raise their grandchildren. Yet children were not relinquished without regret and guilt. In oral interviews, rural mothers often commented that they wished they had spent more time with their children, but poverty and the need to work gave them little extra time or energy to devote to their offspring. Daughters also felt this absence. Mable Oxendine of Robeson County, North Carolina, commented that her mother "never did have too much time for us." Family survival was paramount, and mothers had no choice but to leave their children.[26]

Kin have always been important in the South, meeting needs far beyond simple child care. Immediate and extended family members often serve as a rural woman's most important source of community and emotional support, especially when friends and neighbors live far away. Observers have found close families common in Appalachia, which perhaps has changed less than other areas of the South. As recently as the 1960s, some outsiders described mountain families as "clannish and familial." Such closeness, however, can foster intrusiveness and also wear thin.[27]

Rural women have always worked at paid and unpaid jobs, performing household and farm chores from the time they were little. Young girls collected eggs, swept the yard and house, collected trash, twigs, and firewood, and hauled water. As they matured, they often did the cooking, ironing, and cleaning and watched younger siblings while their mother worked in the field or at a job out-

25.   Anne Moody, *Coming of Age in Mississippi* (New York: Dial Press, 1968), 11–12; Richard Rhodes, *Farm: A Year in the Life of an American Farmer* (New York: Simon and Schuster, 1989), 106–8; Pete Daniel, *Standing at the Crossroads: Southern Life Since 1900* (New York: Hill and Wang, 1986), 223.

26.   Eula McGill Oral Interview, 1974, Southern Oral History Program Collection, SHC; Mable Oxendine, "Mable's Story," in *Picking Up the Pieces: Women in and out of Work in the Rural South,* ed. Helen M. Lewis et al. (New Market, Tenn.: Highlander Research and Education Center, 1986), 15–16.

27.   James K. Crissman, *Death and Dying in Central Appalachia: Changing Attitudes and Practices* (Urbana: University of Illinois Press, 1994), 10–11.

side the home. Farm wives rose as early as 4:00 A.M. to prepare breakfast for their large families. They hoed, planted, and harvested; cleaned house; washed, ironed, and mended the family clothes; fed and cared for domesticated animals; milked cows; churned butter; raised vegetables and nurtured fruit trees; cooked, baked, and canned; picked berries; and sewed clothes for the entire family. Work was constant, from sunup to sundown.

Until the mid-1950s, the absence of electricity in many rural homes meant that these women lacked bright light and indoor running water as well as labor-saving devices such as washing machines and electric irons. While urban families enjoyed the benefits of electricity, even by World War II service had not yet reached many southern farms. For instance, only 15 percent of rural homes in Mississippi had electricity in 1939. This meant that every household task required an enormous amount of time and hard work. Farm women had to complete most chores before sunset. The Rural Electrification Administration began a major effort to install electric lines in the South during the 1930s, a process that continued for more than two decades. Only the disruption of World War II and the fact that many families could not afford a hookup to their homes or were unwilling to modernize hindered the effort.

Oral interviews show that electrification had an unforgettable effect on rural southern women who vividly recalled the exact moment when their homes received electricity. They mentioned how bright their houses suddenly became. One mother noted that lights revealed the dinginess of her kitchen walls, and she immediately scrubbed the entire room. Others described standing in a kitchen or hallway during the first few days with electricity and repeatedly turning the light switches on and off. Electricity had a positive effect on schoolwork, as youngsters who had once crowded around a single kerosene lamp could now study long after the sun had set. Women also were freed from the daily task of cleaning the soot from the glass globes in kerosene and oil lamps.[28]

Electricity brought not only brighter light but, for those who could afford them, modern appliances that lessened the drudgery of women's chores. Homes now could have an electric pump to bring running water inside rather than hauling the water into the house from outside. Barns could be lighted so that chores could be accomplished even at night. A freezer allowed women to preserve foods without the arduous tasks of canning, drying, or salting them. Instead of an ice-box—which required regular ice delivery—or putting fresh milk and butter into the well to keep cool, rural families might purchase a refrigerator. Women could store food, eliminating the tasks of milking the cow twice daily or constantly harvesting fruits and garden vegetables. Women, especially those with paid jobs outside the home, spent less time and energy on their chores. Yet not all found

---

28. For women's reactions to electrification, see Constantinos and Ward, *Living History;* Oral Histories of the Southern Oral History Program Collection, SHC.

modernity totally beneficial. A realistic Lena Boyce observed that despite her labor-saving devices, "it seems that other work comes to take the place; you stay just as busy."[29]

Before a family owned a washing machine, weekly laundering was a woman's most exhausting, time-consuming chore. In nice weather, washing was done out of doors near a spring, a well, or a river, or under a shady tree. Water had to be hauled to the site, poured into a huge iron pot, and heated over a fire or wood or coal stove. As recently as the 1950s, some farm women routinely made their own soap from lard and ashes. Every article of dirty clothing was scrubbed on a wash-board, rinsed several times, wrung by hand, and hung to dry outside. Mothers with large families found laundering especially exhausting. One Virginia woman recalled that, as a child, she had to stay home from school one day each week to help her mother do the wash. Farm women remember with great happiness the day they finally acquired a wringer washer. Mrs. W. D. Elliott called her electric washer "one of the greatest woman-savers ever been invented."[30]

Maintenance of clothing did not end with laundering. Though less physically demanding, ironing consumed several hours each week. In the past, a heavy iron was heated atop a stove and used until it cooled; the process then was repeated. Old habits die hard. One woman was so accustomed to this procedure that when she first used her electric iron, she unplugged it each time it had heated, ironed clothes until it cooled, and then plugged it in again to reheat.

Some rural women continued to use wood stoves for cooking and baking despite modern gas and electric appliances. They insisted that the food tasted better and that baking was more accurate. Women made good use of their stoves, not only for heating an iron but also for heating water. Families without running hot water inside their homes kept a large bucket of water beside the stove, which gradually warmed for nightly washing and weekly bathing.

Sewing and mending clothes were never-ending tasks, though after World War II, southerners began to purchase more store-bought clothes. Improved roads made it easier for rural residents to get to town to shop, and families with more disposable income could afford such items. Nonetheless, Home Demonstration agents noted that during the 1950s, home sewing actually rose in popularity, in part because a larger selection of material and patterns was available. Home sewing also became the celebrated duty of ideal motherhood, an image

29. Lena Boyce, Oral Interview, 1984, Southern Oral History Program Collection, SHC. For comments on women's domestic work and the changes resulting from new labor-saving devices, see Ruth Schwartz Cowan, *More Work for Mother: The Ironies of Household Technology from the Open Hearth to the Microwave* (New York: Basic Books, 1983).

30. Nancy Robinson, "Nancy's Story," in *Picking Up the Pieces: Women in and out of Work in the Rural South*, ed. Helen M. Lewis et al. (New Market, Tenn.: Highlander Research and Education Center, 1986), 26–28; Mrs. W. D. Elliott, Oral Interview, n.d., Southern Oral History Program Collection, SHC.

heralded throughout this decade. Not all women sewed, however, for many families could not afford a sewing machine. These mothers had no choice but to purchase inexpensive clothing for their children or depend on hand-me-downs and secondhand goods. In some counties, Home Demonstration agents tackled this problem by purchasing used sewing machines and establishing county sewing clinics. Yet the impoverished never benefited from such opportunities and made do with whatever was on hand. One mother found that she could not clothe her children when fertilizer prices rose because she had used the burlap fertilizer bags for her family's clothing. Rural women once spent hours patching and mending family apparel and darning socks. These tasks have gone the way of many chores, and today, women often dispose of tattered items or purchase replacements.[31]

Buying new shoes was a luxury that many poor families could not afford. Going barefoot as a child was not unusual in the rural South. When young, civil rights activist Fannie Lou Hamer and her siblings went barefoot in the summer and wrapped their feet in rags during the winter. Children might not attend school or church because they had no shoes. A common sight along country roads was black family members carrying their shoes as they walked to church. They did this not only to preserve precious leather but because the shoes usually were ill-fitting. Stores in the South rarely allowed blacks to try on a pair they wished to purchase.

Rural southern families spent a good deal of time out of doors, and the yard and porch became an important area for family socializing and relaxing. Women had responsibility for maintaining the yard, and with special long-bristled brooms they swept (or "ironed") their hard-packed dirt. In the 1950s, Home Demonstration agents began to encourage southern families to plant grass so as to bathe counties in a sea of green and get rid of "ugly, bare yards." This campaign met resistance, at least in South Carolina, for many families preferred low-maintenance dirt or sand and enjoyed its tidiness. Farm women also took pride in their gardens and spent a good deal of time tending fresh vegetables.[32]

Women worked hard; as Annie Perry stated simply, "We worked all the time." Southern rural females had multiple responsibilities both in the field and in the home. Young mothers who had to juggle many duties sometimes carried their babies to the field so they could breast-feed and tend them as they farmed and, at noontime, rush home to prepare dinner for the entire family. "There was always something needing to be done. *Always*," commented Mrs. Elliott.[33]

31. For a discussion of women's domestic chores in the past, see Susan Jonas and Marilyn Nissenson, *Going, Going, Gone: Vanishing Americana* (San Francisco: Chronicle Books, 1994).

32. Richard Westmacott, *African-American Gardens and Yards in the Rural South* (Knoxville: University of Tennessee Press, 1992), 80.

33. Sarah Elbert, "The Farmer Takes a Wife: Women in America's Farming Families," in *Women, Households, and the Economy,* ed. Lourdes Beneria and Catharine R. Stimpson (New

By following the lead of their hardworking mothers, rural girls from early childhood learned that work and hardship were the norm. In numerous oral interviews, younger women mentioned their mothers' amazing strength and the unspoken lessons they absorbed by watching them hold the family together. Elaine Tiller Duty of Cane Creek, North Carolina, described her mother as "almost a slave." Like her own mother, Anne Moody began cleaning houses when she was only nine years old, and she continued to work throughout high school and college. Emma McCloud labored endlessly to ensure her children's survival. "This life has been kindly rugged here," she said in looking back. "I have never seen too much happiness. My road has been pretty bumpy."[34]

Conditions in Appalachia created a group of tough, worn women. As Eula Hall commented, "I don't think that in Appalachia there's anything worse than being a woman." Mothers raised their children, survived on little money, were without electricity and running water until recent decades, and often handled the men in their family who were depressed and upset by low-paying, dangerous, or otherwise exploitative work. If a husband or father was disabled by hazardous work conditions, a woman probably was the one to take care of him. Men overwhelmed by their bleak existence and lack of economic opportunity too often turned to alcohol and took out their frustrations on their wives and children. Women's recollections indicate that heavy drinking and physical abuse were, and are, common in this part of the world.[35]

One Appalachian woman hardened by life is Darlene Leache, who grew up in an extremely poor Tennessee family. Sometimes her family had no food, and the children gathered polk salad, which her mother fried for breakfast. Her father abandoned the family when she was thirteen. Leache quit school in the eighth grade because she had no shoes or decent clothes, and she married to ease her family's situation. She soon discovered that her husband was an alcoholic; he drank constantly for the next thirteen to fourteen years. He was unable to hold a job and beat her constantly, so severely that once she was hospitalized for a blood clot. Another time, she and her children spent the night in jail to escape his wrath. In his desperation for alcohol, he would steal the money she earned. He resented the birth of each of their six children but refused to let Leache use birth control pills. She worked constantly—waitressing in restaurants, picking blueberries to buy baby clothes, hauling wood and coal—whatever it took to keep

Brunswick, N.J.: Rutgers University Press, 1987), 173–95; Ann Sutton, "Annie's Story," in *Picking Up the Pieces: Women in and out of Work in the Rural South,* ed. Helen M. Lewis et al. (New Market, Tenn.: Highlander Research and Education Center, 1986), 19; Mrs. W. D. Elliott, interview.

34. Elaine Tiller Duty, Oral Interview, 1976, Southern Oral History Program Collection, SHC; Daniel, *Standing at the Crossroads,* 223.

35. Eula Hall interviewed by Dorothy Hall Peddle, "To Do What's Right," *Southern Exposure* 11 (March–April 1983): 39–42; Jeanne Kennedy, "Justice Denied," *Southern Exposure* 20 (Winter 1992): 39–42.

the family alive. Sometimes she held two jobs, laboring seven days a week for nine hours a day. At one desperate point, she sold their television set and car for money to feed her children. The tiny home she purchased was destroyed by a flood. Yet Leache found strength in her deep love for her children and from her grandmother, who finally convinced her to divorce her abusive husband. She also found help from a nun who ran the local Crazy Quilt Community Center. Here, Leache gained a sense of self-worth, earning her high school equivalency diploma, and got a job managing the center's accounts.[36]

Appalachian women have witnessed startling changes in their formerly quiet mountain life. In the 1930s and 1940s, the outside world began to encroach on mountain communities. Federal and state governments began to build roads, dam rivers, and construct new schools. With the growing demand for coal and timber during World War II, mining and lumber companies flocked to the region. They purchased land as cheaply as possible and proceeded to denude and exploit the mountains. Some areas and communities changed forever.[37]

One mountain woman who dealt with such change was Becky Simpson, who grew up on Cranks Creek, Kentucky, in a family that was "as poor as you can get." Her mother never attended school but worked hard and found strength in her deep belief in God. Becky quit school after the third grade, and when she was fourteen, she and her brothers sold coal and hauled anything that needed moving. In 1953, her father was disabled, so she and her twin brother started cutting timber. Strip mining came to the area and destroyed their farmland. Her family released all its cows, hogs, and chickens because it could not feed them. Their topsoil washed away during a flood, making farming impossible. Runoff from mining polluted their drinking water, and the farm became unlivable. Becky married in 1956 and moved off the farm. In 1962, her husband lost his eyesight, leaving her as the sole provider for him and their six children. In the 1970s, when mining companies once again destroyed their land, Becky reached her limit. She organized the local community to demand compensation and reclamation from the mining company. The community finally won its case and received a financial settlement, though no one could ever regain the land and way of life that had been lost.[38]

In addition to work and family, the church has always been an important institution for rural women, who traditionally have made up the majority of its members. Conservative, fundamentalist churches, especially in southern mountain regions, appeal to a good number of rural women. Many women find per-

---

36. Darlene Leache, Oral Interview, 1980, Southwest Research Institute for Research on Women, Oral Histories of Low Income and Minority Women, 1970–92, SHC.

37. Phillip Moffitt, "The Power of One Woman," *Esquire,* January 1985, 11–12.

38. Becky Simpson, "Becky's Story," in *Picking Up the Pieces: Women in and out of Work in the Rural South,* ed. Helen M. Lewis et al. (New Market, Tenn.: Highlander Research and Education Center, 1986), 9–10.

sonal strength and a sense of community by regularly attending church and Bible classes. Quiet moments for reflection or reading favorite biblical passages offer comfort to deal with life's difficulties. Revivals and camp meetings also provide meaningful moments for spiritual renewal. Women often hold God responsible for their fate and feel that their deep faith will help them confront life's difficulties. As Mrs. Wright, member of a Free Will Baptist Church, commented, "I love the Lord. He's taken me through thick and thin."[39]

Although the sense of community and shared activities, often developed through church attendance, are so important to women, some rural women lived in isolation most of their lives. Loretta Lynn described her family's cabin in Butcher Holler, Kentucky ("the most backward part of the United States," she said), as situated far from everything, accessible only by a dirt road and narrow path. During severe snowstorms, the family could be isolated for weeks. Many of her relatives never ventured more than ten miles beyond home. For entertainment, Lynn and her siblings rode ten miles to a mining camp to see a movie once a month. It was here that she first saw Christmas lights decorating the community. She saw her first flush toilet just before she married.[40]

Of course, a good number of rural southern women were not, and are not, impoverished, desperate, or lonely but enjoyed a middle- or upper-class lifestyle. Since farming was the predominant livelihood in the South until recent years, southerners of all backgrounds earned their living off the land. Some families earned a good income; others did extremely well and owned extensive acreage for growing tobacco, cotton, wheat, peaches, sugarcane, or marijuana, or, in the Southwest, the raising of horses and cattle. Well-to-do families owned several hundred acres of land and had tenant farm families or paid laborers to assist them. Wealthy Texas ranchers count their acres in the thousands; beautiful horse farms in Virginia, Kentucky, and Tennessee occupy extensive and valuable land. Most of these privileged women were, and are, the wives of successful farmers or ranchers, though a small percentage owned and managed property on their own. Because they could afford household help and modern appliances, their daily lives were far easier than those of the majority of tenant farm wives, factory workers, and Appalachian women. A task many often remember was being responsible for the daily needs of their tenants and maid, including giving their help leftover scraps and the family's used clothing, finding medical care if needed, and perhaps even paying the doctor's bills.

It was to these middle-class and well-to-do rural women that the *Progressive Farmer* was addressed. This popular southern farm journal, published in Birmingham, Alabama, printed separate editions for different areas of the South. Its

39. Bruce Roberts and Nancy Roberts, *Where Time Stood Still: A Portrait of Appalachia* (New York: Crowell-Collier Press, 1970), 26.
40. Lynn, *Loretta Lynn*, 1.

substantial "Home Department," later an entire section called "The Progressive Home," had its own female editor who focused on the concerns of white farm women. Illustrated monthly features included recipes; tips for sewing, quilting, and preserving; the annual selection of southern women of the year; advice on health and beauty; home management information; and descriptions of Home Demonstration projects. The editor sought not only to dispense information but to make homemakers feel comfortable with their duties and celebrate their domestic and farming capabilities. The magazine also presented the Master Farmer and his family, who epitomized the values most prized by rural southerners. Families periodically chosen for this honor by state Farm Extension programs were carefully screened and received special attention in the women's section. For instance, the J. Calvin Rivers family of Chesterfield, South Carolina, represented the ideal in November 1956. Elizabeth Rivers was a happy farm wife, raising five children, encouraging their pursuit of music, teaching Sunday school, and creating a home life that exuded "serenity and well being."[41]

Women's contributions to farm production often have been invisible because for decades the Census of Agriculture included only one respondent (invariably, census takers chose the male) for each farm. Such information usually overlooked women who worked alongside a father or husband. Historians are beginning to examine the female experience more carefully and to study farming from women's perspective. The most significant change that has affected modern farm women is the decline in the number of farms in the South after World War II as a result of mechanization, overseas competition, government price supports, and economies of scale that benefited large farmers. Mechanical cotton pickers, tractors, and combines began to render human labor less essential, especially the contributions of women.[42]

Until recent decades, the majority of rural southern women actively participated in farmwork. The smaller the farm, the more likely a woman was to help and the more essential was her involvement. Sharecropping and tenant farming often demanded an entire family's participation. Gender had little meaning when it came to completing essential chores. Wives usually did the bookkeeping and bill paying because they often were better educated than their husbands. Rural women described themselves as doing "a man's work" on the farm, able to handle nearly every chore that a male performed. Irene Nixon of Lee County, Georgia, labored as a field hand on the same farm for decades. Her father had

41. Information from issues of the *Progressive Farmer*, 1940–65; Johnson and Hardin, introduction to *Times Down Home*.

42. Elbert, "The Farmer Takes a Wife," 173–95; Rachel Ann Rosenfeld, *Farm Women: Work, Farm, and Family in the United States* (Chapel Hill: University of North Carolina Press, 1985); Marshall R. Colberg, *Human Capital in Southern Development, 1939–1963* (Chapel Hill: University of North Carolina Press, 1965), 9–11; Max J. Pfeffer and Jess Gilbert, "Gender and Off-Farm Employment in Two Farming Systems," *Sociology Quarterly* 32 (Winter 1991): 593–610.

been a sharecropper; as a child she worked six days a week and was accustomed to constant labor. This tiny woman hauled her firewood, raised vegetables, and kept her own house, in addition to her many farming duties. A Kentucky woman, Mabel Scott, worked her fourteen-acre farm and sharecropped an additional two hundred acres. Her husband, who hated farming, taught school and returned home only once a month. She raised tobacco and hay with the help of their three children. Scott never owned a tractor but plowed the land with a team of horses. Like Scott, southern women were more likely to own or farm their own land than women nationwide. According to the 1978 Census of Agriculture, 53 percent of all female-operated farms were in sixteen southern states. Many of these female farmers tended to be older, often African American women, and possessed fewer acres than did male farmers.[43]

With the overall decline of farming in the South and greater availability of paid jobs, the number of rural residents has decreased. For instance, according to the federal census, those people identified as rural in 1940 included 80.2 percent of all Mississippi residents, 75.5 percent of South Carolinians, 72.7 percent of those in North Carolina, 69.8 percent in Alabama, and 70.2 percent of Kentucky residents. By contrast, 1980 census figures indicated that 53 percent of the population in Mississippi was rural, 45.9 percent of the residents of South Carolina, 52 percent of those in North Carolina, 40 percent in Alabama, and 49.1 percent in Kentucky. Texas had only a 20.4 percent rural population in 1980. The southern population was 63 percent rural in 1940 and only 33 percent rural in 1980. Women were partially responsible for this change as they left home to seek paid jobs and perhaps a more exciting life. As Mary Harrington noted, she and her sisters moved off the family's Virginia farm as teenagers to find work. "We just ventured out because we didn't have a lot to do out in the country," she remarked.[44]

Women's farm chores have altered with the decline in farming. For instance, women traditionally were in charge of poultry production, slaughtering, and cleaning, and they preserved meat for family consumption or sale. While south-

43. Sherry Thomas, *We Didn't Have Much, But We Sure Had Plenty: Stories of Rural Women* (Garden City, N.Y.: Anchor Press/Doubleday, 1981), 3–5; Sachs, *Invisible Farmers*, 106; Judith Z. Kalbacher, *A Profile of Female Farmers in America* (Washington, D.C.: U.S. Department of Agriculture, Economic Development Division, Economic Research Service, 1985), v, 2, 10; Rosenfeld, *Farm Women*, 10–11, 25; C. Milton Coughenour and Louis Simpson, "Work Statuses and Occupations of Men and Women in Farm Families and the Structure of Farms," *Rural Sociology* 48 (Spring 1983): 23–43; William H. Friedland, "Women and Agriculture," in *Toward a New Political Economy of Agriculture*, ed. William H. Friedland, Lawrence Busch, Frederick H. Buttel, and Alan P. Rudy (Boulder, Colo.: Westview Press, 1991), 319–20.

44. Mary Estelle and Edward Harrington, Oral Interview, 1979, Southern Oral History Program Collection, SHC. For statistics, see U.S. Department of Commerce, Bureau of the Census, *1980 Census of Population: Characteristics of the Population, Number of Inhabitants, United States Summary* (Washington, D.C.: U.S. Government Printing Office, 1983), 55–56.

erners still raise pigs, turkeys, and chickens, meat production and meat processing have become agribusinesses, conducted in factories on a huge scale, with mass feeding and slaughtering and the employment of thousands of workers. Women once milked the cows and churned butter. Now they easily can purchase both milk and butter at the market.[45]

It is not merely economy of scale and mechanization that have affected female labor. Today's global economy and federal farm policies have an impact on female farmworkers. For instance, in one Florida county, the collapse of shade tobacco in the 1970s created a crisis for female field hands who harvested the crop. Demand declined because of the production of synthetic cigar wrappers and a growing preference for imported cigars; these Florida women lost their jobs. In one area of the North Carolina piedmont, women's farm employment declined by more than half between 1970 and 1980 as a result of federal tobacco support programs that encouraged larger farms and mechanized harvesting and curing operations. Mechanization, which usually demanded physical strength to run heavy farm equipment, displaced more female than male farm laborers.

Not all is bleak in southern farming. Some farmers survive and do well, especially if a spouse is employed elsewhere or is a major participant in the farm operation. One successful Missouri farm family demonstrates the advantages of a married couple's equal participation. They have farmed their 337 acres of extremely rich land for more than two decades. In 1980, their net worth was $450,000, and they enjoyed annual profits of $20,000. The wife learned to run the combine and did all the family laundry, mowed the lawn, drove trucks back and forth to storage bins and elevators, hauled animal feed, kept the farm account books, and paid the bills. When her husband was incapacitated by surgery, she ran the farm with the help of a neighbor. An observer commented that they make an incredible team.[46]

Although the South has a strong agrarian tradition, the region has become far more industrialized in recent years. Rural women today are more likely to have paid jobs outside the home than to work on a farm. The shift from farm to factory work began with World War II as southern farms mechanized and industries demanded workers.

For more than a century, the region has attracted a large number of low-wage industries that traditionally have hired women. Historically, the region's chief source of paid labor was rural women and children who were the first generation of mill workers in the late nineteenth century. More than a century ago, textile industries moved to the South to get closer to the raw product and take advantage of cheap labor and minimal union conflict. Rural poverty, the decline of

45. Barbara Goldoftas, "Inside the Slaughterhouse," *Southern Exposure* 17 (Summer 1989): 25–29.

46. For an account of this family farm operation, see Rhodes, *Farm,* 18–20, 105–9. Rhodes spent a year living with this family and observing their experiences.

farming, and the lack of alternatives in the region provided a ready labor force. Companies that went south were primarily engaged in textiles, apparel manufacturing, food processing, mining, and furniture making. In recent decades, state governments have welcomed their presence and actively competed for national and international corporations.[47]

With the decline in farming and growth in industrial production, rural women replaced their farm labor with "public work"—that is, paid employment in a factory, business, or service industry. Southern women, both single and married, have always worked outside the home in greater proportion than women outside the region. This is true today as well, for the South is a region where the majority of rural residents depend on off-farm jobs. Nearly two-thirds of all textile and apparel workers in the South are women, and 58 percent of them reside in rural areas. Though women no longer predominate as industrial workers, they still are a significant portion of the South's paid laborers. According to a recent *Atlantic Monthly* article, one of the nation's two largest clusters of working mothers today lives in the Southeast. Women's high labor force participation varies and depends on the availability of jobs. In some areas of the South, these are plentiful.[48]

North Carolina has become the most industrialized state in the region. It also has the greatest percentage of women in the work force, the largest percentage of married women working, and the greatest percentage of working mothers with children under six years old. While feminists might celebrate such statistics, the data do not reflect major advances for rural women. North Carolina females are not necessarily more enlightened or more demanding of equity with men. Rather, these figures reflect the fact that so many industries have moved to that state and need workers. In general, where jobs are available, women will take advantage of them. Most of those who work in factories or service jobs do so out of need rather than self-fulfillment. The low salaries women earn often do not put them above the poverty level.[49]

Women's attitudes toward factory work depend on their particular job assignment, factory conditions and salary, and the management style of a supervisor. Rural women with few employment options and a family to support have lit-

47. Jerry R. Skees and Louis E. Swanson, "Farm Structure and Rural Well-Being in the South," in *Agriculture and Community Change in the United States: The Congressional Research Reports,* ed. Louis E. Swanson (Boulder, Colo.: Westview Press, 1988), 238–317; James L. Walker, *Economic Development and Black Employment in the Nonmetropolitan South* (Austin: Center for the Study of Human Resoures, University of Texas Press, 1977).

48. Shelley Louise Pendleton, "Women's Employment in Rural Environments: A Case Study of North Carolina" (Ph.D. dissertation, University of North Carolina, 1984), 10; President's National Advisory Commission on Rural Poverty, *Rural Poverty in the United States* (Washington, D.C.: U.S. Government Printing Office, 1968), 19; Roger Doyle, "At Last Count: Mothers and Jobs," *Atlantic Monthly* 271 (May 1993): 69.

49. Southeast Women's Employment Coalition, *Women of the Rural South,* 24–25.

tle choice about what particular job they perform. Many women found their first job through personal contact, usually a friend or family member. As Barbara Britt of Gilead, North Carolina, commented on her ease in finding textile work, "I think lots of it had to do with having kin there, I really do." Rural women who entered factory work enjoyed the gossip and camaraderie that developed with their co-workers and felt pride in bringing home a paycheck.[50]

Oral accounts and research show that female factory employees found work conditions worsening after World War II, a trend that had begun at least a generation earlier. Management introduced efficient cost-cutting methods, and supervisors pressured employees to work more rapidly. Bosses insisted on new techniques to streamline production and increase profits. The work environment became more impersonal. Workers sensed that they counted for little, unlike earlier years when employees often knew the factory owner and felt that they were part of a family.[51]

Despite the benefits of a regular paycheck and the chance to leave a lonely farm, public work has its downside. Women who enjoyed farming duties complained that factory work was tedious, demanding, stifling, and unhealthy. Families engaged in textile work and mining often lived in factory-owned villages that fostered a sense of community but also stigmatized those who lived there. Mill families were often called "lintheads" and "cotton mill trash." Few female factory employees in the past completed high school because a job was more important to their family than an education. Female workers today are better educated because state laws require that they stay in school until a certain age, and laws establish a minimum age for employment as well. Southern women receive some of the lowest manufacturing wages in the country. For a family to have a decent income and raise young children today, a wife and husband may work different factory shifts. Until recently, there were limits to how far a black or white woman could advance in a company, for supervisory positions were reserved for white men, who earned higher wages and obviously enjoyed better working conditions. Today this has changed, though top management remains predominantly male and white.

Like farmworkers, female employees have always faced a fluctuating, uncertain marketplace as well as hazardous working conditions, exploitation, and harassment. Typical of an unsafe work environment was the Hamlet, North Carolina, chicken processing plant where, in December 1991, a fire broke out and killed scores of workers because management locked fire doors to prevent theft. Oral interviews revealed the prevalence of sexual harassment. Textile workers

---

50. Barbara Britt, Oral Interview, 1977, Southern Oral History Program Collection, SHC.
51. For a discussion of women and textile work in the early twentieth century and this sense of change in the workplace, see Jacquelyn Dowd Hall et al., *Like a Family: The Making of a Southern Cotton Mill World* (Chapel Hill: University of North Carolina Press, 1987), which argues that these changes began during World War I. See also Frankel, "Women, Paternalism, and Protest," 80.

commented that supervisors rewarded female employees with a promotion and raise if they "dated" them. Poor women who often had little choice about a job endured both dangerous and low-paid work. Global markets also affect female workers. For instance, in the 1980s, southern textile companies began to face significant competition from foreign mills that produced yarn, fabrics, and clothing cheaper than American companies. In the mid-1980s, 43 percent of all clothing sold in this country was produced abroad. Southern mills today also face competition at home from the scores of urban sweatshops that hire immigrants who are virtually enslaved. This foreign and domestic competition has forced some southern plants to close, others to cut back positions and fire workers. Automation has also closed less productive factories, thereby eliminating jobs. Today, computers and robots, rather than humans, oversee much of the production in these industries. Such sophisticated technology demands a better-educated work force. Women, who constitute two-thirds of all textile employees, have felt the brunt of these changes through layoffs and lost jobs.[52]

Factory jobs also foster chronic health problems and physical disabilities, and women, especially single mothers, often cannot afford health insurance premiums to obtain medical assistance. Until recently, management has often ignored these concerns and resisted government regulations to control the work environment and ensure worker safety. The most widespread health problem in textile mills has been brown lung disease (byssinosis), acquired by breathing lint dust for years. Afflicted workers struggle with breathing problems and pulmonary disease. The deafening noise from machines causes hearing loss. Female workers in furniture manufacturing and meat processing plants performed repetitive tasks that caused severe tendon disorders. For instance, Donna Bazemore became incapacitated by her working conditions in a chicken processing plant. Living in an area of rural North Carolina where job opportunities were scarce, she felt fortunate to have paid work. Conveyor belts moved chicken carcasses at rapid speed; the work was tiring, filthy, smelly, and repetitive. Like other poultry workers, Bazemore developed pain in her hands, but the company ignored her complaints. Instead, a nurse distributed Advil and bandaged employees hands each morning so they could perform their jobs. Such conditions left many employees crippled with carpal tunnel syndrome.[53]

Race is a factor in paid employment in the South, though its significance has declined over the past fifty years. In the past, when northern industries relocated to the South, most avoided areas where large numbers of people needed jobs. Instead, corporations preferred a white, better-educated, more highly skilled group of workers than they felt could be found in the Mississippi Delta, eastern

52. Colberg, *Human Capital*, 11–12; Mary McNamara, "Drastic Changes for Rural Wage Earners," *Ms.* 15 (August 1986): 30; Frankel, "Women, Paternalism, and Protest," 110.

53. Eric Bates, "The Kill Line," *Southern Exposure* 19 (Fall 1991): 22–29; Bob Hill, "I Feel What Women Feel," *Southern Exposure* 17 (Summer 1989): 30–33.

Kentucky, or southern Alabama. Some scholars conclude that factory owners avoided areas where they would compete for farm laborers. Many industries did not wish to hire black workers except for low-paid, undesirable work such as janitorial and cleaning positions, grubby jobs in tobacco plants, jobs with exposure to hazardous or unhealthy materials, or as scabs during a strike. Textile mills did not drop the color bar until the early 1960s, when they faced a labor shortage and pressure from civil rights activists. Yet even today in the rural South, black women often seem invisible as they struggle to hold on to a home and job and raise their children.

Until the 1960s, the majority of southern black women employed outside the home worked as domestic laborers—as maids, cooks, laundresses, and child minders. As long as Jim Crow laws and widespread racism existed in the South, domestic labor was often the only option (aside from farmwork) available to black women. Until factories ended white-only hiring practices in the 1960s, some 45 percent of all wage-earning black women in the South were domestic servants. For instance, in South Carolina in the early 1960s, 48 percent of all black female workers were household employees, but by 1970, only 28 percent worked in service and household labor. White families needed domestic help, and extremely low wages—as little as $1 to $3 a week for cleaning a house in the 1940s—meant that many whites could afford to pay a maid to clean regularly. One black woman reported that she earned $2 a day for cleaning homes in 1962. Anna Mae Dickson of rural East Texas began housework at the age of thirteen and labored for forty years as a domestic, earning $2.50 to $3.00 a week in 1938 and $10 to $12 a week by the 1950s. With more job options and better pay today, the number of black domestics has declined significantly.[54]

Oral interviews with black maids and their white employers reveal some relationships that were exploitative and frustrating and others that were close and affectionate. Some black women expressed deep loyalty to the white women they worked for; many remained with the same family for decades. Celeste King was a maid for nearly twenty years; this was her only choice because textile jobs were closed to her when she began working. She became head cook in a boarding-house in 1951, and during the nineteen years she worked for her female employer, she missed only two days of work. Her boss always gave her leftover food and helped her make her mortgage payments. Some white women admitted that they felt closer to their maids than to their own mothers or sisters. But maids often resented the way white women addressed them and the requirement that they enter the house by the back door. As a teenager, Anne Moody defiantly

---

54. Southeast Women's Employment Coalition, *Women of the Rural South*, 25, 38; Susan Tucker, "A Complex Bond: Southern Black Domestic Workers and Their White Employers," *Frontiers* 9 (Fall 1987): 6–13.

showed up at one employer's front door and walked out on a domestic job when poorly treated by a white woman.[55]

Appalachian women have experienced a difficult employment situation. For years, most Appalachian families depended on a single income, usually that of the man, who typically worked for a mining or timber company. Because of tradition and the physical demands of extractive work, these were considered male jobs until recently. In contrast to North Carolina, areas of West Virginia, eastern Kentucky, and Tennessee have the lowest percentage of female employment in the nation. This is not because mountain families need only one income to survive or because Appalachian women enjoy a leisurely home life. Rather, these southern mountain areas have not benefited from industrialization. Because job opportunities were limited, most Appalachian women in the past found few paid jobs. In recent years, mountain women who find employment often have to drive a long distance to get to work.[56]

Most industries did not regard Appalachia as an attractive area in which to locate because of its terrain, the difficulty of travel, and a less educated population. In the 1950s and 1960s, with so few job opportunities, many Appalachian women migrated out of the region to search for work and a better life elsewhere, creating an unusual situation with a male majority in many mountain counties. In some areas today, however, the number of jobs available to mountain women is increasing. The development of tourism and more jobs in the service sector, government agencies, and small factories—such as manufacturers of outdoor clothing and camping equipment—have increased female employment opportunities in the region.[57]

Handicraft work and homemade goods also provide income for rural women. Much of this work is done in the home. Some homemade production has evolved into full-scale businesses such as bakeries, catering services, and quilt and craft cooperatives. For instance, a group of black female quilt makers in Alabama created the Freedom Quilting Bee during the civil rights movement. A white minister visiting the area saw the beautiful quilts made by black farm women, and he urged them to produce several quilts, which he then sold in New York City. Recognizing the market for such unique handiwork, he encouraged the women to expand. They began to produce numerous quilts that were sold in exclusive stores. With their profits, the quilters erected their own building in 1969, where as many as sixty women could labor. Unfortunately, success also

55. Byerly, *Hard Times Cotton Mill Girls*, 87–95; Moody, *Coming of Age in Mississippi,* 158.

56. William W. Philliber, "Wife's Absence from the Labor Force and Low Income Among Appalachian Migrants," *Rural Sociology* 47 (Winter 1982): 705–10; Patricia L. Gagne, "Appalachian Women: Violence and Social Control," *Journal of Contemporary Ethnography* 20 (January 1992): 387–415.

57. Florin, "Varieties of Southern Women," 96.

brought problems. So popular were the quilts that department store representatives came south to teach the women how to mass-produce their product. In mass production, the uniqueness was lost. With the growing popularity of the "country look," competition increased as foreign mills began to produce quilts for less cost than these Alabama women could make them. Appalachian women also have used their talents to make handicrafts. In recent years, various women's organizations and institutions, such as the Mountain Women's Exchange and the Penland School in North Carolina, have tried to promote female skills. Berea College's Churchill Weavers developed into a thriving Kentucky business. The Southern Highland Handicraft Guild has been successful as well. Though these efforts are not exclusively female, they support artists and promote the integrity of rural, handmade goods.[58]

Today, the biggest growth areas in employment for rural southern women are the service sector and government. Nearly two-thirds of all service workers in the region are women and, though many of these jobs are located in urban areas, some 36 percent of employed women in the rural South work in service industries, especially in educational institutions and health care. Even though rural women are "the lowest paid workers in the lowest wage region of the country," analysts detect some improvement over working conditions and job opportunities in the past. More southern women now work on a continuous basis; they receive better wages and work fewer hours; more unions and laws protect their rights; and some women enjoy a respite from household duties because husbands today are more likely to assist with household and child-rearing duties.[59]

Before starting a family and assuming new household responsibilities, acquiring an education was, and is, an important part of southern girls' lives. Region, class, and race affect the amount of schooling a female acquires. In general, rural southern women have been less well educated than urban women and their rural counterparts elsewhere. The proportion of college graduates in the rural South is 40 percent below the national average. Over the past century, however, females have been better educated than rural southern males because a girl's contribution to family farming was less essential than a boy's so females could attend school longer. While Jim Crow laws and segregation prevailed in the South, black parents also believed that an educated female was less threatening to whites than an educated male, and they were more likely to encourage a daughter to attend school than a son.

The view of southern parents toward education varied, but their feelings often determined the number of years a girl attended school. Parents sometimes perceived little need for children to acquire more than a basic education because

58. "Hard Times for Freedom Quilters," *Christian Century* 106 (March 1989): 317–18.

59. Smith, "Women in the South," 4; Florin, "Varieties of Southern Women," 15; Frankel, "Women, Paternalism, and Protest," 121.

nothing seemed to promise a better life. Many assumed that daughters would follow in the steps of their mothers. Some mothers were ashamed to send their children to school because their clothing was ragged or they had no shoes. In contrast, parents who were ambitious for their children's future often dreamed that an education was the means for daughters to escape poverty and dead-end jobs.

Not only parental views influenced the amount of education a young woman acquired. Many girls stayed in school only as long as was legally required or until the law allowed them to work in a factory. Oral interviews also show that teenage girls left school when they discovered they were pregnant or they wanted to get married. Others had no choice but to quit to go to work. Annie Viola Fries had to leave school and find a paid job when her father abandoned the family and her mother could not struggle alone. Later in life, women often expressed regret about their decision to leave school and begin work when so young, but there was little they could do except to hope for a better life for their children.

Merely attending school also could prove difficult. In the past, when many rural youngsters had to walk to school, the distance could make attendance nearly impossible, especially in winter if children had no shoes. One Fayette County, Tennessee, woman recalled that in the early 1940s, she walked five miles each way to school. An East Texas woman remembered walking three miles to school, carrying her lunch in a half-gallon syrup bucket. Loretta Lynn and her seven siblings walked two miles each way to attend their one-room schoolhouse. County school buses transported some rural white children but avoided those living in the most remote areas; buses did not carry black children. One vivid memory of African American youngsters was seeing shiny school buses, filled with white children, pass them as they trudged to school.[60]

Other explanations for rural southern girls' limited education were associated with the school system itself. Rural schools were never as well served as urban schools. They received less funding, and white schools always had more money and better facilities than black schools, at least until the 1950s and *Brown v. Board of Education*. Rural school buildings might be so dilapidated, so cold in winter and hot in summer, or the classroom so overcrowded that children found it difficult to learn and had to repeat a grade. Viola McFerren remembered attending a school with one teacher and as many as one hundred children crowded into a single room. Annie Perry attended school for thirteen years, beginning when she was seven and leaving when she turned twenty-two. She only completed the seventh grade, however, because her attendance was so sporadic. Apparently none of her teachers had more than a seventh-grade education either. Completing this grade level and earning a teacher's certificate were all that some

60. Robert Hamburger, *Our Portion of Hell: Fayette County, Tennessee, an Oral History of the Struggle for Civil Rights* (New York: Basic Books, 1973), 31.

rural counties required of their instructors. Rural children also had a reduced school year because of a shortage of county funds and having to leave school when it was time to harvest crops. During World War II, when farm laborers were in short supply, public school teachers routinely dismissed all southern schoolchildren by noon to help on the farm. Because many southern counties had no high school for rural black children, these teenagers had to board with a family in town if they were to acquire more education.

While studies and surveys indicate that rural women usually were not as involved in political matters and that they participated less often as voters and activists than urban women, this has not been true of southern women in union organizing and the civil rights movement. Historically, efforts to form unions and protest wage and working conditions were not successful in the South, for industrial and community leaders have been less receptive to unions than company owners elsewhere. Violent battles, blacklisting, and jailings often resulted when southern factory owners resisted strike efforts and enlisted local and state troops to restore order and force employees back to work. According to oral accounts, ministers often sided with management and urged strikers in their churches to return to work. Nonetheless, southern women were active participants in union organizing, for their own and their family's survival depended on adequate wages and decent working conditions. Union leaders often encouraged women to protest because the police were less likely to attack them than male protesters.[61]

Sarah White, a college-educated woman who worked in a Mississippi catfish processing plant, was one such determined union activist. In 1990, she organized female co-workers to join a union when company management failed to deal with dangerous and unhealthy working conditions and sexual harassment. Low wages kept many women living at a bare subsistence level. Nine hundred women went on strike when the company ignored their grievances. This effort ultimately became the largest strike ever held by black female workers in Mississippi. When the company still failed to meet their demands, the women launched a nationwide boycott of catfish, which hurt company profits. It was a thrilling moment when management finally relented and met their demands. As White stated, "You talking about proud, you talking about filled with joy—to see for once that we could stand together and fight this company." Although many southern women have been reluctant to take action against an employer for fear of losing a job they desperately need, these women had reached their limit.[62]

Wives of men involved in strikes also have protested. In 1976, members of the United Mine Workers (UMW) at the Stearns Mine in Kentucky went on strike against the mining company, demanding better safety regulations. For the first

61. Haney, "Women," 128.
62. Eric Bates, "Something as One," *Southern Exposure* 19 (Fall 1991): 30–33.

time in their lives, wives formed a committee to support their husbands. They picketed the company and boycotted local stores that refused to support the coal miners. During the lengthy struggle, women like Betty Dixon reported that family and friends turned against them. Dixon commented that her mother was ashamed of her activism, and Opal Foster said that her boss would not rehire her when she needed a job because of her involvement. They received threatening phone calls and survived on a minimal allowance from the UMW. According to the women, the UMW finally tired of the three-year protest and settled with the mining company, leaving many in the community without jobs and alienated from kin and former friends.[63]

In addition to labor protests, many black southern women became involved in civil rights activism. While much of what we know about the civil rights movement focuses on events in southern cities such as Birmingham, Greensboro, and Nashville, many black female civil rights workers lived in rural areas where they also experienced oppression and racism firsthand. As children, they knew what it meant to have no schoolbooks or to receive only discards from white schools. Their teachers were poorly paid and their school buildings run-down. Paved roads, electricity, sewage systems, and streetlights extended to white housing long before they ever reached black communities. Parents early on taught their youngsters the meaning of Jim Crow so they could accept segregated movie theaters, lunch counters, drinking fountains, and stores. Southern blacks learned to keep their heads lowered and to step aside when passing a white person. Many rural blacks had no idea that they had a constitutional right to vote. For decades, many believed that it was best to accept this way of life and not create trouble.

Black participation in World War II, a growing number of legal challenges to Jim Crow laws, and rising expectations by the 1950s, however, encouraged southern blacks to begin to question decades of oppression. As some began to protest, women asserted themselves in both bold and subtle ways. For instance, in 1949, Mrs. Neal finally tired of the familiarisms that whites commonly used when addressing African Americans. One day, she and her husband went to buy a truck, and the salesman, like so many southern whites, called her husband "uncle" and her "auntie." She looked him in the eye and calmly asked, "How is my sister doing?" "What?" asked the puzzled salesman. "Well, you must be my sister's son because I only have one sister and if I'm your aunt, you must be her son." Such behavior would have been unthinkable a decade earlier.[64]

Rural women also became civil rights activists. As was true in union organizing, female involvement was less risky than for men, who were more likely to get hurt or killed. One of the most famous female civil rights workers from the

---

63. Opal Foster (pseud.) and Betty Dixon (pseud.), Oral Interviews, 1980, Southwest Institute for Research on Women, SHC.

64. Richard A. Couto, *Ain't Gonna Let Nobody Turn Me Round: The Pursuit of Racial Justice in the Rural South* (Philadelphia: Temple University Press, 1991), 292.

rural South was Fannie Lou Hamer, born in 1917, raised in poverty in Montgomery and Sunflower Counties, Mississippi, the youngest of twenty children. Hamer often slept on a mattress of dry grass or corn shucks. By the age of six, she was picking cotton. The family often had nothing more to eat than greens and flour gravy. Hamer learned about racism when white men poisoned her family's three mules. She eventually acquired a sixth-grade education, attending school between cotton plantings for a few months each year. Her father died in 1939; her mother lost her sight in an accident, and Fannie cared for her until she died. In 1944, Hamer married a sharecropper, and they lived in a frame house with no hot water or indoor toilet. She cleaned house at night for the white family on whose land they lived and worked in the fields during the day. Fannie found strength through her deep belief in God and through her mother, who taught her that hating makes you as weak as those people who are filled with hate.[65]

Hamer's active commitment to civil rights commenced when she attended a meeting at which she first learned that she could register to vote. The effort to register cost her their farm tenancy and livelihood; whites also beat her because she worked for the Student Nonviolent Coordinating Committee. Her most visible moment was attending the 1964 Democratic Convention as a member of the newly formed Mississippi Freedom Democratic party. Here, she demanded the right to be seated as a true representative of the state. Her nationally televised speech stirred those who heard her inspiring words. Hamer continued her efforts for civil rights until her death in 1977.

Another civil rights worker, Anne Moody, also grew up in rural Mississippi. She became aware of white injustice with the murder of fourteen-year-old Emmet Till in 1955 and the burning of a black family's home outside her town. She was fortunate to be able to attend college on a basketball scholarship, and it was here that she joined the NAACP. She and a friend held their own sit-in at a local bus station, and Moody worked during Mississippi's Freedom Summer to encourage blacks to register to vote. Her activism placed her on the wanted list of the racist White Citizens' Council. Moody's autobiography, *Coming of Age in Mississippi,* is a telling portrait of her civil rights work; of a young girl's understanding of injustice, prejudice, and hate; and of her frustration in trying to change black attitudes and fear after centuries of oppression. "I wonder . . . ," she asks at the end of her memoir, questioning if racism will end and life will ever change for southern blacks.

At the same time, political activism and all that it implied frightened many rural women who had no desire to become involved or even associate with those who participated in union activities or the civil rights movement. Activist women saw their children harassed and beaten and their families' lives endan-

65. The most recent and complete biography of Fannie Lou Hamer is Kay Mills, *This Little Light of Mine: The Life of Fannie Lou Hamer* (New York: Dutton, 1993).

gered. Many women in rural communities feared becoming involved in anything controversial, losing a job, and seeing political action affect how others in the community viewed them. Ann Sutton of Somerfield, Alabama, was one of a dozen black girls who faced such pressure when they integrated an all-white high school. She was called names and taunted daily; dead rats were placed in her school locker. Female activists in Fayette County, Tennessee, were surprised by the number of women who opposed their civil rights work and who openly shunned them because of it. Anne Moody's mother begged her daughter to cease her activism; she finally forbade her from coming home when whites threatened Moody's life. When Viola McFerren's husband became involved in voter registration drives, their friends turned against them, believing that any contact with the couple would endanger their own lives. Often blacks turned against civil rights activists or shouted "whitey" at black students who integrated formerly all-white high schools. Being involved in changing lives and improving conditions for the oppressed demanded an enormous amount of courage.[66]

Women in the rural South have struggled, as women have for centuries everywhere, to ensure family survival. It is difficult to generalize about such a vast and varied population, especially without the benefit of greater chronological distance. Yet during this last half-century, significant changes have come to the rural South and have affected the lives of the region's women. "We have seen more change than any generation of people I can think of," commented Mrs. W. D. Elliott of Tyner, North Carolina.[67]

One of the most important of these changes is the transition of many females from their traditional role as tenants and farm wives and laborers to paid employees outside the home. Some mothers hold more than one job or work at a paid job in addition to farming and raising their children. Yet even with a regular income, poverty may be the norm, and women have learned to make do with little and expect less.

Beginning with World War II, the modern world caught up with much of the rural South and changed women's daily lives. Electricity, modern appliances, radio, and television now can be found in most rural southern homes. Young women today are better educated than earlier generations of rural southern women, bear fewer children, and many enjoy better health services. In most cases, such changes have improved their lives. For other women, little has changed as they make sacrifices and struggle to survive, hoping that their children's lives will be better than their own.

The rural South is beginning to attract more scholarly attention. The dual nature of the region and its many contradictions continue to prove fascinating.

66. Moody, *Coming of Age in Mississippi*, 384; Sutton, "Annie's Story," 19; Hamburger, *Our Portion of Hell*, 111.

67. Elliott, interview.

Currently, sociologists, health workers, educators, economists, and academicians interested in women are examining such issues as the effect of a declining farm population and low-wage industries in the rural South; out- and in-migration in rural and mountain areas of the South; the success and failure of local, state, and federal health programs; and the role of women's economic cooperatives and job training programs. In the nation's desire to recapture its rural past, the funding of numerous oral history programs has created a personal view of the lives of thousands of rural women. Future scholars who research rural southern women will find a wealth of primary materials that deserve to be examined and interpreted.

Despite modernization, the rural South remains the poorest region of the country; the majority of its destitute are women and children. While social programs such as Social Security, food stamps, Aid for Families with Dependent Children, the Job Corps, and Medicaid assist women's lives, their condition today is made more difficult by frequent out-of-wedlock babies, sole parenting of their children, and an inferior status in the labor force. Although these problems are evident nationwide, the South's less diversified economy and its low-wage job market make it a challenge for many southern women to earn a decent living. Welfare payments in southern states are below the national average, and rural women generally earn less than their urban counterparts. The situation for many rural southern women remains bleak.[68]

In reading scores of oral accounts of rural southern women, however, one gains a deep admiration for these women and their ability to sacrifice for their families and manage hardship. Although many admit that their rural upbringing was difficult, their experiences also have made them wise. Many women have been able to look at their rural past and realize the effect it has had on their lives. "Actually you had a good life there," commented Mary Harrington. "I wouldn't take anything for the experience of the country life."[69]

68. Southeast Women's Employment Coalition, *Women of the Rural South*, 18.
69. Mary Harrington, Oral Interview, SHC.

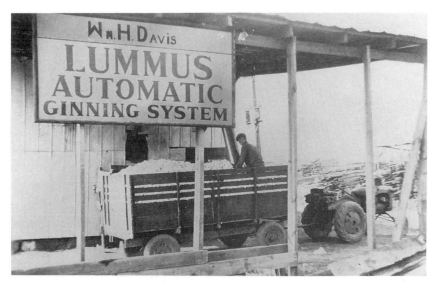

The cotton South changed rapidly after World War II. Competition from Arizona and California, where larger fields, irrigation, and mechanized pickers made cotton production more efficient and profitable, encouraged many southern farmers to diversify. As a result, small-scale cotton ginning businesses soon disappeared from the roadside.

Courtesy Georgia Department of Archives and History

During the mid-1960s, tobacco farmers near Moultrie, Georgia, took their tobacco to the Pidcock Tobacco Warehouse, where it was graded and sold. Tobacco has been a labor-intensive, small-scale crop for many southern farmers. Following World War II, low prices and high labor costs encouraged mechanization and the development of mechanical transplanters, toppers, and harvesters. As health concerns about smoking have increased, tobacco manufacturers have sought new markets abroad.

Courtesy Georgia Department of Archives and History

Southern farmers began to raise more livestock after World War II and to reduce their cotton and tobacco acreage. Hay fields, tractors, and rakes began to change the look of the countryside, while breeding and feeding improvements helped increase livestock production. In 1952, this farmer raked his hay crop into windrows in Chesterfield County, South Carolina.

Cooperative Extension Service Records, Special Collections, Clemson University Libraries, Clemson, S.C.

The poultry industry underwent great change after 1945. In the South, poultry production transformed from a small-scale, supplemental income activity into a large-scale, vertically integrated industry in which farmers had little control over their operations but experienced little financial risk. Southern turkey producers have capitalized on breeding improvements and increased consumer demand to expand production.

Cooperative Extension Service Records, Special Collections, Clemson University Libraries, Clemson, S.C.

During the 1950s, peanut farmers began to mechanize this labor-intensive crop. They adopted an implement that lifted the plants from the soil, removed the dirt, and placed the stalks in windrows. After the peanuts had dried, farmers used another implement to thresh the crop. By the late twentieth century high labor costs and slow technological improvement encouraged many farmers to substitute soybeans for peanut production.

Courtesy Georgia Department of Archives and History

By the mid-1950s southern farmers commonly used crop dusters to spread pesticides over their fields. Large fields and mechanized equipment increasingly characterized southern agriculture by the mid-twentieth century.

Cooperative Extension Service Records, Special Collections, Clemson University Libraries, Clemson, S.C.

County agents had the responsibility of helping farm men and women improve their standard of living. Often they brought new discoveries from the state agricultural experiment stations to individuals or groups. Here, a black home economist demonstrates the proper way to convert a kerosene lamp to electric power. Note the electric fan, coffee pot, radio, and iron on the table. Black extension agents confronted chronic problems of underfunding and organizational support for their work.

Cooperative Extension Service Records, Special Collections, Clemson University Libraries, Clemson, S.C.

Although the mechanical picker became affordable for many large-scale farmers during the late 1940s, black farmers did not have the capital or the acreage to enable them to acquire mechanized implements. Consequently, black extension agents emphasized improvements in subsistence agriculture rather than commercial production.

Cooperative Extension Service Records, Special Collections, Clemson University Libraries, Clemson, S.C.

New Deal agricultural programs encouraged planters to release their tenants and sharecroppers, consolidate fields, and replace workers with mechanized implements. Extension agents, black or white, could neither keep them on the land nor significantly improve their lives.

Courtesy Georgia Department of Archives and History

Southerners have always loved hunting, but blacks and whites usually do not hunt together. Although many poor southerners of both races often hunt for food, fox hunting is an upper-class pursuit in which blacks seldom mingle with whites.

Courtesy Georgia Department of Archives and History

During the 1950s and 1960s, the Ku Klux Klan drew many members from the segregated mill villages. This cross burning occurred in Burke County, Georgia, during the early 1960s, with men, women, and children in attendance. By the late twentieth century, Klan activities had declined, and the organization often drew more attention beyond the South.

Courtesy Georgia Department of Archives and History

Blacks and whites have always worked together in the rural South, although each group clearly understood the boundaries of interracial social contact. In January 1949, this black family helped at hog-killing time on the farm of F. W. Thomas in South Carolina.

Cooperative Extension Service Records, Special Collections, Clemson University Libraries, Clemson, S.C.

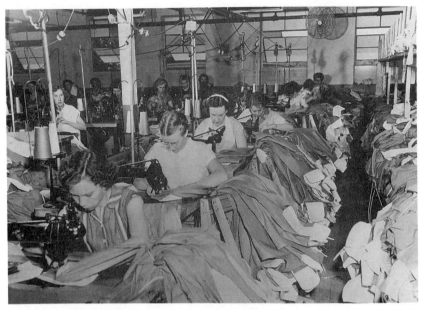

By the end of World War II, most women in the rural South no longer worked in the fields. Tenancy and sharecropping had nearly become an agricultural lifestyle of the past. Government programs and technology had forced people off the land, and many women sought jobs in manufacturing. In 1953, these women worked in a garment factory in Winder, Georgia.

Courtesy Georgia Department of Archives and History

Women in the rural South have been responsible for much of the social interaction of their families, and they have used church, work, and community organizations to help break down isolation. Organizational picnics have always played an important role in the social life of southerners.

Courtesy Georgia Department of Archives and History

During the war years, blacks as well as whites sought relatively high paying jobs in the towns and cities. In 1946, these black women worked for the Easterlin Packing Company in Andersonville, Georgia. Here, they are taking peaches from baskets, removing the pits, and placing the halves on a conveyor belt. Despite this drudgery in segregated conditions, few black women wanted to return to sharecropping.

Courtesy Georgia Department of Archives and History

Hank Williams reigned as the leading country music performer during the early 1950s. Williams sang songs that ran the gamut from blues to gospel, and his music reached audiences far beyond the South. Here, Williams performs at the Grand Ole Opry about 1951. Chet Atkins accompanied on the guitar and Ernie Newton played bass.

Courtesy of the Country Music Foundation

Most country musicians were born and raised in the South, and their music has a distinctly regional and rural sound and theme. Canadian-born Hank Snow, however, was one of the early country music entertainers born outside the region and nation. During the late 1940s, Snow became one of the most prominent country music artists.

Courtesy of the Country Music Foundation

By the early 1980s, some country music performers such as Emmylou Harris had earned the sobriquet of "neotraditionalists." Rejecting the country sound designed to cross over to the top-forty pop charts, she played country music that honored older styles.

Courtesy of the Country Music Foundation

During the late twentieth century, Randy Travis helped preserve an older traditional style of country music, reminiscent of the work of Lefty Frizzel. Although some country musicians have rejected the modern, rather slick country-pop sound with its often shallow and Tin Pan Alley lyrics, others have embraced the opportunity to reach audiences beyond the rural South.

Courtesy of the Country Music Foundation

The Pentecostal churches rapidly increased in number after World War II. Pentecostal worshipers needed only the most basic shelters, such as this church in northern Mississippi, rather than complicated organizational structures.

Courtesy Ted Ownby, photograph by Susan Bauer Lee

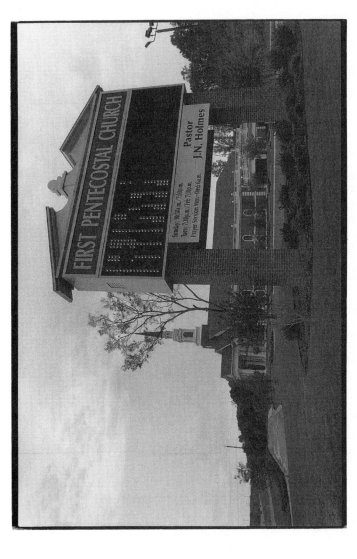

Although financial instability plagues many Pentecostal churches, some communities have sufficient wealth to enable the construction of elegant buildings and support large congregations, such as this church in Arkansas. Wealth, power, and respectability, however, often create fears among the members that the church will become complacent. Indeed, the great fear of Pentecostals, both rich and poor, is that they will become like other successful religious groups.

Courtesy Ted Ownby, photograph by Susan Bauer Lee

Baptisms by full immersion are an important ritual for the evangelical and Pentecostal denominations in the South. This baptism occurred in Harley Barnes's Lake near Ellijay, Georgia, in 1960.

Courtesy Georgia Department of Archives and History

The Democratic party reigned supreme during most of the South's history, but the Republican party gained considerable strength during the late twentieth century by supporting conservative social issues, especially concerning matters of race.

Courtesy Georgia Department of Archives and History

The Voting Rights Act of 1965 enabled the registration and mobilization of African American voters. By the 1970s, the Democratic and Republican parties vied for the black vote in national, state, and local elections. Today voting machines have replaced the written ballots of the past.

Courtesy Georgia Department of Archives and History

During the late 1970s, many southern farmers supported the American Agriculture Movement in its efforts to achieve higher prices. In doing so, they participated in "tractorcades" designed to call attention to their economic difficulties and their demand that the federal government guarantee cost of production prices plus a profit. This demonstration occurred on December 14, 1977, in Statesboro, Georgia.

Courtesy Georgia Department of Archives and History

In 1953, these first- and second-grade children at Matthews School in Barrow County, Georgia, studied the importance of eating a good breakfast while they enjoyed food provided by their parents. The absence of black students attests to the system of segregation at a time when race relations were on the verge of great change.

Courtesy Georgia Department of Archives and History

Moonshine whiskey often is associated with the rural South. Few stills, however, remain active in the countryside today, and most bootleg whiskey is distilled in urban areas.

Courtesy Georgia Department of Archives and History

The Rural South Moves to the City: Country Music Since World War II

BILL C. MALONE

In the fifty years since the end of World War II, musical styles born in the South—gospel (black and white), rhythm-and-blues, rock-and-roll, Cajun, cowboy, and country—have moved into the nation's musical mainstream. While shaping the musical contours of the nation, southern styles have also become some of America's most valuable cultural exports. Although inseparable from the historic poverty, discrimination, and racial injustice of the South, and surviving as living testaments to the abilities of poor people to sustain themselves and to assert their cultural worth, these styles did not flourish commercially until the time of World War II.

The form of music that has best represented the ever-changing social topography of the South—the music that is now called "country"—was not so described until about 1948. The search for an appropriate label reflected the commercial maturation of the genre and the desire among many musicians to abandon the term *hillbilly* that had often been used to describe it. *Country,* however, obscured the fact that the music by 1948 was sustained by people who lived in towns and cities and was disseminated among them by urban forms of communication. The music had begun its commercial evolution in the 1920s at a time of rapid urban growth and had always owed its existence to a peculiarly American blending of urban technology and rural folkways. The massive migration of rural southerners in the 1940s to cities in the South and throughout the nation contributed both to the commercial burgeoning of this music and to its nationalization. Country music endured as the major voice of people who longed nostalgically for a way of life that was gone and who were struggling to adjust to urban industrial life.[1]

---

1. According to Hugh Cherry, the term *country and western* was first used in 1943 by Steve

Country music in the immediate postwar years conveyed a distinctly regional and rural flavor. Country musicians, of course, could be found throughout North America, and a few of them, such as the Canadian-born Hank Snow and Bob Nolan, were among the best-loved entertainers in the United States. Nevertheless, most of the singers and musicians who attained national public visibility and who dominated the jukeboxes and popularity charts came overwhelmingly from the South. The music as a whole conveyed a strong southern flavor in the accents and dialects of its performers and the themes of its songs. Even the most sophisticated of the country singers could scarcely avoid an identification with the rural southern imagery shared by their fans, nor could they easily avoid the performance of songs that embodied such symbolism. Eddy Arnold, for example, the predominant country singer of the mid-1940s, whose smooth style and receptivity to pop innovations soon carried him into nightclubs and on to the leading network radio and television series of the era, called himself the "Tennessee Plowboy." His first widely circulated song, recorded in March 1945, "Mommy, Please Stay Home with Me," was the story of a child who died while his mother was out drinking at a party. This was the kind of song that had been deeply loved by traditional country music fans, but it was far removed from the songs with which Arnold eventually became identified.[2]

Although most country musicians came from rural southern homes, they and their audience should more properly be described as working people with middle-class aspirations. Although many of the musicians had grown up on farms and could recall milking cows or picking cotton, most had spent their young adult lives in military service or as cotton mill workers, coal miners, truck drivers, automobile mechanics, beauticians, or workers in some other blue-collar occupation. The widespread fame attained by a few country entertainers encouraged young amateurs to try their hands at the music business. For example, the commercial success attained in the late 1920s by Jimmie Rodgers, the "Singing Brakeman" from Mississippi who moved from railroad work to a recording career with RCA Victor, and in the 1930s by Gene Autry, the Oklahoma

---

Sholes to describe the hillbilly songs circulated on the Fee-Discs produced for the American Forces Network program in Europe. Sholes, who had been a longtime producer for RCA Victor before he entered military service, may have been primarily responsible for the decision made by the *RCA Victor Record Review* 10 (April 1948): 12, to use *country and western* to advertise similar recordings; see Hugh Cherry, "Joe Allison, AFRTS, Topsy and How They Grew," *Music City News* 7 (April 1970): 28. In June 1949, the national music trade journal, *Billboard* magazine, began using the same designation to describe its hillbilly popularity charts.

2. Arnold's dominance in the late 1940s and early 1950s is documented in the *Billboard* listing of "top ten" country songs, which began in 1948. The listings for the years from 1948 to 1963 appeared in *The World of Country Music* (New York: Billboard, 1963), 187, 189–99. Despite Arnold's prominence in American entertainment, he has never received much attention from writers who specialize in country or any other field of American music. He did write a highly unsatisfactory autobiography, *It's a Long Way from Chester County* (New York: Pyramid Books, 1969).

railroad telegrapher who became the first and most famous Hollywood Singing Cowboy, suggested not only that music could be an escape from manual labor but that it could also be a source of material wealth and comfort. Few musicians, though, could free themselves from wage labor (or "day jobs," as such work is described by country musicians), so most of them performed music at night or on weekends and hoped that a successful record or radio show would launch them into a full-time career in entertainment.[3]

As working people from rural backgrounds who nevertheless yearned for acceptance in middle-class, urban America, country musicians were understandably ambivalent about themselves, the stage personas they hoped to convey, and the success they hoped to attain. Few country entertainers stressed their blue-collar backgrounds in their stage presentations or in their promotional material; instead, they identified most often with a place—a county, state, region, or local landmark. Even Jimmie Rodgers, who did exploit his railroad experiences, stressed the glamorous, rambling aspects of railroading and not the labor that dominated it. He and his promoters emphasized his Mississippi origins as often as his railroading background. Neither the musicians nor their promoters (radio and recording executives, movie producers, booking agents, advertisers) could be certain what the mood of the American public would be at any given moment or what image would be the most effective moneymaker. Should the musicians wax nostalgic about their presumed rural or mountain pasts and dress accordingly in overalls, sunbonnets, and gingham dresses? The public mood certainly inspired such a posture from time to time. Even in the big northern city of Chicago, where the WLS National Barn Dance played to capacity audiences each Saturday night at the Eighth Street Theatre, the hunger for Kentucky Mountain Boys, Arkansas Woodchoppers, and Cumberland Mountain Folk seemed to be insatiable. The fascination with rube hillbillies, which had been a staple in American entertainment long before country music's commercial birth, was also apparent all over America, and most country musicians showed no hesitation in exploiting that comic depiction of their culture for commercial purposes.[4]

3.   Rodgers's story is well told in Nolan Porterfield, *Jimmie Rodgers: The Life and Times of America's Blue Yodeler* (Urbana: University of Illinois Press, 1979). Autry has written an autobiography, with Mickey Herskovitz, called *Back in the Saddle Again* (New York: Doubleday, 1978), but the best account of his impact on American music is Douglas B. Green, "Gene Autry," in *Stars of Country Music: Uncle Dave Macon to Johnny Rodriguez,* ed. Bill C. Malone and Judith McCulloh (Urbana: University of Illinois Press, 1976).

4.   Lewis Atherton long ago noted the popularity of the National Barn Dance among midwesterners in *Main Street on the Middle Border* (Bloomington: Indiana University Press, 1954). John Lair's role in establishing a down-home, and even southern, ambience on the show has not properly been acknowledged, but Wayne Daniel is now working on a book on Lair and his influence in both Chicago and at Renfro Valley, Kentucky. The National Barn Dance has not received the full-scale study that it deserves, but some useful information on its relationship to midwestern broadcasting can be found in James F. Evans, *Prairie Farmer and WLS: The Burridge Butler Years* (Urbana: University of Illinois Press, 1969).

Some early performers (but usually not their promoters) felt that success would be more attainable and more widespread if they abandoned the hillbilly image for a more urbane persona combined with a "progressive" musical approach. Texas fiddler and bandleader Bob Wills had already proved in the late 1930s that large audiences could be won through the fusion of jazz and country styles, and Gene Autry had seen his audiences grow larger when he abandoned his early nasal hillbilly sound and replaced it with the smooth, mellifluous tones of the crooner. During the war, though, the Tennessee Mountain Boy, Roy Acuff, had demonstrated that a huge audience could be won by a musical style suggesting the image and morality of rural Appalachia. Most country performers, however, did not adopt the tradition-oriented and backwoods flavor of the mountains. To a remarkable degree, they instead embraced the romantic, liberating ideal of the cowboy, and from the Canadian maritime provinces to California, from the West Virginia hills to the Texas plains, most country entertainers adopted some semblance of cowboy attire and often gave themselves a western moniker. Consequently, Eddy Arnold could call himself the "Tennessee Plowboy" while wearing cowboy stage garb and using "Cattle Call" as his theme song, and Bob Wills could successfully project the persona of a prosperous rancher while performing a jazz-inflected style of rural music that had nothing to do with cowboys or the West.[5]

Whatever the style or image, country music entered its first great phase of national and international expansion in the years following World War II. As American popular culture invaded the world after the war, country music prospered as an integral ingredient of that invasion. The Armed Forces Radio Network introduced the music to Europeans during the occupation period, and American servicemen carried elements of the music all over the world (one of them, Marshall Louis "Grandpa" Jones, sang with his army buddies in a band called the Munich Mountaineers). At home, many factors fueled the music's postwar boom: the end of rationing and war-imposed scarcity; the prosperity that accompanied full employment; a sense of rising expectations; the movement to the cities; and the maturing sophistication of the American media and advertising complex that skillfully engineered a revolution in consumer purchasing. The recording industry returned to vigorous life, and such older companies as Columbia, RCA Victor, and Decca were joined by a host of newer and smaller

5.   Fortunately, Bob Wills's career and influence have received impressive treatment in Charles Townsend, *San Antonio Rose: The Life and Music of Bob Wills* (Urbana: University of Illinois Press, 1976). Wills's onetime musical partner and co-founder of Western Swing has been well portrayed by Cary Ginell in *Milton Brown and the Founding of Western Swing* (Urbana: University of Illinois Press, 1994). Gene Autry was unquestionably the most popular country singer of the war years even though his career was interrupted by military service. The best treatment of Acuff is Elizabeth Schlappi, *Roy Acuff, the Smoky Mountain Boy* (Gretna, La.: Pelican, 1978). I have discussed the search for usable symbols among country musicians in *Singing Cowboys and Musical Mountaineers: Southern Culture and the Roots of Country Music* (Athens: University of Georgia Press, 1993).

labels that aggressively recorded grass-roots forms like hillbilly, Cajun, gospel, and rhythm-and-blues and made them available to the American public. Close to four hundred thousand coin-operated automatic music machines, known as jukeboxes, provided a powerful market for the record industry, while also providing an inexpensive form of entertainment for thousands of dance halls, cafes, bowling alleys, and other public centers of amusement. The beautifully decorated jukebox, with its bright chrome-and-plastic exterior, neon illumination, and openly displayed record-changing mechanisms became not only a central focus for musical and social experience but also a ready reminder to displaced country folk of American capitalistic ingenuity and success in the postwar era. In many respects, too, the jukebox became a vehicle for and a symbol of country music's dramatic commercial surge during those years.[6]

Records, of course, also became standard fare for radio stations throughout the nation, as disc jockeys steadily replaced the older forms of broadcast programming. Despite the growing allure of "canned music" on radio, live broadcasting continued to be common throughout the United States on both the powerful 50,000-watt, clear-channel stations and the hosts of smaller stations that had only limited coverage. Hillbilly acts appeared on early morning and noontime shows and on Saturday night variety shows that were described variously by such evocatively nostalgic names as barn dances, hoedowns, jamborees, shindigs, or frolics. One of the oldest of these shows, the *Grand Ole Opry,* obtained network affiliation on NBC in 1939 and by the early 1950s was well on the way toward making Nashville the premier city of country music in the United States. Nashville's ascendancy was by no means assured, however, in the years immediately following the war. Other "barn dances" competed favorably in such cities as Shreveport, where the Louisiana Hayride held sway; Dallas, the home of the Big D Jamboree; Knoxville, the locus of the Mid-Day-Merry-Go-Round; Atlanta, the site of the Cross Roads Follies; and Wheeling (West Virginia), the location of the Wheeling Jamboree. All of these shows attracted hosts of adoring and

6. The music's commercial expansion had actually begun in the 1930s with the 50,000-watt radio stations; the national advertising on hillbilly shows of such products as Crazy Water Crystals and Alka-Seltzer; radio transcriptions (which permitted performers to tour while their shows were being broadcast); and, of course, the powerful transmission of the "Mexican border" stations, which could be heard all over North America. See Bill C. Malone, *Country Music, USA* (Austin: University of Texas Press, 1985), chaps. 4–6; Gene Fowler and Bill Crawford, *Border Radio* (Austin: Texas Monthly Press, 1987); Gene Fowler, *Crazy Water: The Story of Mineral Wells and Other Texas Health Resorts* (Fort Worth: Texas Christian University Press, 1991), 40–42; and Louis M. Jones, with Charles Wolfe, *Everybody's Grandpa: Fifty Years Behind the Mike* (Knoxville: University of Tennessee Press, 1984), 90–99. One of the best accounts of the postwar boom and its effects on American habits and assumptions is Godfrey Hodgson, *America in Our Time* (Garden City, N.Y.: Doubleday, 1976). For discussions of jukeboxes, see Vincent Lynch and Bill Henkin, *Jukebox: The Golden Age* (Berkeley: Lancaster-Miller, 1981); Christopher Pearce, *Vintage Jukeboxes* (Secaucus, N.J.: Chartwell Books, 1988); Lewis Nichols, "The Ubiquitous Juke Box," *New York Times Magazine,* October 5, 1941, 22; and John Morthland, "Jukebox Fever," *Country Music* 6 (May 1978): 35–36.

faithful fans, but, in some ways, the most instructive experience exhibited by a country radio show was that of the Renfro Valley Barn Dance. Located about sixty miles southeast of Lexington, Kentucky, the Renfro Valley show lay in a little community that did not exist until after 1939, when John Lair began broadcasting his homespun shows from a big barn that was newly constructed near his old home place. Lair had preserved his affection for the area during his several years as staff member and music librarian at WLS in Chicago. The multitudes who came to the barn dance each Saturday night or who heard the broadcasts of that show and the *Sunday Morning Gathering* were engaged, like Lair, in a trip down memory lane to a rural home that no longer existed or that, in some cases, had never been more than an imaginative construct.[7]

As country music became a national phenomenon with a remarkable commercial appeal, it continued to exhibit its southernness and working-class identity. The music that prevailed from roughly 1945 to 1955 was as transitional in nature as the society that sustained it. Rural southerners were changing their residences and occupations but were not so quickly abandoning their folkways. The crowds who attended the Renfro Valley Barn Dance or the Grand Ole Opry or who otherwise demonstrated their affection for country music did so for a wide variety of reasons. Some of them had no actual experience with rural life but nevertheless identified with musical forms they believed were representative of an older America. More often, though, they were transplanted rural people who were trying to come to terms with lives now spent permanently in cities. Styles of adjustment varied, of course, depending on such variables as the size of the place to which they moved, age, gender, income, education, and race. Some fled the land as if it were a curse and enthusiastically embraced the city and its promises. Others abandoned rural life reluctantly, while more than a few moved with the expectation that urban residence would be only temporary. Women probably made the transition to urban life more easily and willingly than men, welcoming the innovations that made life more bearable. Children also adjusted in varying ways, but, ultimately, they became the most willing converts to urban society.[8]

7.   Useful surveys of radio barn dances include Charles Wolfe, *The Grand Ole Opry: The Early Years, 1925–35* (London: Old Time Music, 1975); Stephen R. Tucker, "The Louisiana Hayride, 1948–54," *North Louisiana Historical Journal* 8 (Fall 1977): 187–201; Ivan Tribe, *Mountain Jamboree: Country Music in West Virginia* (Lexington: University Press of Kentucky, 1984); and Linnell Gentry, *A History and Encyclopedia of Country, Western, and Gospel Music* (Nashville: McQuiddy Press, 1961). Wayne Daniel has authored many articles on country music and a fine book on the country scene in Atlanta, Georgia: *Pickin' on Peachtree: A History of Country Music in Atlanta, Georgia* (Urbana: University of Illinois Press, 1990).

8.   A fine case study of a Virginia mountain family who moved to Washington, D.C., and whose members made country music over a period of seventy years is Ivan Tribe, *The Stonemans: An Appalachian Family and the Music That Shaped Their Lives* (Urbana: University of Illinois Press, 1993). This topic deserves serious academic treatment. Harriet Arnow, in her fine novel about a Kentucky mountain family who moved to Detroit during the war years, *The Dollmaker* (1954; rpr. New York: Collier Books, 1970), paints a vivid portrait of a woman who never lost her longing for the hills of

Dramatic changes in perceptions and worldviews certainly did not occur immediately. In the immediate postwar years, country entertainers, promoters, and fans shared an unspoken, and probably unconscious, assumption that the traditional social relationships that had prevailed in society and were endorsed in the music would endure. Material conditions could be dramatically altered and improved, it was believed, without an alteration of the gender, racial, generational, class, and regional relationships that had long defined American society. Traditional hierarchies, however, had been undermined during the war and were weakened further by the prosperity and accelerated social change that came in the late 1940s and early 1950s. Ultimately, the consumer revolution did the most to transform an already fragile social structure. While promising "things" to people at an unprecedented volume and rate, it obscured the role of class in American life, denied the need for structural change in capitalism, accentuated embarrassment about rural origins, and encouraged (but did not easily create) homogeneity in American society. Country music could not help but be dramatically transformed by such changes, as money flowed into the hands of music purchasers and as women and young people became more assertive of their rights and needs.[9]

It is difficult to pinpoint precisely the moment when country music crossed the threshold into modernity. Well into the age of television, country musicians were still appearing live on early morning radio shows, hawking their picture-songbooks, and making strings of one-night stands on the so-called kerosene circuit in school auditoriums, American Legion halls, movie theaters, churches, and tents. No show was complete without the performance of a hoedown fiddle tune, one or more religious songs, a moralistic recitation, a comedy routine presented by a comedian in baggy pants, floppy hat, and blacked-out teeth, and perhaps a buck-and-wing dance. Country shows were a blend of ingredients that came from virtually every rural music performance idiom of the nineteenth century: minstrel theater, medicine show, circus, religious camp meeting, and tent vaudeville. Some shows, such as those presented by Roy Acuff, the Bailes Brothers, the Louvin Brothers, Molly O'Day and the Cumberland Mountain Folk, and Brother Claude Ely were almost evangelistic in their use of religious material. At the other extreme, a Grand Ole Opry duo called Jamup and Honey performed in blackface in a tent show that traveled through the South until the late 1940s. Fans and performers enjoyed a close relationship during these years that was never again achieved in country music's later history. Bill Monroe, for example, sometimes scheduled baseball games between his own team (composed partially

---

home. Evidence that is admittedly anecdotal, including the recollections of my mother and other women relatives, suggests that women strongly embraced the alternatives presented by city life.

9.   George Lipsitz, *Rainbow at Midnight: Labor and Culture in the 1940s* (1981; rpr. Urbana: University of Illinois Press, 1994), presents a finely nuanced analysis of the ambivalence felt by men and women after the war.

of his own musicians) and teams assembled in the towns where his Blue Grass Boys made music. The Bailes Brothers were not unique in often accepting invitations to eat dinner in the homes of fans who lived in the small towns of western Louisiana, eastern Texas, and southern Arkansas where they often performed.[10]

Although radio programming and musical recording became increasingly uniform, mechanized, and impersonal in the 1950s, disc jockeys with highly personal styles and contrived hayseed demeanors remained common on large and small stations alike. On the powerful Mexican border station XERF, announcer Paul Kallinger, who called himself "your good neighbor along the way," won the confidence of his listeners with down-home charm and folksy patter. Kallinger made sophisticated use of the airwaves, and his shrewd understanding of his listeners sold country music to a national audience while also marketing with great skill the baby chicks, laxatives, and chill tonics of his sponsors. Elsewhere, other DJs built close relationships with fans by reading their cards and letters and by playing requests from listeners and with performers by interviewing them on their programs. It was not uncommon for big-name performer Red Foley to drop by a tiny station in Brookhaven, Mississippi, or for a complete unknown to visit a station and succeed in having his self-produced record played on the daily broadcast. Because of their intimate relationships with fans and performers, disc jockeys often acted as successful booking agents. Elvis Presley, for example, won his first loyal coterie of fans in East Texas through the active booking of DJ Tom Perryman of KSIJ in tiny Gladewater, Texas. Presley was still playing such one-night stands throughout the South as late as 1956 while his manager, Colonel Tom Parker, hawked the star's photographs outside in time-tested carnival fashion.[11]

The music heard in the immediate postwar era also illustrated the transitional nature of country music and its audience. Jazz, blues, and pop sounds often intruded into the music of country performers, but old-time fiddle breakdowns, novelty songs of minstrel parentage, ancient ballads, love songs, and gospel

10. The evidence of the simultaneous coexistence of traditional and contemporary material in country music programming is found in "The Grand Ole Opry, 1944–45: A Radio Log Kept by Dick Hill, of Tecumseh, Nebraska," *Journal of Country Music* 5 (Fall 1974): 91–122; and in the transcriptions of Hank Williams's *Health and Happiness* radio shows, Mercury 314512862-2 (originally produced in 1949 by the makers of the patent medicine Hadacol). A few radio transcriptions survive that capture the mood of evangelism. The best are the Bailes Brothers, Old Homestead OHCS 103 and 104, and the Louvin Brothers, *Songs That Tell a Story*, Rounder 1030. Brother Claude Ely's recordings from that period are clearly evangelistic and are wonderful representations of rural Pentecostal music. Some of his songs were recorded at revival meetings near Whitesburg, Kentucky, in 1953 and 1954 and can be heard on Brother Claude Ely, *Satan Get Back*, King CDCHD456. Neil Rosenberg, *Bluegrass: A History* (Urbana: University of Illinois Press, 1985), 59–60; and the Bailes Brothers' Old Homestead recordings, CS-103, originally recorded in 1948 and 1949, contain commercials, dedications to their "shut-in" listeners, and announcements of personal appearances.

11. Fowler and Crawford, *Border Radio;* Peter Guralnick, *Last Train to Memphis: The Rise of Elvis Presley* (Boston: Little, Brown, 1994), 150–52, 250, 303, 430.

songs from paperback hymnals appeared with great frequency in the repertoires of such performers as the Blue Sky Boys, Grandpa Jones, and Mainer's Mountaineers. Roy Acuff still sang "Wabash Cannon Ball" and "Precious Jewel" each Saturday night on the *Grand Ole Opry,* and country gospel singers still spoke to their listeners in stark, fundamentalist terms about declining morals, a dying world, and the imminent Second Coming of Christ. Nowhere do we find better examples of the divided thinking of that postwar southern generation that, only freshly uprooted from its rural past, was reaching out to embrace the material fruits of the new society while still not sure that it would all last, than in such songs as "This World Can't Stand Long," "Whiskey Is the Devil (in Liquid Form)," "The Drunken Driver," "They Locked God Outside the Iron Curtain," "Cabin in Glory Land," and an extensive body of songs that commented on the atomic bomb as an agent of God's wrath.[12]

Gradually, though, visions of cabins in gloryland gave way to dreams of mansions in heaven and here on earth. An abundant society challenged the fatalistic assumptions of the past, the burgeoning consumer economy weakened the once deeply held conviction of limits, and the city promised opportunities that had never been available in the older rural-village society. Understandably, then, country music continued to reflect the simultaneous impulses of tradition and innovation exhibited in the larger society.[13]

Hank Williams reigned as the king of country music during those first great prosperous years in the early 1950s. His death on January 1, 1953, on first impression, might appear to have been a demarcation point in country music history, a symbol of the similar demise, or coming demise, of the older southern rural society and the music that reflected it. On closer examination, however, Hank's career is best understood as an embodiment of the tensions and contradictions found in country music and as both the fulfillment of traditional country music and the precursor of the modernization that came with great rapidity after his death. Hank was a country boy but never a farmer, who came of age in south Alabama during the unsettling years of World War II. He named his band the Drifting Cowboys, although neither he nor they ever rode the range or sang its rhythms. His intense vocal style rang with the inflections and drawl of the Deep South and was as strongly rooted in the singing of the rural Baptists of his boyhood church as in any other source. Hank's songs ran the gamut from the

---

12. These songs are not collected in a single recording, or in a single publication, but see Charles Wolfe, "Nuclear Country: The Atomic Bomb in Country Music," *Journal of Country Music* 7 (January 1978): 4–21, for a discussion of one genre of topical songs. These songs are placed in a larger perspective by Paul Boyer, *By the Bomb's Early Light* (New York: Pantheon, 1985).

13. Curtis Stewart's "Lord, Build Me a Cabin in Glory," published in 1944 while he was a corporal in the United States Army and printed in numerous paperback hymnals, is the classic statement of rural gospel humility. Such songs are very rare today in gospel music, as are the philosophy and theology that once motivated them. Songs about mansions in heaven are, in contrast, abundant in the gospel repertoire.

blues to gospel, and his stage shows included every type of material with which rural southerners were familiar: moralistic recitations, corny humor, fiddle tunes, love songs (both tragic and happy), blues tunes, and sacred songs.[14]

The overall sound and ambience of Hank Williams's music, however, suggested the influence of the country honky-tonks, the bars where strong drink, dancing, noise, and the hints of violence and illicit sex combined to spawn a style of music that seemed consonant with southerners' evolution from rural to urban blue-collar culture. The honky-tonk was a kind of halfway house between rural and urban life. For some people it provided nothing more than a temporary release from the anxieties of work and daily responsibilities. For others it was an introduction to a world that seemed far more dangerous and sordid than the older rural society. The old-time frolic of rural America (a dance held in rural homes) had virtually disappeared, so many working people sought the honky-tonk as an urban equivalent of that older social diversion. "Honky-tonking" (having a good time on Saturday night and perhaps going to more than one dance hall during the night) became a pastime that provided enjoyment for dancers and listeners while also shaping the tone and sound of country music. In this atmosphere, rustic or pastoral themes became obsolescent—although they never ceased to have periodic nostalgic appeal—and the beat and volume of country instrumentation changed to accommodate the needs of dancers. Obviously necessary in such an environment, the electric guitar was well on the way to becoming the dominant instrument of country music.[15]

Hank's rural and compelling vocal sound and his charismatic stage presence made him the leading performer of country music in the early 1950s. His beautifully crafted compositions such as "Honky Tonking," "Your Cheating Heart," "Cold, Cold Heart," and "I'm So Lonesome I Could Cry" moved across the parameters of song genre and audience taste into the repertoires of such pop musicians as Tony Bennett, Frankie Laine, and Joni James. Thereafter, country musicians never abandoned the dream of having their songs adopted by pop singers

14.   The best biography of Williams is Colin Escott, with George Merritt and William MacEwen, *Hank Williams: The Biography* (Boston: Little, Brown, 1994). Other useful accounts are Roger Williams, *Sing a Sad Song: The Life of Hank Williams* (Garden City, N.Y.: Doubleday, 1970); and Chet Flippo, *Your Cheating Heart: A Biography of Hank Williams* (New York: Simon and Schuster, 1981). George William Koon has provided a very useful assessment of the literature on Hank, while also correcting a few false impressions, in *Hank Williams: A Bio-Bibliography* (Westport, Conn.: Greenwood Press, 1983). The lyrics of Hank's own compositions (without music) have been compiled by Don Cusic in *Hank Williams: The Complete Lyrics* (New York: St. Martin's Press, 1993). Most of Hank's recordings are available, but the most useful album is probably *Hank Williams: The Original Singles Collection* (three compact discs), Polygram 847 194-2.

15.   The honky-tonk's emergence as a factor in country music culture is discussed in Malone, *Country Music, USA*, chap. 5, and in the *Encyclopedia of Southern Culture*, ed. Charles Reagan Wilson and William Ferris (Chapel Hill: University of North Carolina, 1989), 1014–16. A good discussion of the electrification of the country guitar is Rich Kienzle, "The Electric Guitar in Country Music: Its Evolution and Development," *Guitar Player* 13 (November 1979): 30, 32–34, 36–37, 40–41.

or of having their own recordings accepted by the large pop audience. Hank's death at the age of twenty-nine contributed to the creation of the aura of romance that now surrounds his memory, while also suggesting several presumed legacies that later musicians and fans have freely exploited. His talented son, Hank, Jr., who has sung to audiences much wider and more varied than those of his father, has tried to legitimize his own highly publicized rebellion against musical and societal conventions by describing his father as the original country music "outlaw." Other musicians sometimes speak of the "Hank Williams Syndrome," the tendency shown by some country musicians to emulate the lifestyle of the great country singer, to live fast, love hard, and die young. Still others refer to him as an early rockabilly—a precursor of Elvis Presley—and point to songs like "Rootie Tootie," a country boogie tune, as evidence. A few allude to the pop success enjoyed by some of Hank's songs and speculate that he not only would have been pleased with the country-pop style of music that emerged in the 1960s but would also have been a willing participant in the making of such music. An even larger number of fans believe contrarily that, if Hank had lived, he would have remained faithful to his traditional roots and would have resisted the tide toward pop homogenization.[16]

Less than one year after Hank Williams died, another southern country boy, Elvis Aaron Presley, unleashed a revolution that did more than simply lure thousands of youth away from traditional country music; it changed the face of American music. Elvis's early success—before television made him a pop icon of international dimensions—was rooted in the same demographic transformations that subtly changed Hank Williams's music and made country music a national phenomenon. Like other southern working-class youth of his age, Elvis felt the stirrings of change and embraced the promise of the better life that had eluded his parents. His family's move to Memphis in 1948, from his birthplace in Tupelo, Mississippi, certainly did not remove them from the uncertain, hard-scrabble life of the working class, but it did present him with a wide range of alternative life and music styles. Elvis was a child of popular culture and a part of all that he saw and heard. The movies, the hot-rod culture, all forms of popular music, including the country and gospel sounds loved by his parents, and, ultimately, television, bound him to other young people of his age while also providing arenas for a quiet rebellion against the world of his parents. Not untypically,

---

16. While paying tribute to his hero, Waylon Jennings nevertheless says to Hank, "It's no thanks to you that I'm still living today": heard in "Hank Williams Syndrome," in the CD collection, *Too Dumb for New York City/Too Ugly for L.A.*, Epic CD 48982. Hank Williams, Jr.'s various incantations of his father's name include "Standing in the Shadows," on *Fourteen Greatest Hits*, Polydor 0518; "Are You Sure Hank Done It This Way," on *Rowdy*, Elektra 6E-330; and "Family Tradition," on *Greatest Hits*, Elektra 60193-1. There are probably thousands of "amateur" singers in America, performing on weekends in some friend's house or at the VFW hall or some other local venue, who are still singing Hank's songs as close to the "original" style as they can achieve.

Elvis sought both distinctiveness and conformity. From his parents' lives, if not from their reassuring words, he probably received the message that typified a working-class southern view: that little could be accomplished and that one should be aware of limits in this life. In contrast, the American consumer culture defined the pursuit of happiness as the acquisition of material goods and promised liberation and fulfillment in such a quest.[17]

The story of Elvis's emergence as a singer in July 1954 and his consequent ascent to international stardom is too well known to be repeated here. But his swift rise to fame should not obscure his role in country music history. His career and musical style are as deeply rooted in southern working-class history as are those of Hank Williams, and his effects on country music may ultimately be seen as having been far more profound than the influence exerted by the young Alabama singer. Hank had opened up new windows of opportunity for aspiring country singers, and he had attracted younger audiences to country music. But though he could sometimes sing with abandon and delight his listeners with songs of honky-tonking, rambling, and hedonistic glee, Hank Williams could never fully escape the fatalistic vision of his rural forebears or his own sense of personal foreboding. The tragic dimensions of Hank's lifestyle colored both the lyrics and style of his music. Greil Marcus called him a "poet of limits, fear, and failure" and said that "he went as deeply into one dimension of the country world as anyone could, gave it beauty, gave it dignity."[18]

Although Elvis's final years and death were ultimately as tragic as those of Hank Williams, his music never conveyed the themes of resignation, alienation, defeat, or even self-pity. From the time of his first Sun recordings in 1954 until the very end of his life, Elvis's songs held out the possibilities of personal liberation and joyful fulfillment. He somehow suggested the possibilities of escape from the restrictions of the southern past, while also remaining resolutely loyal to the culture that gave him birth.

Although Elvis revolutionized American music, no revolution was ever begun so innocently. Early interviews reveal a young man who seemed genuinely surprised, but delighted, at the almost delirious enthusiasm evoked by his music. Probably neither Elvis nor his young female fans fully understood the sexual dimension of their relationship or the degree to which such conduct challenged the social orthodoxy of the South. Although Elvis skillfully exploited the relation-

17.   Peter Guralnick's *Last Train to Memphis* is the first of two volumes devoted to the singer. Greil Marcus, *Mystery Train: Images of America in Rock 'n' Roll Music,* 2d rev. ed. (New York: E. P. Dutton, 1982), devotes a lengthy section to Presley and continues to be one of the finest analyses of those southern cultural tensions that gave rise to both Presley and Hank Williams.

18.   Although the transformations wrought by Elvis Presley have never been matched by any other country singer, he has not been named to Nashville's Country Music Hall of Fame. See Marcus, *Mystery Train,* 155.

ship and, consequently, enjoyed extraordinary commercial success, he never intended to defy his parents' culture or the larger one to which he aspired.[19]

Elvis was a part of, and prophet to, the youth community that emerged after World War II. Although this community did much to fuel the growth of the modern consumer economy, its rise and influence were disquieting to the nation's moral arbiters and cultural custodians. They resented Elvis's role as the first powerful musical representative of the youth culture. Not only did his music and stage act suggest a loosening of traditional moral standards, but he also represented and encouraged a new assertiveness among young people, African Americans, women, and working-class southerners. As a white southerner of blue-collar parentage who successfully fused elements of black and white music, Elvis seemed to be redefining American culture in an alarming way.

The young southern men and women who emulated Elvis when they took up guitars and pursued musical careers or who did so through the encouragement of their record companies have usually been described as rockabillies. Like Elvis, most of them adapted black or black-sounding music to country string instruments or otherwise made their music palatable to youthful audiences by blending the traditions of African American and white country music. Although a few women, such as Wanda Jackson, Janis Martin, and Rose Maddox, could rock with the best of the singers, rockabilly was essentially a musical genre performed by white men, and it provided an outlet for impulses that were embedded deeply in the culture of the working-class South. Carl Perkins, Jerry Lee Lewis, Charlie Rich, Gene Vincent, Johnny Cash, Bob Luman, Roy Orbison, Buddy Holly, the Everly Brothers, and a host of other performers projected aggressive, sexually tinged styles that captured not only the modern cravings of youth everywhere but also the hedonism that too often served as a legitimization of manhood in the rural South. It is difficult to accept the assertion that their traits in any way "expressed contempt for the American dream," but Stanley Booth is otherwise right on target when he compares the young southern workingmen of Elvis's generation with the rebels of 1861: "You even see their sullen faces, with a toughness lanky enough to just miss being delicate, looking back at you out of old photographs of the Confederate Army." For the most part, however, the rockabillies' aggressiveness was contained in their music, and, as was true of other "Good Old Boys" in the South, a strong streak of religious guilt infused their character and value system. Few singers so strongly embodied the contest between piety and hedonism (with the latter usually winning) as did Jerry Lee Lewis, the extraordinarily talented singer and pianist from Ferriday, Louisiana, but virtually all of the rockabilly men and women gravitated as easily toward the church as toward the dance hall. If their dress, hairstyles, demeanor, and musical styles often

19. Guralnick, *Last Train to Memphis*, 162.

seemed menacing to polite, middle-class society, the rockabillies nevertheless were not rebelling against larger society that had always excluded them. And for a brief moment in American history, these singers carried the music of the working-class South into the mainstream of American life.[20]

No facet of American popular music remained unaffected by the rock-and-roll revolution. The style of music performed by such singers as Bing Crosby, Frank Sinatra, Perry Como, and Jo Stafford lost its dominance. By 1957, Elvis's impact on traditional country music seemed equally devastating. Except for an occasional song, such as the version of "Crazy Arms" recorded by Texan Ray Price, fiddles and steel guitars virtually disappeared from the music heard on jukeboxes and radio shows and from the industry popularity charts. In the quest for a new Elvis, or for someone who could command the same popularity among young people, the record companies emphasized youth and sex appeal as much as talent. Older performers, male and female, had once appeared frequently in country music; it now seemed inconceivable that someone like Uncle Dave Macon, who had first recorded when he was fifty-six years old, could ever again obtain a recording contract. By the end of the 1950s, it also seemed doubtful that any singer could thrive commercially unless he or she demonstrated an ability to rock. Consequently, almost every singer, including such hard-core honky-tonkers as George Jones, recorded a few songs that contained the rollicking beat of rockabilly.[21]

Elvis and the rockabillies evoked a variety of responses among country musicians, most of which have had permanent consequences. Many fans and performers of traditional country music bitterly opposed the rockabilly genre, perceiving it as a threat to both conventional morality and musical purity, but elements of the style nevertheless moved into country music and have remained there ever since. Many former rockabilly musicians and fans eventually became sidemen or singers in country bands, disc jockeys on country radio stations, or journalists for country music publications. Country music became a haven for aging or failed rockabilly singers, and a few of them, such as Jerry Lee Lewis and

20. Probably the single best summary of these musicians is Nick Tosches, "Rockabilly," in *The Illustrated History of Country Music*, ed. Patrick Carr (New York: Country Music Magazine Press, 1979), 217–37. See Robert K. Oermann and Mary A. Bufwack, "Rockabilly Women," *Journal of Country Music* 8 (May 1979): 65–94. The classic exposition of that dualism in southern working-class men is still W. J. Cash, *Mind of the South* (New York: Knopf, 1941). Ted Ownby discusses the efforts made by the evangelicals in the late nineteenth century to tame the wild side of southern masculinity in *Subduing Satan: Religion, Recreation, and Manhood in the Rural South, 1865–1920* (Chapel Hill: University of North Carolina Press, 1990). See also Stanley Booth, *Rhythm Oil: A Journey Through the Music of the American South* (New York: Pantheon, 1991), 61. Lewis has attracted a fairly large number of chroniclers, but Nick Tosches has written the best account of him in *Hellfire: The Jerry Lee Lewis Story* (New York: Delacorte, 1982) and in *Country: The Biggest Music in America* (New York: Stein and Day, 1977), 57–84.

21. Malone, *Country Music, USA*, 251–52, 480–81.

Conway Twitty, became major country entertainers. More interesting, though, are the even younger musicians and singers such as Gary Stewart, Tanya Tucker, Marty Stuart, Travis Tritt, and Dwight Yoakam, who came to country music long after the exciting period surrounding Elvis's Sun sessions and for whom rockabilly conveyed no hint of scandal or controversy. They were too young to have heard preachers denounce Elvis from their pulpits or to have read the condescending or outraged remarks of establishment critics. To these singers, rockabilly was nothing more than a "traditional" form of country music.[22]

The country music industry initially responded to the rock-and-roll threat by trying to produce a body of music that would preserve a country ambience while employing pop instrumental sounds and group vocal backing. Sometimes described as the "Nashville Sound" because it was engineered in that city by producers such as Chet Atkins and popularized by a small group of sessions musicians there, or as "country-pop" because of its fusion of down-home informality and urbane smoothness, the style seemed designed for people who cared for neither rock-and-roll nor the older varieties of country music. With the fiddle and steel guitar temporarily abandoned and vocal groups supplying background support for the featured singers, the architects of country-pop produced a body of music that was politically and stylistically middle-of-the-road. Ironically, this music sounded much like that performed by Elvis Presley after he moved to RCA in the late 1950s. The country-pop "compromise," as it was also described, won great commercial success for the record companies that produced it, while also solidifying Nashville's reputation as "Music City, USA." At its best, country-pop resulted in the superb music of such singers as Jim Reeves and Patsy Cline. At its worst, it produced a bland, predictable, and overstylized product that was neither good nor country.[23]

While the country music industry made its various accommodations with rock-and-roll and the youth market, certain country performers made their own adjustments, often oblivious to market considerations and with little conscious effort either to revive or to alter traditional musical forms. They merely made the music they wanted to make. We have learned to describe their styles as "traditional," but in some cases their contributions were intensely innovative and, in every case, their music reflected all of the broad currents of sound that swirled around them in modern America. Throughout the rock-and-roll period and dur-

22. Several contemporary singers, such as Dwight Yoakam, Marty Stuart, Travis Tritt, and Hank Williams, Jr., move freely and easily from rockabilly to honky-tonk and perform creditably in either genre. A very instructive article is Karen Schoemer's "Marty Stuart Doesn't Need a Big Hat to Be Country," *New York Times,* July 12, 1992, 22.

23. Malone, *Country Music, USA,* chap. 8. Bill Ivey defended the country-pop genre in "Commercialization and Tradition in the Nashville Sound," in *Folk Music and Modern Sound,* ed. William Ferris and Mary Hart (Jackson: University Press of Mississippi, 1982), 129–41, and in his essay "Chet Atkins," in *Stars of Country Music: Uncle Dave Macon to Johnny Rodriguez,* ed. Bill C. Malone and Judith McCulloh (Urbana: University of Illinois Press, 1976), 283–87.

ing the country-pop phase that followed, strongly individualistic singers and musicians managed to create or preserve styles that differed markedly from the sounds heard on Top 40 radio. The quintessential honky-tonk singer George Jones preserved his hard-edged, soulful vocal style through every successive change and instrumental variation in country music. Another veteran of the Texas honky-tonk scene, Ray Price, competed favorably with the country-pop singers by combining his smoky tenor voice with a highly electrified instrumental sound that fused country fiddling and pedal steel guitar phrasing with the shuffle beat of jazz. A few years later, a transplanted Texan named Alvis Edgar "Buck" Owens took the style popularized by Price, added the vigorous beat of rockabilly, and made his own name and Bakersfield, California (where he established a mini-empire), synonymous with that of honky-tonk revivalism.[24]

Long before the modern honky-tonkers began making their vital innovations and well before Elvis launched his revolution, Bill Monroe from Rosine, Kentucky, had been building his own staunchly individualistic style of country music. Since 1939, he had been a fixture on the *Grand Ole Opry* with a band called the Blue Grass Boys, named in honor of his home state of Kentucky. This was a string band with a difference—the sky-high tenor of Monroe and a hard-driving ensemble instrumental sound powered by his blues-inflected mandolin playing. Exhibiting the influence of Jimmie Rodgers, black blues, gospel, minstrel, and old-time string band music, Monroe clung resolutely to the acoustic sound throughout the 1940s and 1950s when almost everyone else was adopting electrified instruments. He and his music were already virtually sui generis when in 1944 and 1945 guitarist Lester Flatt and banjoist Earl Scruggs joined the Blue Grass Boys. Flatt's supple singing and guitar backup style were widely copied, while Scruggs's sensational syncopated, three-finger banjo style made the Blue Grass Boys even more distinctive and attracted a growing legion of fans all over the nation. This was the band the young Elvis Presley heard and from whom he borrowed "Blue Moon of Kentucky."[25]

24.   Biographies and autobiographies of country musicians have proliferated since the 1970s. Their worth and reliability vary widely, but the more creditable ones include Dolly Carlisle, *Ragged but Right: The Life and Times of George Jones* (Chicago: Contemporary Publications, 1984); Bob Allen, *George Jones: The Saga of an American Singer* (Garden City, N.Y.: Doubleday, 1984); Merle Haggard with Peggy Russell, *Sing Me Back Home* (New York: Quadrangle, 1981); Loretta Lynn with George Vecsey, *Loretta Lynn: Coal Miner's Daughter* (Chicago: Henry Regnery, 1976); Tammy Wynette with Joan Dew, *Stand by Your Man* (New York: Simon and Schuster, 1978); Hank Snow with Jack Ownbey and Bob Burris, *The Hank Snow Story* (Urbana: University of Illinois Press, 1994); and Steve Eng, *A Satisfied Mind: The Country Music Life of Porter Wagoner* (Nashville: Rutledge Hill Press, 1992). The immensely influential Ray Price and Buck Owens have not yet been the subjects of biographies or autobiographies. Their work lives on, however, in the performances and repertoires of singers like Dwight Yoakam and Alan Jackson and, of course, in the singing of countless unknown musicians throughout America.

25.   The best short treatment of Bill Monroe is Ralph Rinzler, "Bill Monroe," in *Stars of Country Music: Uncle Dave Macon to Johnny Rodriguez*, ed. Bill C. Malone and Judith McCulloh (Ur-

By the end of the 1950s, the term *bluegrass* was being attached to any band whose musicians had once played with Monroe or whose sound resembled that of Monroe's seminal band. Preserving the acoustic sound, singing in the high-lonesome style of the backwoods, and featuring old or old-sounding songs, the proliferating bluegrass style was soon perceived as the most "traditional" sub-genre of country music. But bluegrass dates from as recently as the mid-1940s, and one need only compare the bluegrass version of a song with its original hill-billy counterpart (e.g., Monroe's and Charlie Poole's versions of "White House Blues") to discern how much bluegrass music diverged from earlier country styles. It is no wonder that Monroe did not seem particularly displeased in 1954 when Elvis recorded his supercharged and radically altered version of "Blue Moon of Kentucky." After all, Monroe had tampered with older hillbilly songs when he forged his own dynamic sound.[26]

Whatever Monroe's motives may have been, the musical style that he and the Blue Grass Boys created became a retreat for old-time country music fans and musicians. It must have been surprising to Monroe, Flatt, Scruggs, and other pi-oneer bluegrass performers to learn that their fans did not live solely in the towns and hamlets of the South where the early bands played or where their radio broadcasts reached. Bluegrass music also touched the lives of young people in other parts of the nation who were attracted by the musicianship they heard or by the mistaken belief that bluegrass was a traditional, Appalachian form of mu-sical expression. By the end of the 1950s, the style was being heard on college campuses and in folk clubs and parks well outside the South, and as early as 1957, bluegrass began to spawn "progressive" offshoots when a group of young musicians in Washington, D.C., the Country Gentlemen, extended the repertoire of bluegrass into the realms of jazz, blues, pop, rock-and-roll, and urban folk music.[27]

Bluegrass profited commercially from its association with the urban folk mu-sic revival of the late 1950s and early 1960s. Folk music had made inroads into the North, especially New York City, as early as the 1930s when such southern

---

bana: University of Illinois Press, 1976), 202–22; Neil Rosenberg, of course, devotes extensive atten-tion to Monroe in his comprehensive *Bluegrass: A History* (Urbana: University of Illinois Press, 1985). Another fine and provocative treatment of bluegrass music is Robert Cantwell, *Bluegrass Breakdown: The Making of the Old Southern Sound* (Urbana: University of Illinois Press, 1984). Charles Wolfe is currently working on a full-scale study of Bill Monroe and his legacy. See also Gural-nick, *Last Train to Memphis,* 121–22.

26. The term *bluegrass* was apparently coined by John Cohen, who produced and filmed a doc-umentary of the same name, dealing with Roscoe Holcomb and other mountain singers in Kentucky. Charlie Poole and the North Carolina Ramblers recorded their influential version of "White House Blues" for Columbia in 1927. It can be heard today on *Charlie Poole and the North Carolina Ram-blers,* County 505. Monroe's version was recorded for Decca in 1954 and can be heard on *The High, Lonesome Sound of Bill Monroe,* Decca DL 4780.

27. Guralnick, *Last Train to Memphis,* 121–22; Rosenberg, *Bluegrass,* 158–61.

rural singers as Woody Guthrie, Leadbelly, and Aunt Molly Jackson captured the hearts of young, socially conscious intellectuals and singers such as Pete Seeger and Cisco Houston. Periodically, self-styled folksingers like Burl Ives, the Weavers, and Harry Belafonte made the nation conscious of ballads and folk songs, but no flurry of interest came close to equaling that which followed the emergence of the Kingston Trio in 1959 and their widely popular recording of an old North Carolina murder ballad, "Tom Dooley."[28]

The Trio's performance of "Tom Dooley" was essentially a smooth, pop interpretation of traditional material, and the song reached the number one position on the pop music charts. It generated a national enthusiasm for folk and folklike material, most of it performed by young singers who had no experience with the traditions about which they sang. The folk revival, as it was soon called, won adherents in every segment of society and was particularly strong on college campuses around the nation. To most singers and fans, folk music was an innocent diversion that provided pleasure and little intellectual absorption. A small number of people, though, both in and outside of academia, soon became dissatisfied with the poppish and often sanitized interpretations of folk songs heard on radios and jukeboxes, and they began searching for both authentic representations and sources of such music. Earlier in the 1950s, the Folkways company in New York had produced a series of albums called *The Anthology of American Folk Music,* composed of blues, hillbilly, Cajun, gospel, cowboy, and other southern grass-roots songs originally recorded commercially in the 1920s and 1930s on 78 rpm records. For many young Americans, who usually discovered the collection in college or public libraries, the *Anthology* was their first introduction to the recorded music of the grass-roots South. Distributed by the prestigious Folkways company and labeled as "folk" music, the songs reached an audience that otherwise would have had no contact with them. The term *folk* lent the music a respectability among educated listeners who otherwise might have rejected "hillbilly" or "country."[29]

28. For accounts of the folk revival in the 1930s, see R. Serge Denisoff, *Great Day Coming: Folk Music and the American Left* (Urbana: University of Illinois Press, 1971); Joe Klein, *Woody Guthrie* (New York: Knopf, 1980); Archie Green, notes to Sara Ogan Gunning, *Girl of Constant Sorrow,* Folk-Legacy FSA-26; Neil Rosenberg, ed., *Transforming Tradition: Folk Music Revival Examined* (Urbana: University of Illinois Press, 1993); and Norm Cohen, *Folk Song America: A 20th Century Revival,* Smithsonian Collection of Recordings RD 046. The most influential early attempt to link bluegrass music with the folk revival was Alan Lomax's article "Bluegrass Background: Folk Music with Overdrive," *Esquire* 52 (October 1959): 103–9.

29. *The Anthology of American Folk Music,* 3 vols. (Folkways Records FA 2951-FA 2953), included recordings taken from the private collection of Harry Smith. The folk revival was paralleled by the emergence of a group of scholars, many of them in folklore, who began probing the origins of such commercial southern grass-roots styles as country, Cajun, blues, and gospel. Such scholars as D. K. Wilgus, Archie Green, John Greenway, Ed Kahn, and Norm Cohen were sometimes described as the "hillbilly folklorists." The first significant compilation of their research appeared in a special

The circulation of the *Anthology* and the burgeoning of the folk revival had enormous consequences for country music. The revival did not simply provide a forum for bluegrass musicians and a consequent entrée to a national audience; it also contributed directly to a renewed interest in the roots of country music. Mainstream country songwriters began dabbling with story songs about real or pseudo-historical events, and a few singers, such as Johnny Cash, became active on the folk revival circuit. Cash began building a relationship with young non-country fans that surpasses that of any other country singer and lasts until this day.[30]

More important, perhaps, were the musicians who styled themselves as folk-singers and who performed songs from the repertoires of Uncle Dave Macon, the Carter Family, Charlie Poole, and other musicians featured in the *Anthology*. Spurred by the *Anthology,* musicians, fans, collectors, and scholars began dipping into other recorded collections while also trying to persuade the recording industry to release such material from its vaults. If it was exciting to hear this music for the first time, it was even more exhilarating to learn that some of these performers were still alive. Buell Kazee, Maybelle Carter, Tom Ashley, and other pioneer hillbillies were rediscovered and introduced to revival audiences throughout the country. The search for these performers had other unexpected but fortuitous consequences. While looking for Tom Ashley, a banjo player and singer from Tennessee, two northern enthusiasts, Ralph Rinzler and Eugene Earle, found Arthel "Doc" Watson, a young blind musician from Deep Gap, North Carolina, whose extraordinary talents as a singer and guitarist have dazzled audiences ever since.[31]

Country music not only survived the emergence of rock-and-roll and the often agonizing readjustments of the late 1950s; it evolved in the succeeding decades as a force of great economic power. Some purists, of course, have argued that country music died with Hank Williams or that it did not survive the movement to the cities. The insistence that country music still lives is not merely an acknowledgment that a body of music continues to be commercially marketed

issue of the *Journal of American Folklore* (the "Hillbilly Issue") 78 (July–September 1965). The relationship between the folk revival and academic scholarship is explored in several essays in Rosenberg, ed., *Transforming Tradition,* but the best book-length account of the revival is Robert Cantwell, *When We Were Good* (Cambridge Mass.: Harvard University Press, 1995).

30.   Malone, *Country Music, USA,* 283–85; Johnny Cash's CD collection of 1994, featuring the singer alone with his acoustic guitar, and simply entitled *Cash,* American 45520-2, inspired a renewed interest in his music among youthful and rock-oriented fans.

31.   Doc Watson was first introduced to folk music fans on an album released in 1961, *Old Time Music at Clarence Ashley's,* Folkways FA2355. The most influential revival string band, the New Lost City Ramblers, recorded several albums for Folkways and made many early hillbilly songs available through Mike Seeger and John Cohen, eds., *The New Lost City Ramblers Songbook* (New York: Oak Publications, 1964).

under such a title but also an indication of the organic evolution of the music and of its intimate relationship to the lives of an evolving southern working-class culture.[32]

It is not easy, however, to generalize about a music whose dimensions have become so vast and whose audience now resides in every corner of the globe. On one hand, country music has become an industry whose leaders speak of producing a "product" for a mass market. Their goal is a commodity shorn of regional identification and class connotations that will appeal to the broadest spectrum of listeners and move readily across the barriers that supposedly separate musical categories. This quest for new audiences has been accompanied by the movement into country music of performers who have had no experience with southern, rural, or working-class life. Country music now embraces pop has-beens, former rock-and-roll stars, and alumni of the folk revival who have added new dimensions while simultaneously making it more difficult to define the genre.[33]

On the other hand, neither industry leaders nor entertainers could always accurately gauge public tastes or determine what music would sell. The homogenized sound of country-pop sometimes evoked boredom or discontent, as did the corporate, almost assembly-line methods of modern record making and merchandising. The realization also emerged frequently that markets could be found not only in various age and demographic segments of American life, but also that songs about working-class life, rowdiness, the South, cowboys, and even rednecks could be commercial. Even more surprising, perhaps, was the realization that many younger listeners, some of whom had been weaned on rock music, were among the most passionate of the fans of the older varieties of country music.[34]

Nashville never lost its economic dominance, and the Grand Ole Opry re-

32.   A young collector from Australia, John Edwards, popularized the idea of "the golden age of country music," the period running roughly from 1920 to 1940. After his death in 1960, his extensive collections of early country recordings and related materials became the basis for the John Edwards Memorial Foundation, a repository of American grass-roots music, originally housed at UCLA and now located at the University of North Carolina at Chapel Hill. The trustees of the foundation have been much more catholic in their musical tastes than Edwards was.

33.   The most prominent converts to country music have included John Denver, Kenny Rogers, Anne Murray, Emmylou Harris, Mary Chapin Carpenter, Nanci Griffith, Donna Summer, and Neil Diamond. Some of them, of course, like Summer, have made only occasional experiments with the genre.

34.   Gram Parsons is probably the best example. Before he assumed his stage name, Parsons grew up in Florida as Cecil Ingram Connors, an heir to great wealth who was nonetheless attracted to the music of the Louvin Brothers, Merle Haggard, and other working-class musical heroes. As the leader of the country-rock band the Flying Burrito Brothers, Parsons strove to incorporate country music into a rock format and to attract other young people to the old-time country sound. Excellent examples of his musical style can be heard in the Byrds' *Sweetheart of the Rodeo,* Columbia CS9670, the Flying Burrito Brothers' *The Gilded Palace of Sin,* A&M SP4175, and his own collection, *GP,* Warner Brothers 0598. See also Ben Fong-Torres, "Gram Parsons: The Spirit of Country," *Esquire* 96 (December 1981): 96–98.

mained an almost holy mecca for multitudes of fans. Nevertheless, alternative centers of musical production emerged in the 1960s and 1970s that provided Nashville with healthy competition while also injecting vital and divergent musical strains into American life. A few, like Memphis and Muscle Shoals, Alabama, and Macon, Georgia, became vital recording centers that demonstrated the pervasive role of the blues in the making of southern music. Austin, Texas, did not become a recording capital, but in the early 1970s it became a thriving haven of live music making where the traditions of rock, blues, and country music became intertwined under the romantic canopies of the Texas mystique and cowboy imagery. When music legend Willie Nelson arrived in 1972, he found a scene that was already booming and experimental and one in which the styles of western swing, honky-tonk, blues, and rock all coexisted comfortably and intermingled freely.[35]

Amid country music's commercial revitalization, and in large part as a consequence of it, came an unprecedented politicization. By the early 1970s, country music had gained a widespread reputation as the voice of the "Silent Majority," or of conservative Middle America. While many earlier songs had conveyed a workingman's populism, country music as a whole had expressed no explicit political agenda or ideology. The new conservative political identification arose from certain preoccupations strongly identified with southern history, especially racism, and from others generated by perceived threats to traditional moral values and the old hierarchical structure that had defined life and preserved order. These concerns gradually intersected with similar anxieties felt by other Americans. When a host of country singers endorsed or attached themselves to George Wallace in the late 1950s, they were endorsing the racial values upheld by the Alabama governor and also linking themselves to a feisty, populistic southerner who talked and behaved as they did. Even though the virulently racist and under-the-counter songs that came out of Crowley, Louisiana, with such titles as "Nigger Hating Me" and "Kajun Ku Klux Klan," had only regional circulation, as the 1960s dawned, the racism explicit in southern society began to match the mood of many dissatisfied white northerners as well.[36]

35.   The Austin musical scene has been much written about. See, for example, Jan Reid, *The Improbable Rise of Redneck Rock* (Austin: Heidelberg Press, 1974); Archie Green, "Austin's Cosmic Cowboys: Words in Collision," in *And Other Neighborly Names: Social Process and Cultural Image in Texas Folklore,* ed. Richard Bauman and Roger D. Abrahams (Austin: University of Texas Press, 1981), 152–94; Nick Spitzer, "Bob Wills Is Still the King: Romantic Regionalism and Convergent Culture in Central Texas," *John Edwards Memorial Foundation Quarterly* 2 (Winter 1975): 191–97; Clifford Endres, *Austin City Limits* (Austin: University of Texas Press, 1987); and Willie Nelson, with Bud Shrake, *Willie: An Autobiography* (New York: Simon and Schuster, 1988).

36.   Malone, *Country Music, USA,* 317–19; Neil Maxwell, "The Bigotry Business: Racist Records, Books Are Hits in the South," *Wall Street Journal,* April 20, 1967, 1, 12; Dan Carter, *The Politics of Rage: George Wallace, the Origins of the New Conservatism, and the Transformation of American Politics* (New York: Simon and Schuster, 1995), 314–16.

The challenge to traditional lifestyles, racial values, older moral presumptions, and masculine dominance posed by Supreme Court decisions and Great Society legislation gradually provoked a conservative backlash that lacked clear regional connotations. The polarization inspired by the Vietnam War and student protests only strengthened the conviction that America was threatened by a breakdown of authority and disintegration of moral values. The country songs that attacked the protesters, such as Merle Haggard's "Okie from Muskogee" and "Fighting Side of Me," or ridiculed welfare recipients ("Welfare Cadillac"), or called for a revival of patriotism ("God Bless America Again"), won enthusiastic audiences all over the nation and provided functional forums in which middle-class conservatives and working-class populists could unite in a common complaint against elitists, intellectuals, and well-to-do students. Jingoistic defenses of war and militant attacks against critics of U.S. foreign policy—from Vietnam to the Persian Gulf—provided public and acceptable ways for musicians like Hank Williams, Jr., and Charlie Daniels to impart their machismo apart from the normal avenues of boozing, fighting, and womanizing.[37]

Cultural anxieties explain much of country music's drift to the right, but a quest for public acceptance also prompted the actions of a music community that wanted simultaneously to be working class and middle class, southern and American. That craving for legitimacy could translate into support for a southerner and Democratic candidate for president in 1976 but more often has gravitated toward Republicans in the elections that followed. The conservatism in country music cut across stylistic categories and, seemingly incongruously, was represented by the poles of musical expression, whether that of Hank, Jr.'s hedonism or Ricky Skaggs's pietism.[38]

As the political stridency of the Vietnam years subsided, the corresponding tone also diminished in country music. An enduring legacy of that prior political involvement, however, and one widely repeated in the popular press and in country music journalism, was the explicit linking of country music with the patriotism and conservative moral values of working-class America. Popularly de-

37. The disaffection of many traditional Democrats from their party's liberal orientation began as early as World War II. Three articles in the *Journal of American History* describe the disintegration of the New Deal liberal consensus: Arnold R. Hirsch, "Massive Resistance in the Urban North: Trumbull Park, Chicago, 1953–1966"; Thomas J. Sugrue, "Crabgrass Politics: Race, Rights, and the Reaction Against Liberalism in the Urban North, 1940–1964"; and Gary Gerstle, "Race and the Myth of the Liberal Consensus" 82 (September 1995): 522–87. Merle Haggard, "Okie from Muskogee," Capitol 2626; Haggard, "Fighting Side of Me," Capitol ST 451; Guy Drake, "Welfare Cadillac," Royal American 1; Hank Williams, Jr., "Don't Give Us a Reason," Warner/Curb 26453-2; Charlie Daniels, "Simple Man," Epic EK 45316.

38. Although his songs have consistently voiced right wing political positions, Hank, Jr., has made no explicit political endorsements. Ricky Skaggs, in contrast, has been a vocal supporter of the religious right and of Pat Robertson's quests for the presidency. Skaggs has also become a prominent performer of contemporary Christian songs.

picted as "poets of the common man," the singer-songwriters Tom T. Hall and Merle Haggard lent to the music an identification that was proudly accepted by the country music industry and echoed by many writers. Consequently, the music became more explicitly working class in its self-depiction than ever before in its history. Throughout the 1980s and 1990s, songs like Alabama's "Forty-Hour Week for a Living," Travis Tritt's "Lord Have Mercy on the Working Man," and Aaron Tippin's "Working Man's Ph.D." praised the worker's pride and independence and complained about the burdens under which he labored as a wage earner and family man. Some of these songs seemed little more than reassertions of masculine authority, and one usually had to look beyond the ranks of the male country stars, and even outside of country music (to such rock singers as Bruce Springsteen and Billy Joel), to find expressions of a more inclusive compassion for working people. Dolly Parton, for example, sang about all kinds of workers in her album *9 to 5,* and Hazel Dickens, the great but sadly underrecognized singer from West Virginia, sang about women's issues and the problems of coal miners and other industrial workers with a biting commentary not heard in American music since the days of Woody Guthrie. But there were no Woody Guthries in the commercial country music of the 1990s.[39]

Country music's identification with working people was accompanied by a heightened reassertion of southernness. The Civil Rights Acts of 1964 and 1965 and the eruption of racial turmoil in the North may have permitted a renewed glorification of the South without the accompanying guilt that existed earlier. The national mood of conservatism also may have inspired a rediscovery of the mythic South as a region of contentment, stability, and bucolic values. But the equally old fascination exhibited by Americans for eccentric southern characters and exotic southern places may have done more to fuel the fad for the down-home humor and gothic backwoods drama that appeared so often in movies and on television in the 1970s and 1980s. Since the 1960s, country singers and song-writers have turned often to southern themes, sometimes resurrecting Confederate imagery to express an aggressive southern nationalism or a personal mode of machismo. They often submit willingly to the stereotypes of a simple and fun-loving people with songs and humor about "Good Old Boys" and rednecks but more frequently revive the revered idea—first voiced by Stephen Foster and the poets of Tin Pan Alley—of a warm, harmonious, and placid rural region. Most of these songs steered clear of politics, but on occasion a veiled plea for racial tol-

39. See, for example, John Buckley, "Country Music, American Values," *Popular Music and Society* 6 (Fall 1979): 293–301; Paul DiMaggio, Richard A. Peterson, and Jack Esco, Jr., "Country Music: Ballad of the Silent Majority," in *The Sounds of Social Change,* ed. R. Serge Denisoff and Richard A. Peterson (Chicago: Rand McNally, 1972), 38–55; and Richard A. Peterson and Paul Di-Maggio, "From Region to Class, the Changing Focus of Country Music: A Test of the Massification Hypothesis," *Social Forces* 53 (March 1975): 497–506. Dolly Parton, *9 to 5 and Odd Jobs,* RCA AAL1-3852; Hazel Dickens, *Hard Hitting Songs for Hard Hit People,* Rounder 0126.

erance could be heard, as in "Catfish John," and at least one song, "The South's Gonna Rise Again," envisioned a modern South barren of cotton fields and filled with skyscraper-dominated cities where the children of poor whites and blacks lived in harmony. A few songs even touched lightly on the theme of class consciousness, as did Johnny Russell's "Rednecks, White Socks, and Blue Ribbon Beer," which noted that "we don't fit in with that white collar crowd." Southern cities appeared occasionally in country songs, but, more often, the songs called singers and listeners back to the society described in "Mississippi, You're on My Mind" or "Sunday in the South," a region of small towns and villages where life was lived simply, close to the healing balm of nature and amid the reassuring warmth of friends, family, and church. Such songs have obvious appeal to southerners, but Americans everywhere can identify with the simple charms celebrated in their lyrics. Living in a highly competitive society, where neither abundance nor progress seems any longer assured, Americans can easily embrace the fantasies conveyed by "Rocky Top, Tennessee," and "Luckenbach, Texas," where life is lived free from smoggy smoke and telephone bills and "where ain't nobody feeling no pain."[40]

Country music has remained alive in the fifty years since the end of World War II because it addresses, with evocative language, singable melodies, and danceable rhythms, the basic longings, frustrations, aspirations, and prejudices of America's working people. It has not simply prevailed; it has become a powerful economic entity in the most intensely urban nation in the world. Its endurance gives testament to the survival strength of rural folkways through successive generations of urban change and adjustment and to the power of the rural myth among a people who have persistently moved to cities while never fully accepting their adopted domain.

Country music speaks in many languages and dialects, but its central voice is that of the South, and many people judge its authenticity by the degree to which southernness endures. The young performers of today come principally from the

40. Larry King discussed, with reservations, the attempts to convert the redneck into a romanticized pop figure in "Redneck!," *Texas Monthly* 2 (August 1974): 50–64. The contemporary fascination with the South and the consequent embodiment of that impulse in various styles of music is discussed by Paul Harvey in "'Sweet Home Alabama': Southern Culture and the American Search for Community," *Southern Cultures* 1 (Spring 1995): 321–34. A good overview of southern themes in country song lyrics is Melton A. McLaurin, "Songs of the South: The Changing Image of the South in Country Music," in *You Wrote My Life: Lyrical Themes in Country Music*, ed. Melton A. McLaurin and Richard A. Peterson (Philadelphia: Gordon and Breach, 1992), 15–35. Unfortunately, these songs are not readily available in any one place. The interested reader or listener must search for them in individual collections: "Catfish John" and "Red Necks, White Socks, and Blue Ribbon Beer," for example, can be heard on Johnny Russell, *Greatest Hits*, Dominion 3141-2; Tanya Tucker sang "The South Is Gonna Rise Again" on Columbia KC 33355; Stoney Edwards sang "Mississippi, You're on My Mind" on Capitol ST-11401; the vocal group Shenandoah recorded "Sunday in the South" on Columbia 386892; the Osborne Brothers' hit recording of "Rocky Top" was on Decca 32242; Waylon Jennings's "Luckenbach, Texas" was on RCA 10924.

South or from regions to which southerners have migrated. Many are the grand-children of the people who left the rural South fifty years ago to take up new resi-dences and occupations in the region's urban centers or in industrial areas else-where in America. Transformation came slowly, and the marks of the rural past endured on the automobile assembly line and in the steel mill and at other sites where industrial or blue-collar work was done. And they persisted in the housing projects and even in the suburban developments when economic opportunities permitted the move to more comfortable residences. Education and exposure to the national media blunted, but could not completely obliterate, the imprints of those rural beginnings, and traces lingered into the third generation.[41]

The young descendants of the rural South grew up hearing the music of that older society, usually as performed by professional musicians but sometimes in the singing and playing of their parents or grandparents. Often they rejected what they heard and embraced instead the musical styles fashionable among youth everywhere in America. Among those who have chosen to follow country music careers one still hears, amid the elements borrowed from Merle Haggard, Lefty Frizzell, George Jones, Willie Nelson, or other traditional country stars, strains absorbed from Bob Dylan, the Rolling Stones, the Eagles, Motown, Billy Joel, the Allman Brothers, or other rock influences.[42]

The country musicians of today pay homage to the rural past, or show evi-dence of it, in a variety of ways. Many of them have supported FarmAid, the movement launched and sustained by Willie Nelson to generate financial aid and legislative support for the nation's endangered family farmers. In supporting this cause, they of course link themselves to America's most cherished myth and one that conveys no hint of controversy. Similar crusades for the nation's equally em-battled steelworkers and coal miners have not been forthcoming. Endangered country styles have also evoked support from a large number of country singers who, since the early 1980s, have been described as "neotraditionalists." A few of these performers, such as Emmylou Harris, Ricky Skaggs, Dwight Yoakam, and Marty Stuart, have consciously articulated defenses of older styles and the vet-eran musicians who personified them while also performing music that honored these sources. Most of the neotraditionalists, however—such as George Strait, who contributed to the revival of Western Swing, or Randy Travis, whose vocals recall the sound of Lefty Frizzell—have preserved the older styles and demon-

41.   James Gregory has ably discussed the transplantation of country music in one of these areas, southern California, in *American Exodus: The Dust Bowl Migration and Okie Culture in California* (New York: Oxford University Press, 1989).

42.   Examples of these influences can be heard in a variety of tribute albums recorded by country singers: *Common Thread: The Songs of the Eagles,* MCA 924531-3; *Skynyrd Frynds* (a tribute to the southern rock band Lynyrd Skynyrd), MCAD 11097; *Come Together: America Salutes the Beatles,* Liberty CDP 31712; and *Rhythm Country and Blues* (songs performed by soul and country singers), MCAD 10965.

strated their commercial viability without crusading or drawing invidious distinctions between the various approaches available to country musicians. Nevertheless, they have all demonstrated that a hunger for the older styles exists and that such performances can be commercial.[43]

We should understand, however, that the southernness of country music is not defined by the rhetorical postures assumed by performers, or by the symbolism and imagery that surround the music, or even by the style of music that is played. Neither support for FarmAid nor neotraditionalism, for example, really defines either ruralness or southernness, nor does the wearing of a cowboy hat prove that its singer had a western or country origin. Musical nostalgia for the South, the western plains, or the old rural home place has been a staple of American popular music for well over a century, and it has often been purveyed by writers and singers who have never been south of the Mason-Dixon line, never been near a horse, and have no familiarity with rural society. The love for traditional music similarly has not been confined to southerners with a rural heritage. Some of the best performers of old-time music, in fact, have been northern-born musicians of urban origin. Country music, in contrast, displays its southernness in the lifestyles of its performers, most of whom are southern-born and southern-bred, and in the values they convey through their songs. While they sometimes succumb to nostalgia about a way of life they have never known or reverentially revive older songs and styles, most modern country singers and songwriters concentrate on the problems and concerns of today. Their accents and dialects betray their southern origins, and their songs often reflect preoccupations and values, such as individualism, religiosity, home-centeredness, the sense of place, and a faith in simple solutions, that are rooted in the rural past.[44]

When country music began its impressive national expansion after World War II, it spoke as the voice of a people who were moving away from agriculture and rural life to take up lives as wage earners in the towns and cities of America. In many ways, it was the "language of a subculture." It now speaks to, and for, a vast constituency that has no memories of tenant farms, coal camps, mill villages, Farm Security camps, or even housing projects. Many of its fans, of course, have left the ranks of blue-collar labor. But even though the specific loci

43. The first significant discussion of the neotraditionalists appeared as "The Old Sound of New Country: A JCM Special Report," *Journal of Country Music* 11 (Spring 1986): 2–25.

44. Mike Seeger, for example, the son of the famous ethnomusicologists Charles and Ruth Crawford Seeger and brother of the legendary Pete Seeger, has been an indefatigable champion, scholar, and performer of traditional country music. One of his most representative albums is *Tipple, Loom and Rail: Songs of the Industrialization of the South,* Folkways FH 5273. Excellent discussions that assay the relationship of modern country musicians to the South are Melton A. McLaurin, "Songs of the South: The Changing Image of the South in Country Music," 15–35; Richard A. Peterson, "Class Consciousness in Country Music," 35–63; and James C. Cobb, "From Rocky Top to Detroit City: Country Music and the Economic Transformation of the South," 63–81, all in *You Wrote My Life,* ed. McLaurin and Peterson.

of country music support can no longer be precisely determined, the music still carries the imprints of its earlier history. As the music of a people torn between tradition and modernity, who have struggled to make sense of their experiences, country music has bequeathed a style and message that finds resonance in the hearts of millions of Americans everywhere who are still trying to understand and come to terms with a complex society that increasingly seems beyond control.[45]

45. Gregory, *American Exodus*. Bruce Feiler describes modern country music as the voice of the suburbs in "Gone Country: The Voice of Suburban America," *New Republic* 214 (February 1996): 19–24. Of about thirty entertainers mentioned in the article, however, twenty-five come from the South.

Struggling to Be Old-Fashioned: Evangelical Religion in the Modern Rural South

TED OWNBY

F ew sights reflect continuity in the lives of rural southerners as clearly as a small country church, isolated from all other buildings and surrounded on a Sunday morning by just a few cars and trucks. The people inside, we might imagine, are hearing, saying, and singing the same words and performing the same rituals as generations of white and black southerners have done before them.

Historians have been slow to investigate how accurate this picture might be. Southern historians interested in modern religion have been drawn primarily to the roles of churches in the civil rights movement, the rise of the New Right in politics, the growth of the electronic church and its heroes and villains, and the fundamentalist-moderate controversies in the Southern Baptist Convention. None of those issues relates specifically to rural religion, although a group of fieldworkers and anthropologists have produced some lively and insightful analyses of the nature and meaning of rural white and African American religious life at the level of the individual and the congregation. Most of the field studies are sympathetic to their subjects, treating religious southerners with far more respect than one would have found in past generations.[1]

---

1. See, for example, Nancy Ammerman, *Baptist Battles: Social Change and Religious Conflict in the Southern Baptist Convention* (New Brunswick, N.J.: Rutgers University Press, 1990); Ammerman, ed., *Southern Baptists Observed: Multiple Perspectives on a Changing Denomination* (Knoxville: University of Tennessee Press, 1993); Ellen M. Rosenberg, *The Southern Baptists: A Subculture in Transition* (Knoxville: University of Tennessee Press, 1989); William Martin, *A Prophet with Honor: The Billy Graham Story* (New York: William Morrow, 1991); Hunter James, *Smile Pretty and Say Jesus: The Last Great Days of PTL* (Athens: University of Georgia Press, 1993); Joel Alvis, *Religion and Race: Southern Presbyterians, 1946–1983* (Tuscaloosa: University of Alabama Press, 1994); James F. Findlay, *Church People in the Struggle: The National Council of Churches and the Black*

The only problem with most of these works of folklife and anthropology is their lack of attention to historical change. By painting pictures of contemporary churchgoers and, often, by suggesting the power of the past in their forms of worship and belief, fieldworkers often seem to suggest that not too much has changed in the country churches. This is also the conclusion of many of the major works on the modern South. For scholars as different as John Boles, Dewey Grantham, and John Shelton Reed, the continuing importance of evangelical religion stands as one of the constants that makes the South the South.[2]

If the evangelicals themselves were asked if their religion is static, they would answer a resounding no. Evangelicals always hope to change things by fighting sinfulness in themselves and in other people, by witnessing to the world, by making some things better while believing that many things—maybe most things— are getting worse. For them, there can be no ideal past, not only because of Adam's sin but also because progress in some form is always demanded. Southern religion, nonetheless, has a profoundly old-fashioned side. That side lies not in the ways evangelicals have repeated the religious traditions of older generations but in the ways they have consciously adopted approaches they identify as being old-fashioned. Perhaps the unifying theme of recent southern religion is that attempt to define and then to pursue the old-fashioned. The best of the folklife

Freedom Movement, 1950–1970 (New York: Oxford University Press, 1993). Among the many excellent field studies of recent southern rural religious life are Jeff Todd Titon, *Powerhouse for God: Speech, Chant, and Song in an Appalachian Baptist Church* (Austin: University of Texas Press, 1988); Troy D. Abell, *Better Felt Than Said: The Holiness-Pentecostal Experience in Southern Appalachia* (Waco: Markham Press, 1982); Peter D. Goldsmith, *When I Rise Cryin' Holy: African-American Denominationalism on the Georgia Coast* (New York: AMS Press, 1989); Sally Suzanne Graham, " 'Right Now Lord!': Pastor Carolyn King and the Noah's Ark Holiness Church" (M.A. thesis, University of Mississippi, 1993); Steven Michael Kane, "Snake Handlers of Southern Appalachia" (Ph.D. dissertation, Princeton University, 1979); Joel Brett Sutton, "Spirit and Polity in a Black Primitive Baptist Church" (Ph.D. dissertation, University of North Carolina, 1983); M. Jean Heriot, *Blessed Assurance: Beliefs, Actions, and the Experience of Salvation in a Carolina Baptist Church* (Knoxville: University of Tennessee Press, 1994); Walter F. Pitts, *Old Ship of Zion: The Afro-Baptist Ritual in the African Diaspora* (New York: Oxford University Press, 1993); Carol J. Greenhouse, *Praying for Justice: Faith, Order, and Community in an American Town* (Ithaca: Cornell University Press, 1986); Bruce T. Grindal, "The Religious Interpretation of Experience in a Rural Black Community," in *Holding on to the Land and the Lord: Kinship, Ritual, Land Tenure, and Social Policy in the Rural South,* ed. Robert L. Hall and Carol B. Stack (Athens: University of Georgia Press, 1982), 89–101; Howard Dorgan, *Giving Glory to God in Appalachia: Worship Practices of Six Baptist Subdenominations* (Knoxville: University of Tennessee Press, 1987); Faye V. Harrison, " 'Give Me That Old-Time Religion': The Genealogy and Cultural Politics of an Afro-Christian Celebration in Halifax County, North Carolina," in *Religion in the Contemporary South: Diversity, Community, and Identity,* ed. O. Kendall White, Jr., and Daryl White (Athens: University of Georgia Press, 1995), 34–45.

2. John B. Boles, *The South Through Time: A History of an American Region* (Englewood Cliffs, N.J.: Prentice-Hall, 1995); Dewey W. Grantham, *The South in Modern America: A Region at Odds* (New York: Harper Collins, 1994); John Shelton Reed, *One South: An Ethnic Approach to Regional Culture* (Baton Rouge: Louisiana State University Press, 1982).

scholars, Jeff Todd Titon, summarizes this idea in his study of a white church in rural Virginia: "Religion at the Fellowship Independent Baptist Church is not a compensation for powerlessness and poverty, but . . . it involves the deliberate use of inherited traditions to make life meaningful."[3]

What traditions have evangelicals tried to uphold? Samuel Hill, professor of religion at the University of Florida, has offered four basic characteristics of evangelicalism—the forms of Protestantism found among Baptists, Methodists, and Presbyterians and the many groups that split from those three. For evangelicals, he writes, "(a) the Bible is the sole reference point of belief and practice; (b) direct and dynamic access to the Lord is open to all; (c) morality is defined in individualistic and personal terms; and (d) worship is informal." We can identify from these points three principles evangelicals in the rural South considered old-fashioned and wished to keep alive. First, old-fashioned interpretations of evangelical religion place the conversion of the individual at the center of thought, feeling, and behavior. Nothing in theology, politics, economics, morality, church government, or anything else should threaten that central belief. Second, old-fashioned religion seeks to uphold especially strict standards of personal morality. Third, old-fashioned religion values a face-to-face, almost familial, religious community. In yearly homecoming services and in many other ways, evangelicals try to keep alive the old metaphor of a church family in which people call each other brother and sister, strive to avoid sustained conflicts, and hope, through conversions, to bring "new births" into the family.[4]

In a sea of dramatic economic, demographic, and political changes, rural evangelicals who identified themselves as old-fashioned interpreted what was best and worst about their lives through these three lenses. Rural church life has changed in four ways, however. First, the growth of pockets of prosperity in some towns and areas near cities has resulted in wealthier and larger churches. Second, technological and governmental revolutions in agriculture and the ensuing depopulation and widespread economic crisis have challenged the ability of many churches to grow and even to survive. Third, political changes have had religious consequences, both in the increased political participation of many African American churches during and since the civil rights movement and, more recently, in the rise of conservative activism in many white churches. A fourth major change—no less significant than the others—has been the dramatic increase in the number of Pentecostal churches and church members.

One of the greatest challenges evangelical religion has faced is success. In the minds of many evangelicals, a church that became large and well funded and its members respectable and powerful was likely to face a crisis of complacency.

---

3. Titon, *Powerhouse for God,* 448.
4. Samuel S. Hill, "Religion," in *The Encyclopedia of Southern Culture,* ed. Charles Reagan Wilson and William Ferris (Chapel Hill: University of North Carolina Press, 1989), 1269.

They feared the members might take for granted the basic goals for which they once struggled—the single-minded commitment to saving souls, the belief in high standards of personal morality, and the comfort of a congregation based on face-to-face, almost familial relationships. On one hand, church growth and increasing social and political respectability suggested that evangelicals in the South were successfully expanding the number of converted Christians. On the other, many evangelicals feared the possibility of becoming worldly and only moderately committed to their beliefs.

The pockets of wealth in the modern South include many towns and areas that have only recently felt the influence of nearby cities. These areas provide new opportunities for growth in the size of churches. The story of two, no-longer-small Methodist congregations illustrates the effects that population growth and new prosperity can have on church life. In the early 1960s, ninety members met in a wooden church building about forty-five minutes from Charlotte, North Carolina. Just twelve years later, following the rapid growth of the area around that city, the church had three hundred members meeting in a large new brick building. Another church, thirty minutes from Knoxville, Tennessee, had about one hundred members in the 1940s but grew to four hundred by the 1970s. In both cases, most members belonged to households in which at least one person worked in the nearby city. Growth resulted in increased wealth as well as church membership, and, in both cases, a shiny new building seemed to represent a successful church life.[5]

To many evangelicals, rapid increases in church membership, numbers of churches, funding, new church buildings, and the complexity of church activities were reasons for celebration and calls for dedicated efforts to achieve even more growth. Southern Baptists led the way with a confidence that could border on the bombastic. The largest Protestant denomination not just in the South but in the United States, the Southern Baptists far outnumber other religious groups, making up almost half of the total churchgoing population of some states. In the post–World War II period, Southern Baptists have thought in big, round numbers. The Southern Baptist Convention decided its churches should strive to add a million new members to its Sunday schools in 1954. With the theme song "A Million More in '54," this crusade challenged Baptists to reach "every unenrolled person in your church community." A year later, a Southern Baptist publication proudly called its group "the fastest growing denomination in the United States" that set an "All-Time Record in 1954."[6]

5.   Lyle E. Schaller, *Hey, That's Our Church!* (Nashville: Abingdon Press, 1975), 75–80.

6.   On Southern Baptists' numerical dominance, see the essays on various states in *Religion in the Southern States: A Historical Study,* ed. Samuel S. Hill (Macon: Mercer University Press, 1983); J. N. Burnette, *The Pull of the People* (Nashville: Broadman Press, 1953), 16. Inside the front cover is a copy of W. Hines Sims, "A Million More in '54 Enrolled in Sunday School"; *Baptist Record,* February 3, 1955, 1.

Southern Baptists were not alone in the breadth of their vision. In 1989, the Sycamore Church of Christ in Cookeville, Tennessee, planned a nationwide campaign its members called "One Nation Under God." The church placed a full-page discussion of Church of Christ belief in the *Reader's Digest,* helped sponsor a week-long series of television broadcasts, and encouraged the fourteen thousand Churches of Christ throughout the country to sponsor simultaneous revival meetings. Most amazingly, the church tried to mail material on the Church of Christ to every household in the country.[7]

For evangelicals, adding new members expanded the number of souls saved from damnation. The goal of all of church life was to bring people to the altar to have life-changing experiences and thus to increase the number of converted members of the Christian community. As North Carolina Pentecostal Holiness preacher John Hedgepath asked in 1974: "Can we direct our church growth through the local church services to the point where our church will 'add daily' and yes, even more 'begin to multiply' for the Kingdom of God? . . . Nowhere in the Bible have we been excused for a lack of church growth." Paul Rogers, preacher of the Centreville, Tennessee, Church of Christ, allowed, "There is, of course, no wrong in having a small church in a small town, but there is something wrong if the church is not seeking to grow larger day by day."[8]

To pursue the Christian duty of expanding the church, many leaders of rural and small-town congregations adopted practices they associated with the most successful modern bureaucratic and marketing strategies. Paul Rogers made a revealing comparison: "Since World War II, the most innovative idea in merchandising has been the shopping center which enables the customer to park conveniently and have his complete shopping needs satisfied at one location." The church, he reasoned, should offer as many activities as possible—buses to bring people to church; nurseries; Sunday school classes for all ages; radio and television programs; publications; a cassette tape ministry; and classes, programs, and counseling for singles, the elderly, the poor, the sick, the imprisoned, and the "bereaved."[9]

A central part of this expansion of church activities and one of the most startling and often overlooked changes in rural religion has been the increase in the number of services at most churches. In the 1940s, churches commonly met to hear a preacher only one or two Sundays a month. By the 1980s and 1990s, the great majority of churches had preaching services every Sunday, most had two Sunday services, and increasing numbers also had one or two weeknight meetings and numerous seminars, camps, and other gatherings, especially during the summer. A quick survey of the services of more than 300 Southern Baptist

---

7. *Christian Echo,* November–December 1989, 10.

8. *Pentecostal Holiness Advocate,* October 5, 1974, 7; Paul Rogers, *Building Up the Church in a Small Town* (N.p., n.d.), 3–4.

9. Rogers, *Building Up the Church,* 4.

churches in eight rural associations throughout the region shows an enormous change in the frequency of Sunday meetings. In the 1940s, only 36 percent of the churches met weekly and 15 percent still met only once a month. The number of churches meeting weekly had increased to 71 percent by the 1950s and rose gradually after that. By the 1980s, all 359 churches in the eight associations met at least once a week, and all but 25 met at least two times weekly.[10]

Along with these added church meetings came more church employees and activities. Many churches that had long struggled to pay the salary of a full-time preacher now found ways to add a minister of music and even, with a radical growth in programs for children, a minister of education. Leaders of these programs often spoke in the excitable language of unlimited opportunities. As a church leader in Tippah County, Mississippi, reported: "Never in any year have we had so many advances as in 1947. We have had more associational enlargement campaigns than ever; more Sunday School training awards than ever; more churches participating in training than ever; more vacation bible schools than ever; more departments and classes than ever; more real emphasis upon vital promotional features of good Sunday School than ever; more study and planning for the best in the physical equipment than ever; more baby buildings than ever." To attract more people to these Sunday schools, a Southern Baptist manual offered "the laws of growth," which included the goal of keeping a ten-to-one ratio of students and teachers, creating new classes whenever possible, organizing grades by age, and having a building with enough rooms to accommodate a burgeoning Sunday school program.[11]

Sunday schools had been growing since early in the century and were commonplace by the 1940s, but the interest in long-range planning, teacher training, and expanded church facilities reached new heights in the postwar South. One of the clearest signs of the elaboration of church functions was the rapid expansion of vacation bible schools. The number of these summertime events, usually one or two weeks in length, grew quickly after the 1940s. In about three hundred churches in seven Southern Baptist associations, the percentage with vacation bible schools rose from 35 in the 1940s to 60 in the 1950s to 86 by the 1980s. Even in African American churches in the Upper Mississippi Conference of the United Methodist Church, which experienced dramatic declines in numbers of churches and members, vacation church schools became almost commonplace. Slightly

10. These figures come from a study of the association minutes from the following eight Southern Baptist associations between the 1940s and the 1980s: Broad River (South Carolina), Saluda (South Carolina), Alachua (Florida), Suwannee Missionary Baptist Association (Florida), Hardeman County (Tennessee), Sevier County (Tennessee), Anson (North Carolina), and Three Forks (North Carolina).

11. Tippah County (Mississippi) Baptist Association Minutes, 1947, 26, Mississippi Department of Archives and History, Jackson, Miss., (hereafter MDAH); Burnette, *Pull of the People*, 39–48.

fewer than a quarter of those churches had vacation church schools in 1945, almost half did so in 1955, and 62 percent did in 1965.[12]

A new church building was a dramatic sign of growth and a proud symbol of success. Whether a congregation constructed an entirely new church house or added a building to existing ones, the act of building made an important statement that the church was growing and planned to grow more. Church leaders loved to report to associations or denominational newspapers that they had completed—and paid for—an impressive modern structure. Church members often described their new buildings either in the breathless language of real estate agents or in the balance sheet language of accountants. The program celebrating the centennial of the First Baptist Church in Columbia, Mississippi, described a new educational building completed in 1950: "Built and equipped at a cost of $140,000, it contained refinements of soundproofing, space, and equipment for visual education, and room for church activities from Sunday School to large banquets. Two hundred fifty people could be seated in the assembly hall while the second floor auditorium held 400. The modern nursery contained germicidal lamps."[13]

The fascination with new buildings went well beyond downtown Baptists, Methodists, and Presbyterians. Members of a Pentecostal Holiness church in Waycross, Georgia, reported that their new building was "constructed of red-faced jumbo brick, with cathedral glass windows, asphalt tile floors, fluorescent lighting, oak pews and pulpit furniture with harmonizing woodwork on the interior." African American church leaders had the same interest in building in spite of extreme economic insecurity. Whereas a study in 1950 found that 87 percent of the rural African American churches in the South were wooden frame structures, forty years later C. Eric Lincoln and Lawrence Mamiya discovered that only about 20 percent were wood and more than three-quarters were brick.[14]

Why such an interest in building? First, an enlarged building indicated a commitment to the array of activities intended to make the church even more attractive. A Sunday school divided into at least fifteen different grades—the ideal number, according to Southern Baptists—needed a great deal of space for all

12.   Statistics come from a survey of the following Southern Baptist associations from the 1940s through the 1990s: Broad River (South Carolina), Saluda (South Carolina), Alachua (Florida), Suwannee Missionary Baptist (Florida), Hardeman County (Tennessee), Sevier County (Tennessee), Three Forks (North Carolina), Southern Baptist Historical Library, Nashville, Tenn. (hereafter SBHL); Upper Mississippi Conference, United Methodist Church, Minutes, 1945, 1955, 1965, J. B. Cain Archives, Millsaps College, Jackson, Miss.

13.   "A Christ Centered Century, May 14, 1883–1983," program of the centennial celebration of the First Baptist Church, Columbia, Miss., 9.

14.   Pentecostal Holiness Advocate, July 8, 1954, 3; Ralph A. Felton, These My Brethren: A Study of 570 Negro Churches and 1542 Negro Homes in the Rural South (Madison, N.J.: Author, 1950), 79; C. Eric Lincoln and Lawrence H. Mamiya, The Black Church in the African American Experience (Durham: Duke University Press, 1990), 102–3.

those classes to meet. Obviously, building a new gymnasium or "family life center" indicated a desire to keep members in and around the church as much as possible. Second, in a period of rapid mobility in the rural South, putting up a new church building was a sign of a congregation's intention to stay in an area. Always important as one of the few buildings African Americans owned and controlled in many parts of the South, a church was an investment that suggested stability in an often mobile population. Many congregations also saw a new structure as an impressive advertising tool in attracting new members. Church publications often described "the need for attractive meetinghouses in good communities" and the desirability of a building "of such material and construction as to be attractive to outside people of the community, and one on which all will look with a degree of satisfaction—one to which members and friends of the church will not be ashamed to invite others."[15]

Church growth, however, threatened all three of the basic points rural evangelicals identified as parts of old-fashioned religion. Many wondered if their interest in increasing numbers of members might bring into the churches people who lacked genuine conversion experiences. In the complexity of their programs of cassette tape ministries, multigrade handbell choirs, family life training seminars, and vacation church schools, could they continue to see themselves as simple people coming together to preach the word of God to the unconverted? What of their high standards of personal morality? Might the effort to increase membership require compromising traditional beliefs about acceptable and unacceptable behavior? Less often discussed, but also troubling, was the possibility that church growth would lead to congregations whose members were strangers and did not view each other as brothers and sisters.

The general evangelical belief in the likelihood of moral decline made any apparent successes questionable. Selling out, to some, meant using dubious methods to attract members into their shiny brick buildings. A member of a Church of Christ in rural Mississippi noted that in the early twentieth century, "the pure and simple Gospel was preached and it could produce nothing but love and harmony among the members." But since the 1950s, he said, "liberals" who thought they could "change God's law" tried to increase church membership by holding church socials, watermelon cuttings, barbecues, hay rides, and other amusements that detracted from the true purpose of the church. Other church members interpreted selling out for growth as allowing members to get away with things that might not have been permissible in earlier years. For example, the First Baptist Church in Sevierville, Tennessee, passed a resolution in 1949 recognizing "that we are surrounded with modernistic views being introduced into

15. Burnette, *Pull of the People,* 52–53; Lincoln and Mamiya, *Black Church,* 105; quoted from Robert Hooper, *A Distinct People: A History of the Churches of Christ in the 20th Century* (West Monroe, La.: Howard, 1993), 184; Church of God of Prophecy Bible Training Camp, *Lessons in Bible Training, Volume One* (Cleveland, Tenn.: White Wing Publishing House, 1954), 66.

our churches and that in many churches that under the guise of being 'broad-minded' and with liberal views the leaders have chosen by example and by teaching led our young people astray and utterly failed to warn them of the dangers of engaging in card playing, gambling, dancing, cocktail parties, mixed bathing, immodest dress, and other worldly things."[16]

For many evangelicals, the emphasis on increasing church numbership and expanding activities was most dangerous because it distracted members from the traditional concentration on the conversion of individuals. If, as Martin Marty, professor of religion at the University of Chicago, has argued, evangelicalism is attractive mainly because its vision of life is not "chopped up" into disconnected pieces, many have understandably feared that a busy bureaucracy might be consuming their churches. As Zeno Tharpe, Church of God preacher from Greenville, South Carolina, said in 1954: "We are pushing and prospering in practically every department of the church except along evangelistic lines. . . . We have an unending number of records pertaining to administration and governing the church, but we have none for evangelism." Church leaders have thus felt the need to stress that the immediate purpose of almost all activities is to save souls.[17]

Many churches have tried to turn every activity into an effort to convert the unconverted. Numerous Sunday school teachers and writers have reminded themselves and others that the goal of Sunday school is not to create a religious version of public schools but to convert children to Christianity. As a Church of God of Prophecy manual made clear: "The supreme business of the Sunday School is to win the lost to Christ. . . . These people in the Sunday School are at the best age for evangelism." At the end of camps for church youths, leaders urge children to consider having conversion experiences. An association of Tennessee Baptists that opened a pregnancy crisis center to suggest alternatives to abortion reported in 1991 that "a Christian witness is shared with each person with at least 2 making a public profession of faith. To God be the glory!" In funeral services Appalachian Baptists ask people to examine themselves and convert if necessary.

New church buildings also generated some fears about complacency. The confidence about new church structures was accompanied by a note of sometimes barely audible concern that new buildings and physical comfort might cause people to stray from old-fashioned notions of simplicity in worship. Mem-

16.   Claude Gentry, *"Wolves in the Fold": A History of the Church of Christ at Baldwyn, Mississippi* (N.p.: N.p., 1971), 3, 10; Harold Ownby, *Forks of Little Pigeon Church* (Sevierville, Tenn.: First Baptist Church, 1989), 88.

17.   Martin E. Marty, "The Revival of Evangelicalism and Southern Religion," in *Varieties of Southern Evangelicalism,* ed. David Edwin Harrell, Jr. (Macon: Mercer University Press, 1981), 7–22; Minutes of the Church of God General Assembly, 1954, p. 13, Hal Bernard Dixon, Jr., Pentecostal Research Center, Cleveland, Tenn. (hereafter PRC).

bers of one Baptist church in eastern North Carolina renovated the exterior of their old wooden church with bricks partly, as John Forrest writes, "to see if the members were sufficiently committed to the church to risk the financial burden of a fulltime preacher." Members decided not to change the building's interior because they took pride that "entering the church is like stepping back a century."[18]

That members of some growing churches wished to maintain old-fashioned interiors may be seen in the countless congregational histories members have written to celebrate their churches. Very often, the writer emphasized the special strength of character of the earliest members of their churches who met in rough, uncomfortable wooden structures. Church historians often reminded congregations that "the little pine-pole meeting house was good enough for them. It may, however, seem very simple to the reader of the present day, who has known only the comfort and luxuries which wealth brings." A history of an African American Baptist church stressed that the freed people had no resources to build a church house and thus, "in their humble and contrite manner, they built brush arbors and pitched tents in an effort to keep the first commandment—'Thou Shall Have No Other Gods Before Me.'" Repeatedly, such historians urged contemporary church members to emulate and not to forget the example of those who had it so hard.[19]

Another sign that church members were trying to remember old-fashioned virtues in the midst of increasing church sizes and complexity was a growing fascination with church camps for children. As part of the general expansion of activities for the young, countless church organizations established camps in remote areas. Camping, especially at camp meetings, was an old tradition among evangelicals, who saw a return to nature as a way to escape the distractions of town life and concentrate on religious essentials. Parents must have decided that towns and cities had grown so complex, perhaps so threatening, and certainly so secular that sending children to an exclusively religious environment for one or two weeks a year was a way to expose them to the face-to-face religious community they may have feared was on the decline. The Church of God in Christ has developed a greater urban membership than many southern churches, but every summer, children can go camping at All Saints Academy in rural Lexington, Mississippi. It was in that town that church founder Charles Harrison Mason delivered the first Church of God in Christ sermon in an abandoned gin building

18. Church of God of Prophecy Bible Training Camp, *Lessons, Volume One,* 124; Nolachucky Association of Baptists (Tennessee), Minutes, 1991, p. 37, SBHL; Dorgan, *Giving Glory to God,* 209; John Forrest, *Lord I'm Coming Home: Everyday Aesthetics in Tidewater North Carolina* (Ithaca: Cornell University Press, 1988), 120, 122.

19. East Fork Baptist Church (Mississippi) Sesquicentennial Celebration Program, August 21, 1960, 7, MDAH; Walter M. Johnson, "History of the Second Baptist Church in Oxford, Mississippi Since 1869," Second Baptist Church File, Office of Historic Preservation, Jackson, Miss.

in 1897, so returning to Lexington is a way to connect children to nearly sacred ground. Publicity for a band camp in 1995 advertised that young church members could "walk where Bishop C. H. Mason walked" and "appreciate their spiritual and historical inheritance."[20]

In contrast, the confidence Southern Baptists showed when they sang "A Million More in '54" had little meaning in rural areas marked by increasing poverty and declining population. Membership dwindled and many churches closed as migration from rural areas challenged those who remained to find ways to keep their churches alive. Migration left many areas without the population to support churches as they once did with their attendance, energy, and finances. The greatest challenge was not merely to survive but to make new converts. Evangelicals who judged the Sunday-to-Sunday success or failure of their church by the number of newly converted believers had real problems trying to fulfill their main reason for being.

Migration had the most dramatic effects on African American churches. One study found that membership declined substantially in the 1930s and 1940s in most of the African American churches in four southern counties. In one county in Arkansas, over 80 percent of the churches lost more members than they gained, and many churches lost more than half of their members. The Mississippi Delta offers a particularly vivid example of the problems facing churches in an area of economic devastation and rapid migration. Because high levels of tenancy necessitated frequent movement within the region, church membership for African Americans had long been less stable in the Mississippi Delta than in many areas of the South. The migration of the postwar period brought dramatic changes in church life. African American churches in the Upper Mississippi Conference of the United Methodist Church—the conference that included Delta churches—saw membership decline almost every year from 1946 to 1957, sometimes by more than a thousand members a year. In the Clarksdale district, the only group of churches completely in the Delta, membership dropped by about a third in the five years after World War II, and the district was dissolved by 1954.[21]

Many of those who left interpreted the migration in religious terms as an exodus from bondage and the northern cities as a potential promised land. To the churchgoers and preachers who stayed behind, migration represented a religious crisis. One Delta minister's report on rural church life in 1948 attributed the loss of twenty-two churches in the Clarksdale district to rapid migration caused by the decline of agricultural labor. Church officials complained that it was difficult to keep and train lay leaders in the churches, that the region attracted only "the

20. *The Whole Truth* (Memphis), Memorial Collector's Edition, 1995, 9.

21. Harry Richardson, *Dark Glory: A Picture of the Church Among Negroes in the Rural South* (New York: Friendship Press, 1947), 49–51, 65–67; Felton, *These My Brethren*, 36; Upper Mississippi Conference, United Methodist Church, Minutes, 1945–57, Cain Archives. Membership in the Clarksdale district declined from 2,208 in 1946 to 1,946 in 1951.

most poorly prepared teachers and preachers," and that members could not afford to keep churches in decent condition.[22]

Methodist leaders in the region called for new efforts to keep and add church members. Minister D. T. Jackson listed statistics in 1955 about the decline of churches and their membership and concluded, "By the above mentioned facts we should be shocked to an awareness that the hour is hastening on when we will either cease to be part of the great army or a fragmentary part of our former selves, greatly reduced in power and influence." Jackson urged prayer, "fervent preaching," and more aggressive use of revival meetings to attract new church members. Another minister, challenging fellow Methodists with the fact that churches in other denominations were not experiencing such decline, blamed "indifference on the part of some of the leaders and poor service on the part of the preachers." He likewise saw the problem of membership decline as a challenge for the rising generation. "Our past history has been glorious, the fathers have wrought well, with their limited preparation for the work, but you are expected to do greater works than they."[23]

The notion that rural church life is in crisis continues to be a popular theme for religious writers and thinkers. According to many such cries from the wilderness, the main elements of the crisis were shrinking populations, low funding, poor preaching by student pastors or city dwellers with little interest in rural people, limited church programs, and dilapidated church buildings. Writing in the 1940s, Kentucky Southern Baptist minister J. C. Dance saw a host of crises in rural churches. Preaching was irregular, poor, and uninspired. Without meaningful sermons, "there is not much reverence," and laypeople gathered for purely social reasons. Sundays schools met only occasionally and lacked trained teachers. Young people, he said, thought only about leaving for cities, and few cared enough about their churches to give them much money.[24]

The idea of rural crisis indicates a significant tension in southern church life. On one hand, evangelicals both rural and urban valued small rural churches for the face-to-face contact they offered church members. That was a significant part of the meaning of old-fashioned and no one wished to give it up. J. C. Dance, for example, followed his criticisms of rural church life by reminding himself, "So often the church yard holds in its bosom those nearest and dearest to us." On the other hand, churches that became too small posed a threat first of

22. Rural Church Report, Upper Mississippi Conference, United Methodist Church, Journal, 1948, 31; Rural Conference Report, Upper Mississippi Conference, United Methodist Church, Journal, 1949, 31, both in United Methodist Collection, Rust College, Holly Springs, Miss. (hereafter UMCR).

23. Report on Evangelism, Upper Mississippi Conference, United Methodist Church, Journal, 1955, 57; Report on Church Membership, Upper Mississippi Conference, United Methodist Church, Journal, 1946, 36, both in Cain Archives.

24. J. C. Dance, "A Voice from the Country," unpublished sermon from 1940s in U. N. A. Lawrence File, Southern Baptist Library and Archives, Nashville, Tenn.

dying but more immediately of failing in religious commitment. In 1945, a Southern Baptist in Chickasaw County, Mississippi, worried not only "that our country churches are becoming depleted and, in many cases, inactive" but especially that numbers of conversions were declining dramatically.[25]

What were the answers? One solution posed by many church leaders was to consolidate rural churches in some way. Combining the efforts of churches in fund-raising, in preachers and preacher training, in revivals, and in projects of many kinds seemed to offer a way out of the problems caused by declining members and funds. In 1950 Presbyterian writer Ernest Trice Thompson, believing that Presbyterianism was fast on the decline in rural areas, called for rural churchgoers to pool their efforts under the "larger parish plan" in which churches could share pastors, projects, and expenses. Disciples of Christ termed the concept "pastoral unities," and Methodists urged members of small churches to adopt what they called the "parish concept." Baptists, especially fearful of too much organization, spoke simply of "consolidation."[26]

In Calhoun County, Mississippi, many church members resisted the idea of consolidation. In the 1970s, the rural county had a nearly unbelievable fifty Southern Baptist churches in a county with fewer than fifteen thousand people. One writer called it "the most overchurched association in the Southern Baptist Convention." Because many churches had only about thirty or forty members, most were poorly funded, and many shared pastors. Some of those pastors believed that consolidation could solve the problems. Calhoun County dramatized the ways churches upheld notions of old-fashioned religion. Few of the county's people worked on farms, many drove everyday to factory jobs outside the county, and most rural institutions had been consolidated in towns. In such an atmosphere, a great many members resisted suggestions that they consolidate their churches. Instead, they preferred to stay with groups of families they had always known and especially refused to leave the sites of family cemeteries. As one preacher said with a bit of frustration, the reluctance of members to leave their churches for larger, better funded, more regularly pastored churches was "simply because of the ties they've had."[27]

A second solution was to attract newcomers. If the sons and daughters of longtime members were moving away, perhaps newcomers to rural areas could

25. Ibid.; North Mississippi Conference, United Methodist Church, Journal, 1974, 179–81, UMCR.

26. On Presbyterians, see Ernest Trice Thompson, *The Changing South and the Presbyterian Church in the United States* (Richmond: John Knox Press, 1950), 67, 80–83; on Disciples of Christ, Edwin Becker, *Disciples of Christ in Town and Country* (N.p.: N.p., 1950), 23; on Methodists, North Mississippi Conference, United Methodist Church, Journal, 1974, 179–81, UMCR; Mississippi Conference (South East) United Methodist Church, Journal, 1969, 192, UMCR; on Baptists, Carl A. Clark, *Rural Churches in Transition* (Nashville: Broadman Press, 1959), 8.

27. George Sheridan, "Is There Really Hope for the Rural Church?" *Baptist Program*, March 1973, 16; Everett Hullum, "Push a Little, Pull Slowly," *Home Missions*, March 1973, 50.

keep the churches alive. Around Boone, North Carolina, a Southern Baptist suggested that churches should do more to attract people moving to the mountains as tourists, retirees, or mining employees. Even in the Mississippi Delta, church leaders tried to search out the rare newcomer as a potential member.[28]

Church members' attachment to the face-to-face community, however, complicated this possibility. In 1973, Southern Baptist writer George Sheridan said that, despite a great deal of enthusiasm from preachers about the possibility of attracting people who moved into the rural South because of new industries or resort areas, actual successes were few. People moving to resorts, he said, were rarely comfortable in evangelical churches. And Sheridan quoted Kentucky missions secretary A. B. Colvin, who feared that "many rural churches are reluctant to welcome such members. They fear that a large group of new members will 'take over.'"[29]

The historian of one church that did not survive gives a particularly poignant picture of the appeal of the face-to-face church community in a time of extreme depopulation. Writing about the decline and ultimate demise of Longshot Methodist Church in a shrinking community in the Mississippi Delta, Barbara Jean Clifton Whittington described the struggles of the church to stay alive. Finally, by 1984, the congregation had dropped to six members, none of them children, and showed no signs of adding new members or attracting new contributions. The last holdouts of the Longshot congregation admitted they could not sustain church services, but they wanted to keep the church building for homecoming services.[30]

The Longshot story illustrates the problems rural church members faced when they tried to keep alive a notion of home when most of the meanings of the church as home were slipping away. Home as nostalgia—seeing old faces and doing old things in old places—was not part of a fully meaningful evangelical religion without the other crucial element of expanding the church family through new births. Unless they were adding new members through conversions, such congregations feared they stood more as monuments than as church homes. If members of evangelical churches believed their goal was to inspire conversions among as many people as possible, members of congregations in decline could not help wondering if they had failed.

At the same time, southern evangelical churches have long had a reputation for having little interest in political issues. From that perspective, the participation of so many churches in political action since the 1960s might seem shocking. In fact, recent political activity built in many ways on earlier precedents. Southern evangelicals have long claimed the right to enter politics to fight the orga-

28. Three Forks (North Carolina) Baptist Association Report, 1976, 20, SBHL.

29. Sheridan, "Is There Really Hope?" 16; Clark, *Rural Churches*, 20–21.

30. Barbara Jean Clifton Whittington, *Brief History of Longshot United Methodist Church* (N.p., 1988).

nized forces of sinfulness and worldliness. African American churches had political visions and served political functions since their origins, hosting political meetings and offering preachers and lay leaders as political leaders. Much of the thrust of African American church life, both under slavery and after it, identified freedom as a religious goal and held out a Promised Land as God's eventual reward for persistence and righteousness. White evangelicals had major political successes trying to unite their society around the defense of slavery in the mid-nineteenth century and the attack on alcohol around the turn of the century. By the mid-twentieth century, many felt comfortable addressing a variety of political issues. Thus the old criticism that southern religion concentrates so much on the conversion of individuals that it avoids earthly and especially political concerns seems invalid.[31]

Two developments stand out as new political emphases in the post–World War II rural South. First, African American churches took increasingly aggressive roles in the civil rights movement and expanded the range of their political and economic activities in the wake of that movement. Second, white evangelicals likewise expanded their political interests into new arenas, even if a great many remained issues of personal morality. In recent years white evangelicals have shown an increasing confidence that their messages and causes may win out in American politics.

Urban churches and their leaders such as Martin Luther King, Jr., are famous for their leading roles in the civil rights movement. Historians have not drawn as clear a picture of the political involvement of rural churches. Those churches, as we have seen, often suffered from declining membership and unsteady leadership. Moreover, they were particularly vulnerable to economic and physical intimidation; between 1962 and 1965, bombs or arson destroyed or damaged numerous African American churches, most of them in rural areas. In his important study of civil rights organizing in Mississippi, John Dittmer confronts a conventional, and possibly too comforting, notion about rural church life. "Perhaps the most inspiring image of the Mississippi movement of the 1960s is the packed Delta church, with hundreds of blacks singing freedom songs and impassioned speakers urging them to join the march to the courthouse the next morning. Yet in Mississippi the institutional church did not stand in the forefront of civil rights activity, and black ministers were conspicuously absent from the

---

31. Lincoln and Mamiya have critiqued the scholars who argue that the African American church has tended to look toward heaven at the expense of political action in *Black Church*, 197–99. Among the more important works that suggest white evangelicals have avoided meaningful political action are Samuel S. Hill, ed., *Religion and the Solid South* (Nashville: Abingdon Press, 1972); Samuel S. Hill, *Southern Churches in Crisis* (New York: Holt, Rinehart and Winston, 1967); John Lee Eighmy, *Churches in Cultural Captivity: A History of the Social Attitudes of Southern Baptists* (Knoxville: University of Tennessee Press, 1972); Ernest Kurtz, "The Tragedy of Southern Religion," *Georgia Historical Quarterly* 66 (Summer 1982): 217–47.

front ranks of movement leadership." Dittmer suggests that ministers consider-ing political activism risked endangering their support from middle-class blacks and any contacts they had with white town leaders. Likewise, in Albany, Geor-gia, an active movement with seven different protest organizations was well un-der way before protesters finally received permission to use the town's largest Af-rican American Baptist church. Two studies from the immediate postwar period found that rural churches were not greatly involved in political affairs. Ac-cording to one, only 12.8 percent of the rural churches hosted or initiated NAACP meetings in the late 1940s and no other group or political activity drew even that much attention. The other study concluded that ministers were "quite dissatisfied with conditions, but they prefer not to change if change involves vio-lence or bloodshed or serious trouble."[32]

Despite this slow beginning, rural churches and especially their members be-came crucial forces in the civil rights movement. Even if the congregations as or-ganized groups and ministers as individuals did not offer early leadership for civil rights activities, most came around to offering support after the movement was under way. By the mid-1960s, small-town churches had become common as meeting sites. Oral histories of the movement stress the role of religion—if not always the role of churches—both in providing inspiration for political action and in offering relief from worrying about the consequences. Tennessean Viola McFerren, for example, recalled that in tense times, "whenever it dawned on me the conditions that was existing, I would just stop right then and there, regard-less of what I was doing—whether I was putting diapers out on the line in back or if I was doing the laundry or whatever—I just stopped right then and I would pray. And I asked the Eternal Father to please remove the fear that I had because I couldn't live with it—it was about to get me down." Charles Payne's study of the Mississippi Delta may help explain how religion could motivate a movement without sustained help from church leaders. He argues that the rural protesters

32. See, among many possible examples, David Goldfield, *Black, White, and Southern: South-ern Race Relations and Southern Culture, 1940 to the Present* (Baton Rouge: Louisiana State Univer-sity Press, 1990); Adam Fairclough, *To Redeem the Soul of America: The Southern Christian Leader-ship Conference and Martin Luther King, Jr.* (Athens: University of Georgia Press, 1987); Taylor Branch, *Parting the Waters: America in the King Years, 1954–63* (New York: Simon and Schuster, 1988), 53; Aldon D. Morris, *The Origins of the Civil Rights Movement: Black Communities Orga-nizing for Change* (New York: Free Press, 1984); Lincoln and Mamiya, *Black Church,* 97. See also Bernice Montgomery Johnson's interview in Youth of the Rural Organizing and Cultural Center, *Minds Stayed on Freedom: The Civil Rights Struggle in the Rural South, an Oral History* (Boulder, Colo.: Westview Press, 1991), 70; John Dittmer, *Local People: The Struggle for Civil Rights in Missis-sippi* (Urbana: University of Illinois Press, 1994), 75; Felton, *These My Brethren,* 97; Richardson, *Dark Glory,* 154. Among other studies that question the idea that the church was at the center of civil rights organizing are Adolph L. Reed, Jr., *The Jesse Jackson Phenomenon: The Crisis of Purpose in Afro-American Politics* (New Haven: Yale University Press, 1986) 41–60; William H. Chafe, *Civili-ties and Civil Rights: Greensboro, North Carolina, and the Black Struggle for Freedom* (Oxford: Ox-ford University Press, 1980).

who were most moved by religious themes and language were women, who made up about three-quarters of rural church membership and "provided the everyday maintenance of the movement." For protesters like Fannie Lou Hamer, religion was more important as a sustaining (and often musical) force than as an organizing agency.[33]

Rural African American churches have become far more involved in political issues since the civil rights movement. According to Lincoln and Mamiya, about half of today's rural churches support civil rights organizations, especially the NAACP. Growing numbers have become involved in programs to fight poverty, to form cooperatives, to treat drug addiction and educate nonusers about drugs, and to help single mothers and their children. In fact, past involvement in the civil rights movement and contemporary involvement in antipoverty programs have become essential parts of the identities of many churches.[34]

For many observers of the religion of white southerners, its great moral failure has been its weakness in taking a stand on issues of race relations. For the most part, the record white rural evangelicals compiled on civil rights issues is far from impressive. Many congregations—it is difficult to determine how many—decided they would not meet with African Americans. For example, members of a rural Baptist church in Mississippi resolved in 1971 "that if during any worship service a black person should visit our church, our policy would be for pastor to have prayer and church be dismissed." Members of the Baptist church Jimmy Carter attended in Plains, Georgia, made news in the 1970s when they turned away African Americans they judged to be trying to join their church only for publicity. A second way many white evangelicals responded to the civil rights movement was to criticize and refuse to use denominational children's literature they found to be biased in favor of civil rights. Even more chilling were groups called the Christian Citizens' Councils, formed in 1947 by groups of Mississippi Baptists and Methodists that wanted "to create an effective army whose force will be exercised to destroy evil and to build up good." Although those groups formed with the goal of opposing the legalization of gambling and alcohol, it seems likely that they served as forerunners to the groups whites in the same state formed seven years later to oppose civil rights activities.[35]

---

33. Viola McFerren, in *Our Portion of Hell: Fayette County, Tennessee, an Oral History of the Struggle for Civil Rights,* ed. Robert Hamburger (New York: Links Books, 1973), 23; Youth of the Rural Organizing and Cultural Center, *Minds Stayed on Freedom;* Howell Raines, *My Soul Is Rested: Movement Days in the Deep South Remembered* (New York: Penguin Books, 1977); Charles Payne, *I've Got the Light of Freedom: The Organizing Tradition and the Mississippi Freedom Struggle* (Berkeley: University of California Press, 1995), 276. On Fannie Lou Hamer, music, and religion, see Kay Mills, *This Little Light of Mine: The Life of Fannie Lou Hamer* (New York: Dutton, 1993), 17–22. On women as constituting three-fourths of most rural congregations, see Lincoln and Mamiya, *Black Church,* 103.

34. Lincoln and Mamiya, *Black Church,* 109.

35. Arm Baptist Church (Lawrence County, Mississippi) Minutes, vol. 4, July 3, 1971, MDAH;

There were exceptions, and they were significant. Such important white reformers as Howard Kester, Clarence Jordan, Will Campbell, and James McBride Dabbs were church figures who interpreted their religious commitments as inspiration to challenge class and racial conventions. David Edwin Harrell, Jr., has suggested that some smaller sects have taken more diverse approaches to race relations than the Baptists, Methodists, and Presbyterians. Pentecostals began at the turn of the century with biracial congregations and a few remain, especially in tiny groups such as the Church of God (Jerusalem Acres), which has integrated congregations and makes no distinction between white and African American preachers. As important, many independent faith healers preached energetically to biracial audiences.[36]

Despite the exceptional Pentecostals and the occasional liberals, most churches in the rural South continue to be institutions for either blacks or whites. In a time of significant religious change, this is continuity.

The general absence of action on issues of race relations has not meant a lack of interest in political issues. Since the 1970s, evangelicals have become increasingly aggressive in using politics to address issues of public morality. This is hardly a new phenomenon. Around the turn of the century, Baptists, Methodists, and Presbyterians sought to make illegal activities they had long found offensive such as drinking alcohol, gambling, using profanity in public, and pursuing numerous recreations on Sundays. Almost always, they emphasized the sanctity of the family as their primary rationale. In the recent South, evangelicals have become more combative and more sophisticated in politics and have begun to address a wider variety of issues.[37]

In many church associations, reports on temperance gave way in the 1960s and 1970s to broader reports on public morals. Alcohol and gambling remained prime targets for legislation and lobbying as well as sermons, and Sunday recreations continued as a familiar if less compelling issue. Many went beyond attacks on alcohol to call for an end to advertisements for alcohol. But evangelical groups expanded their interests to attack the availability of drugs and pornography—widely defined—and to call for the right to public group prayer in schools. Above all, they condemned legal abortion, which to them signified the murder of a child, sex without responsibility, disrespect for the family, and (for some) the damnation of an infant's soul.[38]

Nell Thomas, *This Is Our Story . . . This Is Our Song . . . First United Methodist Church, Greenville, Mississippi, 1844–1994* (Greenville: Burford Brothers, 1994), 70; *Mississippi Baptist,* April 24, 1947, 2.

36.   David Edwin Harrell, Jr., *White Sects and Black Men in the Recent South* (Nashville: Vanderbilt University Press, 1971), 96–98.

37.   Among other sources, see Ted Ownby, *Subduing Satan: Religion, Recreation, and Manhood in the Rural South, 1865–1920* (Chapel Hill: University of North Carolina Press, 1990).

38.   On the rise of the religious right, see, among other works, Robert C. Liebman and Robert Wuthnow, *The New Christian Right: Mobilization and Legitimation* (New York: Aldine, 1983); Mi-

The increasing political aggressiveness has come not merely from the loudest voices in the media, such as Jerry Falwell, who ran the "Clean Up America" campaigns and the Moral Majority movement from Lynchburg, Virginia. It also comes from ordinary churches throughout the South. In 1984, a group of Baptist churches in western North Carolina praised their state legislature for raising the drinking age and defeating a proposed lottery. They also feared that their state "has become the nation's 'smut' capital with more sex outlets (x-rated theaters, etc.) per capita than any other" and urged church members to support Jesse Helms's effort in the United States Senate to "curb dial-a-porn and cable porn that has become so prominent." Finally, the group supported political candidates who pledged to vote against government funding for abortion. This notion of a moral crisis that necessitated political action was not limited to old farming areas. The Florida Keys Baptist Association resolved in 1992 to "take clear public stances on issues" because "public morality declines in such areas as gambling, abortion, alcohol, drug abuse, and sexual promiscuity."[39]

The roots of this increased political activity among white rural evangelicals lay in three major changes. Evangelicals have interpreted the rising influence of news media, the increasing availability of drugs, the dramatic increase in divorce, and Supreme Court decisions about abortion and school prayer as new challenges to their conceptions of family virtue and personal morality. It would be a mistake simply to accept their argument that they have become more politically active because the world has become more sinful. It is clear, however, that these developments have created a sense among evangelicals that social changes, especially in and since the 1960s, require them to work harder than ever to defend old-fashioned conceptions of morality. A second change was the growth in the size, wealth, and confidence of many Baptist and Methodist congregations. The same self-assurance exemplified in the construction of impressive new buildings showed in the effort to wield greater influence than ever on life beyond the church walls. But the most important reason for an increase in the political activity of white evangelicals lay in the development of a two-party South. For most of the twentieth century, southern Democrats did not have to take stands on issues of public morality because, as a monopoly party, they did not need to alienate drinkers or nondrinkers, gamblers or nongamblers, to win votes. With the rise of a competitive two-party system, however, Republicans in many states have gained advantages by appealing to evangelicals on a series of moral issues.[40]

---

chael Lienesch, *Redeeming America: Piety and Politics in the New Christian Right* (Chapel Hill: University of North Carolina Press, 1993); Robert Wuthnow, *The Restructuring of American Religion: Society and Faith Since World War II* (Princeton: Princeton University Press, 1988).

39. Forks Baptist Association of North Carolina Minutes, 1994, 38; Florida Keys Baptist Association Baptist Association Minutes, 1992, 5–6, both in SBHL.

40. The best work on the new two-party political system in the South is Earl Black and Merle Black, *Politics and Society in the South* (Cambridge, Mass.: Harvard University Press, 1987). They have surprisingly little to say about religious issues.

Of course, exceptions abound. Many churches, and many entire denominations, show no interest in politics and never have. Fieldworkers in Appalachia, for example, have found that most churchgoers there "are not particularly interested in the political process." A dichotomy between white churches' activism on issues of personal morality and African American churches' activism on issues of social justice is too simplistic; a great many African American churches share whites' concern over drugs, abortion, and pornography, and some white churches have made new efforts to address poverty and its effects.[41]

The most dramatic development in southern church life in the last fifty years, however, has been the growing popularity of Pentecostal churches. Pentecostals since the turn of the century have drawn both white and African American members primarily from Methodists and Baptists dissatisfied with their churches, their theologies, and their understanding of morality. Their appeal has long been especially powerful among the poor. Evident in the startling growth in size and number of both the organized churches such as the Church of God, the Church of God in Christ, and the Pentecostal Holiness Church as well as completely independent self-named churches, the dramatic success of Pentecostal religion has become as much a southern export to the rest of the country as music with a good beat, fried food, sugary, caffeinated soft drinks, and a certain brand of conservative politician.

Numbers of Pentecostal churches and members are not easy to gather, but it is clear that they are growing rapidly. The Church of God in Christ is clearly the fastest-growing African American church not merely in the rural South but throughout the country, with over 10,000 churches and 4 million members. The development of the Church of God, the group Martin Marty can confidently state "had the fastest growth rate among white churches after midcentury," provides a clear example of Pentecostal growth since World War II. Between the mid-1940s and the late 1980s, the number of churches more than doubled in each southern state. Most dramatically, the 265 Churches of God in Georgia and Florida in 1946 grew to 786 by 1990. Membership increased as dramatically as the numbers of churches, growing from about nine thousand in Georgia in 1948 to over sixty-six thousand by 1985 and from approximately four thousand in Kentucky to eighteen thousand by 1987 (see table). Almost three-quarters of these churches were in rural areas and small towns and a great many began in abandoned schoolhouses and stores, tents, mobile homes, and even abandoned bars.[42]

41.   Titon, *Powerhouse for God,* 157; Abell, *Better Felt Than Said,* 152–53; Dorgan, *Giving Glory to God in Appalachia;* Deborah Vansau McCauley, *Appalachian Mountain Religion: A History* (Urbana: University of Illinois Press, 1995).

42.   Hans A. Baer and Merrill Singer, *African-American Religion in the Twentieth Century: Varieties of Protest and Accommodation* (Knoxville: University of Tennessee Press, 1992), 155; Martin E. Marty, *Pilgrims in Their Own Land: 500 Years of Religion in America* (Boston: Little, Brown, 1984), 469.

Numbers and Members of Churches of God, 1946–1990

State	Year	No. of Churches	Year	No. of Churches
Alabama	1946	157	1990	396
Florida	1946	179	1990	500
Georgia	1948	86	1985	286
Kentucky	1945	75	1987	212
Louisiana	1946	28	1990	60
North Carolina	1945	128	1986	348
South Carolina	1943	143	1984	354
Tennessee	1945	122	1987	324

State	Year	No. of Members	Year	No. of Members
Georgia	1948	9,090	1985	66,735
Kentucky	1949	4,000	1987	18,033
South Carolina	1950	9,179	1989	29,015
Tennessee	1950	10,722	1989	42,364

Sources: Church of God, Minutes of the Annual Assembly, 1946, 90–95, PRC; Minutes of the Annual Assembly, 1990, PRC, 388–404; *The Continuing Generations: A History of the Church of God in Georgia* (Cleveland, Tenn.: Pathway Press, 1986), 20, 261; *The Church of God of Kentucky, a History, 1911–1987* (Charlotte, N.C.: Delmar, n.d.), 160, 164; *A History of the Church of God of North Carolina, 1886–1978* (Charlotte, N.C.: Herb Eaton, n.d.), 96–99; *Tennessee Church of God History, 1886–1990* (Cleveland, Tenn.: Pathway Press, 1990), 84–92; *South Carolina Church of God History, 1914–1986* (Cleveland, Tenn.: Pathway Press, 1986), 53, 76.

Six elements distinguish Pentecostal and Holiness religion from other forms of evangelicalism. First is the crucial doctrine of sanctification, an elaboration of the Wesleyan doctrine of perfectionism or freedom from sin. As the manual of the Church of God in Christ states, sanctification means "that gracious and continuous operation of the Holy Ghost, by which He delivers the justified sinner from the pollution of sin, renews his whole nature in the image of God and enables him to perform good works." A significant step beyond the crucial moment of conversion, sanctification is an experience reserved for adults. Pentecostals often describe the effects of sanctification in the way other evangelicals characterize conversion. One white Church of God preacher said that until a person experiences sanctification, "there will still be things in the world that will glitter in your eyes." After reaching that stage, "you will become a new creature in Christ, and will be living in a new world."[43]

43. The following discussion is based on field studies such as Abell, *Better Felt Than Said;* Graham, " 'Right Now Lord!,' " Goldsmith, *When I Rise,* and works of history and theology such as Vinson Synan, *The Holiness-Pentecostal Movement in the United States* (Grand Rapids, Mich.: Eerdmans, 1971); Joseph R. Washington, Jr., *Black Sects and Cults* (Lanham, Md.: University Press of America, 1972); Lincoln and Mamiya, *Black Church,* 76–91; Baer and Singer, *African-American Religion in the Twentieth Century;* W. J. Hollenweger, *The Pentecostals: The Charismatic Movement in the Churches* (Minneapolis: Augsburg, 1972); John Thomas Nichol, *Pentecostalism* (New York: Harper & Row, 1966); Joseph E. Campbell, *The Pentecostal Holiness Church, 1898–1948: Its Back-*

The second key Pentecostal and Holiness doctrine attracts the most attention from outsiders. Church members describe the baptism of the Holy Ghost as a feeling that comes only to those who have been sanctified. Members of Pentecostal-Holiness churches in Appalachia described Holy Ghost baptism as "the zenith of spiritual experience." That experience is decidedly communal, intense, and joyful. In many churches, sanctification and Holy Ghost baptism are the ultimate goals of the services, just as conversion is the ultimate goal of many other evangelical churches. Preachers often ask congregations for more open signs of Holy Ghost baptism; as one said, "It's awful quiet tonight; it's too quiet for a Pentecostal-Holiness meeting. You act like you don't believe it tonight." During services, church members raise their hands, sway, shake, stomp their feet, shout, weep, hug, and pray with a fervency often expressed through volume. Throughout much of the experience, they sing or keep rhythm with the testimonies of other church members. Percussion, in the services of both whites and African Americans, plays a major role in the music. Such experiences often strike outsiders as anarchy and undirected emotionalism, but the church members themselves say they are using various forms of worship as testimonies about the power of the Holy Ghost. Churches of God and Pentecostal-Holiness churches report conversions, sanctifications, and Holy Ghost baptisms to their state organizations, just as many other churches count new church members.[44]

The notion of Holy Ghost baptism shows in a variety of forms of worship that words seem empty to describe. Two of the major works describing Pentecostal church services, one among African Americans in Georgia and one among whites in Appalachia, stress that the members believe their experiences transcend conventional language. Sally Graham writes that members of Noah's Ark Holiness Church in rural Georgia "say there are no words adequate to explain the experience of being filled with the Holy Ghost and contend the only way an outsider will understand is by becoming open to experiencing the baptism of the Holy Ghost themselves." Church member Doris Pierce told Troy Abell that the experience was "better felt than said." This inability to convey the nature of a spiritual experience helps explain the importance of speaking in tongues—a third and one of the most distinctive parts of Pentecostal and Holiness worship. For Pentecostals, glossolalia is essential in communicating the intensity of the experience of the Holy Ghost.[45]

Fourth, one of the most famous of all Pentecostal forms of worship is snake

ground and History (Franklin Springs, Ga.: Pentecostal Holiness Church, 1951); Mickey Crews, The Church of God: A Social History (Knoxville: University of Tennessee Press, 1990); Robert Robinson, An Introduction to Church of God in Christ: History, Theology and Structure (Little Rock: Author, 1988), 45; J. D. Bright, "Fleeing from and Following After," in Camp Meeting Sermons, ed. J. D. Free (N.p.: N.p., n.d.), 48.

44. Abell, Better Felt Than Said, 35, 126–27.
45. Graham, " 'Right Now Lord!,' " 116; Abell, Better Felt Than Said, 167.

handling, a practice common in only a few Appalachian churches. Like Pentecostalism, handling poisonous snakes as a Christian experience is a twentieth-century innovation, apparently originating in the 1910s. Congregations that handle snakes are most often of independent churches with names such as the Church of God with Signs Following or the Holiness Church of God in Jesus Name. It seems, sometimes, that there may be more filmmakers and ethnographers studying snake handling than there are people actually handling snakes, but the practice remains significant as another form of worship involved in sanctification and Holy Ghost baptism. To snake handlers, the practice is a biblically supported method of showing that a believer has indeed reached a sanctified state.[46]

Many more Pentecostals practice healing. Troy Abell found that almost every service in the Appalachian Pentecostal Holiness churches he attended allowed time for healing, and more than three-quarters of the church members claimed to have experienced Christian healing. At the far edge of this practice was the Tennessee preacher who, in 1981, tried to raise his drowned son from the dead with a three-day service that included the prayer, "I thank You, Lord, that You're a blind-eye opener, that You're a deaf-ear unstopperer, that You're a cancer healer, that you're a tumor disappearer, and You're a *DEAD!* raiser!" Although very few Pentecostals go this far, the practice of healing is common in some form from the smallest African American and white churches to the largest churches in Oral Roberts's healing empire.[47]

Last, scattered among Pentecostals are beliefs in prophesying and casting out demons. Believing strongly in the imminent return of Jesus Christ, many church members tell about dreams and signs they interpreted as suggesting that the Second Coming will occur soon. For members of the Church of God in Christ, the activity and popularity of demons—evil forces sent by Satan—"is a sign of the approaching end of this Age."[48]

No scholar has yet offered a full explanation of the dramatic growth of Pentecostalism in the recent South, and one must be cautious in making such an effort. Pentecostal churches have seen themselves as the latest in the long line of reformed Protestant churches that have tried to shuck established ways of worshiping and begin again along the lines of the original Christian church. More specifically, they see themselves as giving new life to the central importance of

---

46. Kane, "Snake Handlers of Southern Appalachia"; David L. Kimbrough, *Taking Up Serpents: Snake Handlers of Eastern Kentucky* (Chapel Hill: University of North Carolina Press, 1995); Thomas Benton, *Serpent-Handling Believers* (Knoxville: University of Tennessee Press, 1993).

47. Abell, *Better Felt Than Said*, 37–38; Patsy Sims, *Can Somebody Shout Amen!* (New York: St. Martin's Press, 1988), 41; Graham, " 'Right Now Lord!' "; Goldsmith, *When I Rise;* David Edwin Harrell, Jr., *All Things Are Possible: The Healing and Charismatic Revivals in Modern America* (Bloomington: Indiana University Press, 1975).

48. Abell, *Better Felt Than Said*, 38–41; Graham, " 'Right Now Lord!,' " 63–67; Robinson, *Church of God in Christ*, 39.

conversion, of strict personal morality, and of the face-to-face community. Their goal seems to be to keep alive the small, personal congregation and to spread it throughout the world.

Peter Goldsmith's study of a Church of God in Christ congregation in Georgia offers an excellent entry into why so many Baptists have moved into Pentecostal churches. He finds that Baptists who joined the Harlem Church of God in Christ said they were leaving the anonymity of the larger and quieter Baptist church. Every member of the new congregation is *expected* to testify about his or her experiences. That notion of the face-to-face community seems especially important in upholding standards of moral behavior. Church of God in Christ members believe that while they look after and question the behavior of fellow church members to hold them to a high standard, the anonymity of much larger Baptist churches allows their members to be "Sunday Christians" who leave their religious convictions at church.

Encouraging individual creativity in a small, personal communal setting seems crucial to the growing appeal of Pentecostalism. Many smaller churches encourage all members to be creative artists in their own ways. All concentrate on giving spoken testimonies about their own experiences. A great many rural southerners have also produced extraordinary works of visual art dominated by Pentecostal themes of the reality of Satan, the need for conversion and sanctification, and the imminent return of Jesus. One of the clearest examples of a specifically Pentecostal form of religious art is the work of rural Georgian J. B. Murray, who fills his art with a script he interprets as a version of speaking in tongues.[49]

As much as any evangelicals and far more than most, Pentecostals emphasize creativity in music. Perhaps most famous of all was the Assemblies of God church in Tupelo, Mississippi, where eleven-year-old Elvis Presley made his first singing appearance. Sally Graham has detailed four forms of music in Noah's Ark Holiness Church. Along with nineteenth-century spirituals like "I'll Fly Away" and more modern gospel songs such as "This Little Light of Mine," church members sing religious adaptations of modern pop songs like "You Are So Beautiful." Most intriguingly, many church members are "divinely inspired" to create their own songs, and those who do not originate songs have favorite tunes they request from the congregation. The notion of turning church members into a community of performers who testify through their music shows clearly in the popularity of gospel musicians. William Lynwood Montell documented an incredible 812 gospel singing groups in the post–World War II period with their roots in nineteen counties in south-central Kentucky. Not all of those

49. Goldsmith, *When I Rise*, 82; Graham, "'Right Now Lord!,'" 90–94; Judith McWillie, "Writing in an Unknown Tongue," in *Cultural Perspectives on the American South:* Vol. 5, *Religion*, ed. Charles Reagan Wilson (New York: Gordon and Breach, 1991), 107–11.

groups emerged from Pentecostal churches, but almost all came from the small evangelical churches, and hardly any came from downtown First Baptist or First Methodist congregations.[50]

With their concentration on the personal, the face-to-face, and the experiential sides of religion, most Pentecostals have shown little interest in public life and government. Although Church of God in Christ headquarters served as a base for the involvement of Martin Luther King, Jr., in the Memphis sanitation workers' strike, most of its rural churches have remained less politically aggressive than most other African American churches. As Goldsmith writes of a Church of God in Christ congregation in coastal Georgia, "Since the first flowering of Afro-American social action, Pentecostals have been conspicuously absent. . . . Problems of the world are not thought to be soluble through action in the world." Yearly conferences of the Church of God have occasionally made policy statements ranging in topic from segregation to prayer in school to abortion. In general, however, such churches and most assuredly the smaller and less organized Pentecostal groups have not seen political action as a significant part of their mission. Pentecostals prefer to uphold especially strict standards of behavior but believe they can accomplish little through legislation.[51]

It would be a great mistake to see Pentecostals, with their small churches and general disinterest in politics, as uninterested in changing the world. The Churches of God, the Churches of God in Christ, and the Churches of God of Prophecy have all been very active in sending missionaries throughout the country and the world. A sign hanging today outside the first Church of God in Christ ever organized proudly proclaims, "The Movement Has Grown to Cover the Entire United States and 52 Foreign Countries," and the denomination describes itself as "the fastest growing Pentecostal Church in the world." Church of God speaker John Jernigan had similar ambitions in 1946 when he discussed the "great possibilities of becoming the world's leading church," and by 1974 that organization had a goal of establishing one new church everyday. Discussing the international growth of the Church of God of Prophecy, an in-house historian claimed in 1977 that "from the isolated hills of North Carolina, at the beginning of the Twentieth Century, to every nook and corner of the entire world by the end of the same century, the Church of God will achieve what has never been accomplished before in the history of mankind."[52]

50.   Peter Guralnick, *Last Train to Memphis: The Rise of Elvis Presley* (Boston: Little, Brown, 1994), 19–20; Graham, " 'Right Now Lord!,' " 95–103; Goldsmith, *When I Rise;* Otho B. Cobbins, ed., *History of Church of Christ (Holiness) U.S.A.* (New York: Vantage Press, 1966), 399; William Lynwood Montell, *Singing the Glory Down: Amateur Gospel Music in South Central Kentucky, 1900–1990* (Lexington: University Press of Kentucky, 1991), 203–25.

51.   Goldsmith, *When I Rise,* 77; Lincoln and Mamiya, *The Black Church,* 224; Crews, *Church of God,* 161–78.

52.   Robinson, *Church of God in Christ,* 14; Church of God, Minutes of the Annual Assembly, 1946, 17, PRC; Charles W. Conn, *Like a Mighty Army: A History of the Church of God, 1886–1976*

The goal seems to have been to build new churches throughout the world *and to keep them small*. At a time when most evangelical congregations portray growth as the clear sign of success, Pentecostal churches have remained small. This effort to replicate the traditional model of the face-to-face church community shows most clearly in the growth of the Church of God of Prophecy. One of several churches with headquarters in Cleveland, Tennessee, its membership more than doubled in the South from the 1950s to the 1980s, but it did so without abandoning the idea of small churches. In 1952, 672 churches averaged 31.6 members. By 1980, 1,142 churches averaged a still small 39.5 members. Members need not fear becoming lost in a crowd or losing their chance to give their testimony.[53]

As Pentecostals see their place in history, their main goal is to avoid the temptations of complacency that they feel have plagued other reformed groups. John Jernigan's plea to Church of God members in 1946 had a clear sense of history. Previous evangelical churches had challenged existing forms of religion and then enjoyed "large organizations, big congregations, fine church houses, plenty of money, and an educated ministry, with the world patting them on the back." Those churches, "in their backslidden and compromised condition," offered a lesson to Pentecostals. "The devil and the world are bidding for the Church of God. They are offering us a place in society and politics—and the spirit of the world is beginning to invade our borders." The official historian of the Pentecostal Holiness Church issued the same solemn warning in 1951: "Wealth and education are the two greatest enemies of the Church. The proper use of wealth and education is possible but highly improbable. These two factors have been the downfall of others. Our place is to work among the poor, the untutored and disfranchised." Likewise, in an address in 1989, Church of God in Christ presiding bishop J. O. Patterson "lamented over the condition of the present day church" and urged members to avoid materialism, extravagance, and the pride that might come from too much public acceptance. As the Church of God in Christ publication the *Whole Truth* reported, "He raised the issue of what true holiness would do, however our customs have minimized the effects. . . . The laity was encouraged not to conform but rather be transformed from the world."[54]

In many ways, the rise of Pentecostalism shows rural southerners trying to merge their contemporary experiences with their understanding of old-fashioned religion. If movement toward large churches threatened to make many evangelical churchgoers strangers to each other, Pentecostals offered small

---

(Cleveland, Tenn.: Pathway Press, 1977), 373; James Stone, *The Church of God of Prophecy: History and Polity* (Cleveland, Tenn.: White Wing, 1977), 67.

53.   Church of God of Prophecy, Minutes of the Annual Assembly, 1952, 18–24; 1980, 36–37, PRC.

54.   Church of God, Minutes of the Annual Assembly, 1946, 17–18, PRC; Campbell, *Pentecostal Holiness Church*, 175; *Whole Truth* (Memphis), November–December 1989, 1, 7.

churches based on old models of the congregation as family. If churches in areas suffering from depopulation seemed old, listless, and dying, Pentecostals offered a movement that seemed so fresh and alive that so-called pioneers could start churches anywhere. If the growing use of bureaucratic methods made some evangelicals fear they were losing their concentration on the spiritual condition of individuals, Pentecostals made several stages of religious experience the center of their services. And if many evangelicals believed the best way to fight sinfulness was through political action, Pentecostals offered instead the possibility of a sanctified condition in which the temptation to sin had no power. Finally, if modern Pentecostals are worrying that their success might cost them their old-fashioned religious commitment, that concern in itself places them in a long tradition of worrying evangelicals.

Populism Left and Right:
Politics of the Rural South

WAYNE PARENT AND PETER A. PETRAKIS

The unique and often perverse nature of southern politics has long made it an attractive topic for scholars. The classic work *Southern Politics in State and Nation,* by V. O. Key, set the stage for the fifty years of tumultuous politics that are the subject of this essay. Although Key's work is still considered the yardstick by which all others are measured, politics in the South have changed dramatically in the half-century since its publication. Key's insights, although invaluable, have been somewhat supplanted by the enormous changes that have occurred since World War II. He found a one-party, Democratic-dominant South where African Americans participated very little in politics. Key characterized these oppressive politics as a major cause of the widespread poverty, inferior education, and racial strife that plagued the South. In the fifty years since his work, the politics of the region, at least, have been transformed. These fundamental political undercurrents are significant and pronounced. Arguably, the social and cultural forces at work in the rural South since 1945 are at the center of the extraordinary political dynamism of the entire region during this period.[1]

The political reorganization of the South since 1945 is characterized by dramatic partisan upheaval and by African American political mobilization. The partisan realignment is striking. In 1945 all the governors, all 22 United States senators, and all but 2 of the 120 members of the House of Representatives from the eleven states that constituted the old Confederacy were Democrats; by 1994, 6 of the 11 governors were Republicans along with 13 of the 22 United States senators and 67 of the 125 congressmen. In the seventeen presidential elections

---

1. V. O. Key, *Southern Politics in State and Nation* (New York: Knopf, 1949).

between 1880 and 1944, Alabama, Arkansas, Georgia, Louisiana, Mississippi, and South Carolina voted Democratic every time; Florida, North Carolina, Texas, and Virginia voted Republican only once (in 1928); and Tennessee went Republican twice (in 1920 and 1928). In stark contrast, since 1960 the Republican ticket has carried most states in the South most of the time, and by 1992, despite the presence of two southerners on the presidential ticket, Democrats carried only Arkansas, Tennessee, Georgia, and Louisiana.

The spectacular mobilization of African Americans as voters is a story at least as compelling as the rise of the Republicans in the South. Although African American participation outside the South is largely an urban phenomenon, rural African Americans are a significant and unique political factor in the American South. Before the Voting Rights Act of 1965, only 29 percent of eligible African Americans were registered to vote. While the percentage of eligible blacks registered varied widely in the South from state to state, it did not vary by degree of urbanization. Rural blacks were as likely to be allowed to register to vote as urban blacks. Because of the close national scrutiny imposed by the Voting Rights Act of 1965 and subsequent extensions, black voter registration in 1994 roughly equaled white registration across the South. Blacks are a meaningful minority of voters in all eleven southern states and now constitute at least 25 percent of the voters in Mississippi, South Carolina, Louisiana, Alabama, and Georgia. In the fifty years since 1945, there has been an enormous increase in African American voting strength, especially in the five states of the Deep South and certainly in their rural areas.[2]

Partisan change and racial mobilization are not unrelated. Although several forces seriously affected the politics of the region, most scholarly works on the evolution of southern politics emphasize the elemental and conspicuous impact of the civil rights movement. The civil rights bills and equally dramatic court decisions that preceded and followed them altered America forever, but no place has been so radically affected as the South. The forced dismantling of southern apartheid destabilized the traditional political and social order in the region. Alliances, perspectives, and particularly partisanship became fluid variables. The once static and hegemonic forces in the South became dynamic and, in some instances, unpredictable. There have been many attempts to characterize this induced upheaval, and their foci vary immensely. A significant portion of political science has been concerned with the changes in partisanship, be they realign-

---

2. Earl Black and Merle Black, *Politics and Society in the South* (Cambridge, Mass.: Harvard University Press, 1987), 112; Donald R. Matthews, *Negroes and the New Southern Politics* (New York: Harcourt, Brace and World, 1966). Mississippi (with only 5 percent registered), Alabama, South Carolina, and Virginia had the lowest rates. Tennessee, Florida, North Carolina, Arkansas, and Texas had the highest rates. The story of African American successes and failures will not receive the attention it deserves here because it has been so well documented elsewhere, and it logically conforms to traditional theories of mobilization and resistance.

ment, dealignment, or merely the by-product of migration. While there is considerable disagreement as to the scope, degree, and causes of these changes, the overwhelming evidence suggests that there is now, at least to some degree, a two-party South.[3]

It would be superficial to characterize the politics of racial mobilization and racism as the only driving force behind the emergence of the Republican party in the South, but it should be seen as the germinal factor. In 1948, when Hubert H. Humphrey (who had experienced the racism of the Deep South firsthand in his years as a graduate student at Louisiana State University) convinced the national Democratic party to include progressive civil rights stances in its platform, southern segregationists felt that they had been betrayed. In 1964, when Barry Goldwater, the Republican standard-bearer, visibly and vocally criticized the civil rights acts, tides of southern white support began to flow not only away from the Democratic party but distinctly to the Republican party for the first time in southern political history.

Initially southern voters abandoned the Democratic party only in presidential elections, but race began to influence contests even down the ticket. A woeful period of race-baiting divided the Democratic party; moderate Democratic candidates and incumbents began to be defeated by staunch segregationists. This fateful phase waned by the 1970s because with the registration and participation of African Americans it became more hazardous to be openly racist. Race had been the key divisive force in southern politics. It, more than any other single issue, changed the political terrain and opened the door for Republican encroachments.

The contrasting stances of the two parties on race issues was but the first step toward the development of a two-party South. There were economic, cultural, social, and demographic reasons for the rising importance of the Republicans. Two of the best representatives of scholarship in this field are Alexander Lamis's *The Two-Party South* and Earl Black and Merle Black's *Politics and Society in the South*. Lamis focused on traditional economic, class-based cleavages as the primary structural mold for the emerging two-party South. Black and Black conceded the role of these traditional cleavages but emphasized the importance of cultural and social issues, most notably race.[4]

While the debate as to the underlying impetus for change rages on, there does appear to be a consensus that southern politics is at least superficially beginning to resemble the national scene. A two-party system exists in which Republicans and Democrats are highly competitive. The Republican party has not only estab-

3. Jack Bass and Walter De Vries, *The Transformation of Southern Politics: Social Change and Political Consequences Since 1945* (New York: Basic Books, 1976); Black and Black, *Politics and Society in the South*.

4. Alexander P. Lamis, *The Two-Party South* (New York: Oxford University Press, 1984); Black and Black, *Politics and Society in the South*.

lished itself in presidential elections but has attained success at all levels. These advances have been possible because voters in the South are now beginning to respond to what political scientists call "long-term forces." These forces involve the relation between partisanship and the environment a person is reared in, specifically education and socioeconomic status.

One of the most common long-term relationships is the link between a white-collar, higher-income environment and Republican partisanship. This direct and easily understandable relationship, which closely mimics long-term relationships outside the South, has evolved fairly naturally among southern urban and suburban voters since 1945. As the South became more urbanized, southern white-collar workers were attracted to the Republican party. Therefore, the strongest areas of Republican voting strength in the South are the suburban counties surrounding the largest cities. The more complicated and interesting phenomenon in the South is the conversion of *rural* southern whites from fairly regular Democratic voters to ticket-splitters and Republican voters.

The degree to which this emerging two-party system allows Republicans to be truly competitive may be dependent on their fortunes in the rural white South. Their successful appeal here is clearly the key to any effective winning strategy in almost all of the states of the former Confederacy, but especially in the Deep South (Alabama, Georgia, Louisiana, Mississippi, and South Carolina).

The recent political activity of rural white southerners is intriguing because it runs counter to traditional expectations. Traditional explanations of partisanship—long-term forces and economic interest—predict Republican gains in the suburbs and among higher socioeconomic classes. Thus the appeal of the Republican party to rural white southerners cannot be explained by conventional means. In fact, by supporting the Republican economic agenda, rural white southerners appear to be acting against their economic self-interest—a violation of one of the hallmarks of traditional models describing partisanship. What could be driving these southerners to vote Republican?

The key to understanding the politics of this group lies in the recognition of the overriding saliency of social issues in guiding voter choice. The Republican party's stance on social issues such as gun control, abortion, school prayer, gay rights, affirmative action, and welfare is the cornerstone of Republican popularity with rural white southerners.

Cole B. Graham, Jr.'s discussion of partisan change in South Carolina—a notably rural state in which the shift has been most dramatic—provides evidence for the importance of social issues to Republican successes in the South. He argues that before the 1960s, counties with high rural populations supported Democratic candidates because "these counties tend to be poorer and thus potential beneficiaries of federal and state spending." As noneconomic issues became part of the Democratic agenda, however, rural white defection to the Republicans began. Graham explains:

The rural defection is a potentially compelling descriptor of a general partisan shift. The major negative value [in his correlational analysis] is in Humphrey's 1968 campaign. Large numbers of South Carolina's rural white voters in fact supported George Wallace's American Independent party that year. These counties did not return to the Democrats in 1972 and later [as his analysis shows]. Since there were no other significant third-party presidential candidates in the period of this study, much rural support must have become Republican in subsequent presidential votes.

Indeed, Republican conversion in the rural white South often hinged on the character of the Republican appeal.[5]

An example from North Carolina explicitly illustrates the contrast between a Republican appeal to affluent voters through pocketbook issues and to less affluent rural voters through social issues. In North Carolina, the 1984 U.S. Senate race featured incumbent Jesse Helms, who "focused his campaign on the emotional social issues such as prayer in the schools, abortion, and affirmative action." In 1986, the Republican was incumbent James Broyhill, who was from the more "traditional" wing of the party that "tended to stress standard conservative economic and foreign policy issues." This classic contrast of elections in the same state only two years apart allows for an interpretation of the strength of two different Republican appeals. With Helms on the Republican ticket, the rural areas of the state were more likely to vote Republican. The reverse was true in the more urban areas of the state: these counties were more likely to vote Republican with Broyhill as the Republican standard-bearer. Helms won with his stronger rural white support; Broyhill lost without it. These two elections illustrate that the character of the Republican appeal is important to rural white voters. When conservative social stances are emphasized, Republican strength in the rural white South grows; when traditional economic issues are emphasized, Republicans enjoy less advantage in these former Democratic strongholds.[6]

So what lies behind the saliency of social issues? Racial prejudice continues to be a powerful explanation of much of this electoral activity, but racial bias alone cannot explain the potency of gun control, antiabortion rights, school prayer, and other issues. Is the importance of these issues to be condescendingly dismissed as a remnant of southern provincialism, or is there a more powerful explanation, such as the heritage of southern Populism?

Describing such prominent Republican politicians as Newt Gingrich and Dick Armey as populists strikes those familiar with the term as odd. Their connections to big business and promotion of the latest technologies as a source of

5. Cole B. Graham, Jr., "Partisan Change in South Carolina," in *The South's New Politics: Realignment and Dealignment,* ed. Robert Swansbrough and David M. Brodsky (Columbia: University of South Carolina Press, 1988), 168–69.

6. Lamis, *Two-Party South,* 286.

social salvation are antithetical to the Populism of the late nineteenth and early twentieth centuries. Yet the ability of Republicans increasingly to garner the support of rural white southerners—direct descendants of the Populists—lends credence to this ostensible misnomer. The resolution to this apparent contradiction lies in the transformation of the term *populism*. Although the Republican version of Populism draws on sources similar to those of nineteenth-century Populism, it differs in important respects. Nineteenth-century Populism closely linked culture and economics, and its calls for reform addressed both. The late-twentieth-century version, however, has been diluted; it supports traditional values but subscribes to an economic agenda—and an optimism about the future—that is contrary to the original perspective.

A close examination of the redefinition of Populism will provide two important contributions. First, it will enrich the study of rural white voting patterns by illuminating possible causes for the strident saliency of social issues to southerners. It will show that the rigid adherence of rural white southerners to traditional values is not simply reactionary but rather the sole surviving element of the more radical critiques put forth by the farmer movements of 1890–1914. Second, an examination of early Populism will place the more complete critique back into the current public dialogue and perhaps reveal the ersatz character of the new Republican "populism" in the rural South. Social issues are but one aspect of the original Populist critique. Nineteenth-century Populism maintained that the form and substance of economic activity were intimately related to the maintenance and sustenance of traditional values. The Populist agenda of recognizing economic and political limits was not simply backwardness, but rather a profound perspective informed by a skepticism concerning the ultimate benefits of progress—especially concerning its impact on democracy—and grounded in the republican notion of virtue.[7]

A more complete account of Populism may call into question the strength of the Republican appeal to rural white southerners. The conviction that important social issues will continually override economic interest may prove to be a tenuous foundation for party competitiveness in a region as poor as the South.

Populism is a term that is difficult to use with analytical precision, in large part because there is considerable scholarly debate as to what it constitutes. Although common usage has spread to include such individuals as Joseph McCarthy, George Wallace, George McGovern, Jimmy Carter, Ronald Reagan, and now Newt Gingrich, scholars have generally confined the term to the late nineteenth and early twentieth centuries. Reducing the life span of the term, however, only partly clears up the confusion. The agrarian revolts that occurred between 1865 and 1914 were often short-lived, changed names frequently, and pursued di-

---

7. For the linkage of Populism to civic republicanism and civic virtue, see Christopher Lasch, *The True and Only Heaven: Progress and Its Critics* (New York: Norton, 1991), chap. 5.

verse policies. Greenbackers, the Grange, the various Farmers' Alliances, the Farmers' Union, the free silver movement, and even the presidential bid of William Jennings Bryan are regularly identified as parts of the Populist movement. Despite the distinctiveness of these various movements, there is considerable justification for grouping them all under the rubric of Populism because they all share certain basic characteristics.[8]

In the decades following the Civil War it became increasingly clear that the cycle of poverty that plagued southern farmers was in some sense structural. Gilbert Fite notes, "Southern farmers knew well enough that something was wrong with the system that kept them in such a state of poverty. For most of them the American dream of 'getting ahead' economically and of perhaps being able to leave some inheritance to their children remained just that—a dream." The hegemony of cotton as the predominant crop was a major factor in this cycle. The inability of farmers to diversify their crops made them especially susceptible to fluctuations in the market, bad weather, and insects. Even if there had been the impetus to diversify agriculture—which there was not—poor markets, largely impassable roads, insufficient rail lines, and the unwillingness of banks and creditors to gamble on other crops served to reinforce the preeminence of cotton. Scarcity of capital and investment further contributed to the systemic problems of the South—an absence of technological improvements, poor education, inadequate nutrition, the prevalence of disease, and limited communication—and made the cycle of poverty virtually inescapable.

The insular nature of the South also contributed to the financial squeeze on farmers. While this region remained stagnant, the emergence of the modern economy and the volatility of market forces made farming more complex. The time when farmers' chief concern was the price they could attain for their products at market had passed, and "as farming became more commercialized and less self-sufficient, the prices of commodities that farmers had to purchase became increasingly important" to their economic survival. In short, farmers now were required to gauge not just how many acres to plant but also how the price ratios of products to commodities might shift during the months the crops were

---

8. The literature is large, but the most notable works are John D. Hicks, *The Populist Revolt: A History of the Farmers' Alliance and the People's Party* (Minneapolis: University of Minnesota Press, 1931); John Chamberlain, *Farewell to Reform, Being a History of Rise, Life and Decay of the Progressive Mind in America* (New York: Liveright, 1932); Richard Hofstadter, *The Age of Reform: From Bryan to F.D.R.* (New York: Knopf, 1955); Richard Hofstadter, *The Paranoid Style in American Politics and Other Essays* (New York: Knopf, 1965); Norman Pollack, *The Populist Response to Industrial America: Midwestern Populist Thought* (Cambridge, Mass.: Harvard University Press, 1962); Lawrence Goodwyn, *Democratic Promise: The Populist Movement in America* (New York: Oxford University Press, 1976); Robert C. McMath, Jr., *Populist Vanguard: A History of the Southern Farmers' Alliance* (Chapel Hill: University of North Carolina Press, 1975); and Robert C. McMath, Jr., *American Populism: A Social History, 1877–1898* (New York: Hill and Wang, 1993). See also William F. Holmes, "Populism: In Search of Context," *Agricultural History* 64 (Fall 1990): 26–58.

in the ground. This relation of crop prices to commodities and products required to run the farm greatly influenced the importance of managing debt. For instance, if the price of cotton was ten cents a pound when a farmer borrowed a hundred dollars but dropped to five cents by the time the crop came in, his debt doubled. The progression of agriculturists away from subsistence to commercial farming made shifting markets increasingly vital. Most southern farmers had so little margin between cost and production that even mild shifts in prices could throw them into financial ruin. They became aware that they needed more control over the contingency of their situation. Gilbert Fite has written:

> But farmers were in a weak bargaining position to improve the relationship between farm and nonfarm prices. In the first place, business and industry were becoming increasingly better organized and even monopolistic, while farmers remained scattered and individualistic. Furthermore, farmers were exchanging cheap raw materials—cotton, tobacco, grain, and livestock—for expensive manufactured goods. In this situation the terms of trade were fundamentally unfavorable to the farmers except in a few unusual periods. While the issue of farm price parity did not become a major political question until the early twentieth century, farmers were acutely aware of the problem much earlier.[9]

As southern farmers became more intimately connected to the market economy, they realized that other interests were organizing in an effort to compete effectively. Business and industry formed trusts, pools, and corporations, while laborers fought for unionization. The first opportunity for southern farmers to organize appeared when Oliver Hudson Kelley, a Washington bureaucrat, after touring the South for the Department of Agriculture, founded the Patrons of Husbandry in 1867. The Grange, as it was known, focused farmers' attention on monopolies, merchants, and commission agents and attempted to establish cooperatives to eliminate the expenses of middlemen. Members set up cooperatives that were independent of the established financial system and funded through the farmers themselves in an attempt to eliminate the "middling interests" and increase their profit-to-cost ratio. Unfortunately, these efforts were doomed from the beginning because of insufficient capital. A few, like the Texas Cooperative Association, showed early promise, but all eventually went bankrupt. Even large groups of poor farmers could not sufficiently fund independent cooperatives without access to substantial credit. The scarcity of funds underlying the cooperatives merely shifted the vulnerability of costs to prices from the individual to the aggregate level—cooperatives also went broke in even mild

---

9. Gilbert C. Fite, *Cotton Fields No More: Southern Agriculture, 1865–1980* (Lexington: University Press of Kentucky, 1984), 49–50.

economic downturns. Of course, the countervailing interests of merchants and businesses did everything they could to facilitate the collapse of the cooperatives.

As the cooperatives failed and the Grange movement faltered, farmers became more critical of monopolies, big business, banks, and financiers. Cooperatives and other means of reducing the take of middlemen continued to be a prominent issue for farmers, but attention began to shift to the monied interests, transportation, and government. Calls for higher taxes on land speculation, easier and fairer access to railroads, regulation of interstate commerce, and inflated currency became the common battle cries of Populism. Despite the growing consciousness that it was structural restraints that effectively retarded farmers' struggles to escape poverty, subsequent agrarian movements continued to suffer from a lack of organization, coordination, and agreement on goals. Schisms over whether the agriculturists should aspire to political reforms—farmers were by far the most numerous segment of the population at this time—or work to establish effective cooperatives factionalized the movements. Southerners usually pursued political reforms only through the Democratic party. They feared that an independent political party would divide the Solid South and thus open the door to the Republicans and more liberal racial policies. In short, concludes Lawrence Goodwyn, "the received cultural inheritance of white supremacy continued to hold greater sway over southern whites than issues of economic reform did." The fear that an entrenched political party was not a suitable vessel for the radical aspirations of Populism, however, prompted nonsoutherners to push for an independent party. Such disagreements were largely responsible for the failure to achieve Populist reforms. Poor southern farmers painfully witnessed the rise, evolution, and eventual demise of the Grange, Texas Farmers' Alliance, National Farmers' Alliance, Southern Farmers' Alliance, and Farmers' Union. These movements—spasms of frustration and revolt—spanned the period from the 1870s to the eve of World War I, and as each one failed, the anger and resentment of southern farmers grew. They had tried private organization, they had turned to state and federal governments, and they had mounted an important political challenge to the two-party system. Yet despite their numbers and efforts, they had failed to achieve significant reform.[10]

The argument that the Populist movement did not fail but was simply incorporated into the larger and more successful reform movements of the twentieth century is found in John D. Hicks's classic work *The Populist Revolt*. Hicks contended that reform movements evolved and that the Populists' inability to achieve real reform was the by-product of a learning curve. The Populists simply did not know how to organize effectively and manipulate the political system. The incremental reforms attained by the Progressive crusade revealed accruing political skills, but substantial reforms were not achieved until the New Deal.

10. Goodwyn, *Democratic Promise*, 299.

Hicks, then, asserted that all of the reform movements were driven by the same underlying forces. He commented that "a backward glance at the history of Populism shows that many of the reforms that Populists demanded, while despised and rejected for a season, won triumphantly in the end." This belief that the grievances of the Populists led to and were satisfied by the New Deal reforms shows Hicks's captivity to his age. His emphasis on economics set the stage for other interpretations.[11]

The studies that followed Hicks's work were either narrow in focus—examining Populism in a specific state or region—or part of a larger work dealing with several reform movements, most notably Progressivism. C. Vann Woodward's scholarship on southern Populism remains one of the best examples of the former trend.

In *The Origins of the New South, 1877–1913,* Woodward explored southern Populism. With the agrarian resurgence in the 1890s, the debate over sectional versus cooperative political strategies reemerged among southerners. Although southern Alliance men were sympathetic to cooperating with the West, they did not initially follow suit with efforts to form a third party because the Democratic party cooperated with the Alliance movement in the South. On the surface, this cooperative strategy proved successful. In 1890, under the Democratic guise, southern Alliance men won a majority in eight state legislatures, elected six governors, and gained the pledges of more than fifty congressmen to support the Alliance platform.[12]

As Populism gained momentum in the South and third parties erupted in the West, however, Democrats became concerned. Woodward wrote: "In 1890 the movement had been widely regarded as a boon to national Democratic party interests at the expense of Western Republicans," but when Populism presented a real challenge in the South, the cooperative spirit died. The nomination of Grover Cleveland, seen as a concession to monied interests assured the political break, and Cleveland became a symbol of all that the reformers thought was wrong with the Democratic party.[13]

While much of Woodward's work, especially *The Origins of the New South,* sought to undermine oversimplifications like the cliché of the Solid South, he emphasized the seriousness of party defection. Involving much more than simply changing one's mind, abandonment of the Democratic party often led to economic and social ostracism. "It might involve a falling-off of clients, the loss of a job, of credit at the store, or of one's welcome at church. It could split families,

11. Hicks, *Populist Revolt,* 404.
12. C. Vann Woodward, *Origins of the New South, 1877–1913* (Baton Rouge: Louisiana State University Press, 1951), 235.
13. Ibid., 240, 242.

and it might even call into question one's loyalty to his race and his people." Nevertheless, a revolt occurred.[14]

Woodward demonstrates that, contrary to the various caricatures, the leaders of Populism were cut from the same cloth as other political leaders. Some sprang from patriarchal families, others clawed their way up from truly plebeian roots, but most came from the middle class. The rank and file, however, came from the lower economic and social classes. For whites, Populism was strongest among small-scale farmers and thus existed in a somewhat inverse proportion to the population of African Americans. Woodward recognized the significant successes of African American Populism in the South, but he argued that ultimately the white power structure endured.[15]

The most notable exception to the inverse relation between black population and Populist strength was Tom Watson. Although his and a few other Populist strongholds were in the Black Belt, in the main Populism was an effort to wrest control from the rule of the Black Belt Democratic party of the former slave owners. Populists were sober-minded folk, almost exclusively former Democrats, and they challenged the "New-South romanticism head on. . . . They spoke openly of conflicts of sections and class, and ridiculed the clichés of Reconciliation and White Solidarity. The bolder among them challenged the cult of racism with the doctrines of common action among farmers and workers of both races." Populism was not some minor tinkering with the political system of the South but a wholesale challenge; it was a revolt. Woodward wrote: "The political strategy of Southern Populists was based on combinations and alliances along regional, class, and racial lines—first, an alliance between South and West; second, a combination of farmers and city and factory laborers; and third, a combination with Negro farmers and laborers of the South. Every phase of this strategy was a challenge to the New-South system, which had sought to divide all the elements that the Populists were trying to unite." Ultimately, it was this third proposition that proved to be most difficult. Because racism killed most reform movements in the South, alliance with African Americans proved difficult. Indeed, that alliance had "wrecked the Readjusters and had proved a fatal weakness of the Republicans. In the end, it had been the Redeemers, the party of white supremacy, that had been most successful in controlling the Negro vote."[16]

In 1890, Henry Cabot Lodge introduced a "force bill," which gave federal supervisors the power to control voter registration, in a tactical effort to cripple Populism in the South. Fearing a return of "Negro domination," Populists scrambled for cover. They had to align themselves against the bill for the sake of

14. Ibid., 244.
15. Ibid., 246–47.
16. Ibid., 249, 252, 254.

their white voters, resulting in a schism between the white and black Populist movements. In the beginning, many Populist leaders pushed for equal representation for blacks in the movement, and they achieved some remarkable successes. In the end, however, achievements were limited and the old specter of race won the day, especially after the "fusion" with the Democratic party and its nomination of Bryan in 1896.[17]

The Populists had been outmaneuvered during the presidential campaign in 1896, and increasingly their "frustrated impulses toward revolt were to seek newer and stranger outlets in the future." No one exemplifies this shift from early Populism, which offered an innovative critique of the political system, to the pandering and naïve demagoguery of later Populism better than Tom Watson. For Woodward, Watson was a tragic figure. He wrote:

> I do not believe it is accurate to blame Watson for the "sinister forces." . . . To do so would be to assign him far too important a role, a role that belongs to the vastly more impersonal forces of economics and race and historical heritage. To do so, moreover, would be to miss at the same time the deep meaning of his story. He did not produce those forces: he was produced by them. They thwarted at every turn his courageous struggle in the face of them during his early Populist battles, and they led him into the futility and degeneration of his later career.

Although some have not been as forgiving of the Populist demagoguery as Woodward, this basic sentiment has been echoed in several interpretations since Woodward's classic works.[18]

Richard Hofstadter's *Age of Reform* and *Paranoid Style in American Politics* countered Hicks's evolutionary interpretation by focusing on the cultural forces behind the various movements. Hofstadter argued that the Populist and Progressive movements erupted at a time when the cultural and political traditions of America were shifting. He contended that America's unique version of liberalism, with its roots firmly planted in the soil of "indigenous Yankee-Protestant political traditions," was being challenged by the dramatic influx of European immigrants. The immigrants brought very different notions of citizenship and beliefs about the proper role and purpose of government and the function of economics than those held by indigenous Americans. Hofstadter remarked that the Yankee-Protestant "assumed and demanded the constant, disinterested activity of the citizen in public affairs, argued that political life ought to be run, to a greater degree than it was, in accordance with general principles and abstract laws apart from and superior to personal needs, and expressed a common feeling that government should be in good part an effort to moralize the lives of individ-

17. Ibid., 255.
18. C. Vann Woodward, *Tom Watson: Agrarian Rebel* (New York: Rinehart, 1938), viii.

uals while economic life should be intimately related to the stimulation and development of individual character." Hofstadter also noted that European immigrants, whose political and social outlook was "founded upon the European
backgrounds of [those] immigrants, upon their unfamiliarity with independent
political action, their familiarity with hierarchy and authority, and upon the ur-
gent needs that so often grew out of their migration, took for granted that the
political life of the individual would arise out of family needs, interpreted political and civic relations chiefly in terms of personal obligations, and placed strong
personal loyalties above allegiance to abstract codes of law or morals."[19]

Hofstadter contended that the path and pursuits of the reform movements
were shaped by these two competing versions of liberalism. Americans informed
by the Yankee-Protestant perspective, "whether they were reformers or conservatives, wanted economic success to continue to be related to personal character,
wanted the economic system not merely to be a system for the production of sufficient goods and services but to be an effectual system of incentives and rewards." The European immigrants, Hofstadter argued, had no such expectations about the role of economics. They saw the economy as simply a means of
providing for their families and were much more comfortable with the increasing
centralization of the economy and political system. They had a weak attachment
to the individualism and entrepreneurial ethics that had guided previous reform
efforts, from Jeffersonianism to Jacksonianism to Populism. Thus the ambiguity
and faltering of the Populist and Progressive reforms were the result not of any
inherent deficiencies in the strategies of the movements themselves but of the
lack of a uniform driving cultural and political perspective. The New Deal
marked the practical victory of the European immigrants' form of liberalism,
but this did not end the battle waged by these competing visions. Hofstadter asserted that the conservative reaction to the New Deal was actually the continuation of the struggle between these two versions of liberalism. To Hofstadter,
Populism "seem[ed] very strongly to foreshadow some aspects of the cranky
pseudo-conservatism of our time." But, he argued, "Somewhere along the way a
large part of the Populist-Progressive tradition has turned sour, become illiberal
and ill-tempered." Hofstadter believed that returns to the Populist ethos were inspired by antidemocratic tendencies.[20]

In the mid-1970s, the scholarship of Lawrence Goodwyn and Robert C.
McMath, Jr., initiated a major revision of the historical interpretation of Populism and its legacy. Goodwyn's *Democratic Promise* directly opposed Hofstadter's dark views of Populism as the breeding ground of racist and antidemocratic inclinations by arguing that the importance of Populism was precisely its
impact on American consciousness, especially in enhancing perceptions about

19. Hofstadter, *Age of Reform,* 9, 11.
20. Ibid., 11, 20.

democracy. Indeed, Goodwyn praised the Populists not as forerunners of more successful reform efforts, as Hicks and others had done, but as educators. In this regard, he characterized their struggles to establish independent cooperatives as central to the movement, not because they were effective reform ideas but because they inculcated civic responsibility. He stated that "to describe the origins of Populism in one sentence, the cooperative experience within the cooperatives radically altered [the Populists'] political consciousness." Thus Populism "not only created a mass culture of hope and self-respect among the voiceless, but also gave shape to radically new and unsettling perceptions about the meaning of the American experience." Goodwyn also wrote, "For the triumph of Populism—its only meaningful triumph—was the belief in possibility it injected into American political consciousness."[21]

What made Populism unique, however, and perhaps has contributed to the farmers' low esteem, is that their optimism differed from the dominant mood of America, which was an almost total faith in progress. Reined in by an almost inherent awareness of limits, Populists did not subscribe to the belief in salvation through progress. This stance increasingly came to define Populism. Indeed, Goodwyn remarked that they "derived their most incisive power from the simple fact that they declined to participate adequately in a central element of the emerging faith. In an age of progress and forward motion, they had come to suspect that Horatio Alger was not real."[22]

Thus the reforms attempted by the Populists were informed and constrained by a profound skepticism of progress and this newest American dream. It was by no means clear to farmers that the coming industrialized age, replete with its advances in efficiency and productivity, would be beneficial to democracy or, ultimately, to their way of life. Goodwyn was the first to underscore the importance of this aspect of Populism. He explained that "Populists dissented against the progressive society that was emerging in the 1890s because they thought that the mature corporate state would, unless restructured, erode the democratic promise of America." The Populists' hesitancy concerning the fruits of technology and progress are typically pointed to as examples of their provincialism. But Goodwyn pointed out that the traditional dismissive assessments by both the left and the right are not caused by the intellectual bankruptcy of Populism—as is so often portrayed—but rather by a shared and unspoken conviction that progress will ultimately lead to greater human happiness and freedom. It is this presupposition that has prevented adequate appraisals of Populism.[23]

Along with Goodwyn, McMath is the scholar most responsible for reviving

21. Goodwyn, *Democratic Promise*, xviii, xxiii.
22. Ibid., 552.
23. Ibid., xiv.

Populism. McMath's two books on the subject, *Populist Vanguard: A History of the Southern Farmers' Alliance* and *American Populism: A Social History, 1877–1898,* shift attention away from the economic aspects of Populism and toward its social and cultural roots. McMath's major contribution has been his careful analysis of the intellectual, cultural, and social antecedents of Populism. By broadening his examination from the People's party to include the earlier movements such as the Farmers' Alliance, the Grange, and the various other cooperative movements, McMath revealed a uniform and underlying social and cultural perspective. Indeed, he contends that this outlook did not simply appear during the Populist movement but had its roots in pre–Civil War reform movements. McMath connects Populism to both the Jacksonian period and Atlantic republicanism. By putting Populism in its social context, McMath demonstrates that it was not a unique protest movement that spontaneously sprang into action because of dire economic circumstances; rather, Populism was the climax of over a century of rural unrest and discontent. In his latest book, McMath discusses this larger social critique under the rubric of "producerism." Adhering to a labor theory of value, producerism is the assertion that the people who should primarily profit in a society are those who are actively and directly engaged in the production of goods. Obviously, the main justification for such an arrangement is not economic efficiency. Indeed, producerism is motivated by the belief that modern capitalism, which is driven by the accumulation and fluidity of capital, carries severe social, cultural, and political costs. In short, producerism argues that shifting rewards from those who produce to those who finance will erode the democratic ethos. Families, farms, civic organizations, and rural communities will gradually be marginalized. Monied interests will co-opt politics from independent landowners. McMath finds evidence of these sentiments throughout much of American history, and he reveals that in this sense, at least, Populism was not so much unique as it was the last gasp.[24]

Christopher Lasch's *True and Only Heaven: Progress and Its Critics* built on Goodwyn's and McMath's reappraisal of Populism. In his effort to explain the current variance "Right-Wing Populism," he noted that "the conventional identification of democracy with progress makes it hard to see that democratic movements in the nineteenth century took shape in opposition to innovation." Put simply, "the idea that workable small-unit democracy is possible within large-unit systems of economic production is alien to the shared presumptions of 'progress' that unite capitalists and communists in a religious brotherhood." Populism, as understood by Goodwyn, McMath, and Lasch, is not a naïve economic or cultural critique mired in provincialism, but rather a profound questioning of the prevailing faith in progress. Once the skepticism of progress is re-

---

24. McMath, *Populist Vanguard* and *American Populism.*

vealed as the cornerstone of Populism, it becomes clear that "a whole way of life was at stake against industrialism. Workers [and farmers] were defending not just their economic interests but their rights, families, and neighborhoods."[25]

By emphasizing the explicit connection between economics and social issues for nineteenth-century Populism, the movement emerges not as anticapitalist but as antiprogress. In brief, Populists believed that certain forms of economic activity were virtuous while others were not. Moneylenders, leaders of big corporations, commodity speculators, those engaged in the stock market, and middlemen in general all shared the characteristic of not being engaged in the production of tangible goods. Economic activities that did not increase concrete goods were considered to be parasitic. Adhering to such an economic perspective, which has been convincingly linked to producerism, Atlantic republicanism, and civic humanism, Populists were not an outgrowth of the left or the right, as traditionally understood, but the latest bearers of an economic perspective that had been the habitual competitor of liberalism throughout the ages. The Populists believed that as farmers they were involved in virtuous economic activity, while business and financial elites got rich through, in their view, scams and swindles. It was the farmer and the worker who were the backbone of America.[26]

The Populists dared to ask whether the benefits of progress outweighed its destructive influences. Would the supplanting of a culture that closely associated work and virtue by a culture driven by the harsh laws of efficiency and production be advantageous to American democracy? Would not the divorce of economics from virtue result in the destruction of the very social units—family, neighborhood, and community—that gave America its cohesion, stability, and freedom? In the face of the bountiful dynamism of the modern economy, these seemed to be audacious contentions. Today, however, wrote Goodwyn, "against the widespread modern resignation about the fate of mere humans, psychologically trapped by their own technological inventions and in homage to the seemingly rigid and uncontrollable industrial structures that have generated those inventions, the Populist view of human possibility" carries more force and is perhaps more convincing.[27]

The Populists' skepticism about progress and their realization that social issues are intimately related to economic policies and attitudes did not win the day. With the emergence of the New Deal came a narrowing of the dominant discourse. The left and right agreed on certain fundamentals: a faith in progress, efficiency, technology, and, increasingly, capitalism. The contentions about the necessity of centralization collapsed into a discord simply as to its appropriate location; the right sided with big business and industry, while the left promoted

---

25. Lasch, *True and Only Heaven*, 213, 216, 220.

26. Civic republicanism and its competing role in American economics and politics is best presented by the works of J. G. A. Pocock, Gordon Wood, and Bernard Bailyn.

27. Goodwyn, *Democratic Promise*, xiii.

the federal government. Calls for small and substantially independent democratic and economic communities ceased to be pertinent. Small towns became novelties, seen as inefficient, isolated, and economic dead ends; a remarkable migration to the big cities and suburbs ensued. By agreeing on these fundamentals, the Democratic and Republican parties had little to disagree about except the proper role of government and their relative positions on social issues. These have become the defining differences between the two parties, and, according to Lasch, "as 'social issues' came to define the difference between the right and the left, a new breed of 'populists' began to build a political coalition around lower-middle-class resentment."[28]

In terms of practical politics, after George McGovern's disastrous presidential bid in 1972, the Democratic party placed its hopes in "neoliberalism." In an effort to redefine the party, candidates such as Gary Hart, Paul Simon, Paul Tsongas, Michael Dukakis, Al Gore, and Bill Clinton emerged as standard-bearers. The economic perspectives of these candidates were virtually indistinguishable from those of the right, and slowly the calls for lower taxes and smaller, more effective government have become uniform. What did distinguish these candidates, however, was their positions on social issues. Both parties, it seemed, turned their backs on the economic interests of the working class and focused instead on their differing perspectives on social issues. For the Democratic party this strategy, though perhaps understandable in a national context, played directly into the hands of the southern Republicans, especially with regard to rural whites. Lasch points out that "the ideological appeal of the new right depended on its ability not only to emphasize social issues at the expense of economic issues but to deflect 'middle-class' resentment from the rich to a parasitic 'new class' of professional problem solvers and moral relativists." This portrayal of bureaucrats and politicians sitting in Washington and devising complicated schemes to micro-manage the lives of everyday Americans struck a chord among those in whom the Populist sentiment termed "producerism" lingered. The nineteenth-century Populists' accusation that business and financial elites did not produce any tangible goods and were therefore parasitic applied easily and more acutely to this "new class" of technocrats. Nineteenth-century elites did not live at the public expense, but this new class did. This new target was especially advantageous for the right because it "enabled the right to attack 'elites'

---

28. Lasch, *True and Only Heaven*, 505. The brevity of this discussion is not meant to gloss over important early differences on these issues. Obviously, there was, and in some pockets continues to be, serious disagreement on these fundamentals. The populism of George Wallace is an excellent example. He was decried as a "Country and Western Marxist" by many on the right for his advocacy of increased government spending on social security and health care and his calls for government guidelines ensuring more equitable collective bargaining. Despite important exceptions like Wallace and, perhaps, contemporary candidates like Pat Buchanan, however, there has been a growing consensus among policy makers on the left and right that makes this assertion of shared fundamentals creditable.

without attacking big business. Businessmen, it appeared, were responsible and public-spirited."[29]

Thus, by diverting attention from economic policies and refocusing the anger and frustration of the working middle class on this new class, Republicans became credible when spouting Populist rhetoric. Not only did Republicans staunchly support the traditional values so dear to rural white southerners, but they were also engaged in the latest crusade against ignoble elites. Lasch posits that by targeting this new class, Republican populists were able to "obscur[e] the difference between opposition to 'middle-class values' and opposition to business. . . . The political alignments of the seventies and eighties indicated that a defense of values loosely identified with the counterculture was quite compatible with a defense of business and the free market." This obfuscation allowed Republicans to decry the erosion of traditional values and claim responsibility for trying to fix the problem by rooting out technocrats without ever mentioning the corrosive effects of capitalism and progress on traditional values. The Republicans were and are silent on the issue of how relatively unrestrained capitalism, complete with its economic incentives to seek the best opportunities available in a global economy, deleteriously affects families, neighborhoods, communities, and, eventually, civic responsibilities.[30]

While the appeal of Populism certainly resonated with the concerns of rural blacks, the nineteenth-century version systematically maintained a segregated political order. Hence other social forces have been more pronounced in guiding black voters' choices.

After the movements of the 1960s, the struggle for civil rights was still difficult in rural areas. Compared with urban areas, rural areas had fewer concentrations of blacks, scrutiny by the news media was less likely, and white law enforcement was able to be more hostile. Rural black economic dependency on the white small-town and rural elite allowed for a system of white control both before and after the Voting Rights Act of 1965. Before the federal legislation, white government officials used the litany of registration manipulation techniques specifically outlawed by the Voting Rights Act such as poll taxes and literacy tests. After the Voting Rights Act, the manipulation of black voting continued through economic and other forms of intimidation and manipulation. Black and Black explain: "It would be inaccurate to portray this pattern of manipulation in which

---

29.   Ibid., 509, 512. This turning away from working-class economic issues has neither been complete or warranted by empirical evidence. Kevin Phillips found that the middle-class tax revolt of the early 1980s was focused on regressive property taxes, not the federal income tax. He was skeptical about the Republican party's interpretation of these sentiments as support for supply-side economics. Even today many observers warn that this newest Republican revolution should not be misread as public support for Republican economic policies at the expense of social spending. See Phillips, *The Politics of Rich and Poor* (New York: Random House, 1990).

30.   Lasch, *True and Only Heaven*, 515.

rural blacks received nothing for their votes. . . . The key payoff to blacks was more or less 'friendly' law enforcement that minimized hostility and violence toward blacks—no small gain, considering the histories of police brutality, harassment, and intimidation in many southern communities." While rural blacks have indeed seized the opportunity to participate in the political process since the 1960s, systemic social, economic, and cultural forces have often inhibited the translation of this political mobilization into real societal power.[31]

In sum, the political landscape of the rural South has undergone remarkable changes in last fifty years. The roughly one-fifth of the population that was systematically excluded from the political system is now participating regularly and with some effect. African Americans are now voting in proportions almost equal to those of whites, and their vote choices conform to traditional explanations of partisanship. One unique force influencing African American political activity, however, is that they make up a substantial portion of the rural southern population. Nowhere else in America does this situation exist, and hence nowhere else do blacks confront the social, economic, and cultural barriers found in traditional rural environments.

While African Americans normally vote Democratic, many formerly Democratic white voters have radically changed their voting patterns. The one-party, Democratic-dominant South has given way to a two-party system in which Republicans compete at every level. The Republican appeal to rural white southerners has been an integral component of their success in the entire region.

The degree to which Republicans have made inroads into the rural South would be unremarkable if it had been through the traditional Republican constituency of middle- and upper-income voters. The key to Republican success in the South, however, has been the ability of the party to appeal to rural white voters in lower-income brackets. Most scholars of southern politics agree that initially this appeal came almost exclusively from Republican opposition to civil rights legislation. Although studies convincingly portray conservative stances on race-related issues as a continuing source of Republican appeal to lower-income white voters, other forces have also come into play. This constellation of issues can be explained in the latest rendition of Populism promoted by current Republican champions such as Newt Gingrich.

Today's Republican version of Populist appeal to rural voters in the South may not prove as resilient as the party followers might hope. We learn from the nineteenth-century roots of Populism that it must address the economic as well as social and cultural needs of its followers to remain successful. If the Democratic party, which was once dominant in the rural South, is to recapture these voters, it must focus on its economic message. If social issues are emphasized, Republicans are likely to continue their dramatic gains.

31. Black and Black, *Politics and Society in the South*, 119.

Cultural Distinctiveness in the Face of Structural Transformation: The "New" Old South

JEANNE S. HURLBERT AND WILLIAM B. BANKSTON

erhaps the oldest proposition of regional sociology, the hypothesis of southern cultural distinctiveness has intrigued scholars for many years. Throughout the history of the country, the idea that the southern way of life was unique could be taken as a truism. Indeed, as Raymond D. Gastil has noted, much of the history of the nation can be told in the story of the struggle and competition between two very different WASP cultures, those of New England and the South. Ironically for the military victors in this struggle, the crushing defeat and occupation of the South by its competitor did not destroy or even diminish regional distinctions, but instead seemed to contribute to their perpetuation and even to intensify them. Nevertheless, although changes in the economic infrastructure of the South may have proceeded at a slower pace after the Civil War than they did in the North, they have been dramatic. This transition has motivated considerable academic debate over several decades concerning the survival of a culturally distinct South and whether the traits that traditionally set the South apart still persist.[1]

Sociologically, this debate confronts us with the classic Weberian question of the independence of ideal and material dimensions of social organization and institutional change. Although the material foundations of an agrarian feudalism

Data were provided by the Interuniversity Consortium for Political and Social Research and the Louisiana Population Data Center.

1. Raymond D. Gastil, *Cultural Regions of the United States* (Seattle: University of Washington Press, 1975), 5–6; W. J. Cash, *The Mind of the South* (New York: Knopf, 1941); Frank E. Vandiver, "The Southerner as Extremist," in *The Idea of the South,* ed. Vandiver (Chicago: University of Chicago Press), 43–55.

that shaped nineteenth-century southern culture are clearly gone, the continuing survival and influence of the South's unique patterns of social action remain open empirical questions. The analysis presented here will examine the assertion that the South remains an identifiably distinct cultural region, even in the face of diminishing socioeconomic and urbanization differences. This analysis will be accomplished by our use of data from the 1972–1994 General Social Surveys (GSS) to compare attitudes and beliefs of southerners with those of nonsoutherners. We begin by identifying cultural traits that previous research and commentary suggest are typically southern and by selecting measures for them. Where possible, we examine empirically the relationships among these indicators. We then assess whether these traits are more prevalent among southerners than among nonsoutherners. To address the longitudinal question of whether the South has become more similar to the rest of the nation over time, comparisons will be made at three time points during the last two decades.

Beginning with the exploitation of southern resources by northern capitalists in the "colonial economy" during and after Reconstruction, the South began to integrate into the national economy. Though its pace was slowed by the collapse of cotton in the 1920s and the Great Depression of the following decade, the South experienced social and economic development, at least relative to its previous trajectory. The region would remain below the national average on most indicators of social well-being (particularly education and income), but after World War II its isolation declined through increased rural-to-urban migration, the advent of hard-surfaced roads, and the introduction of radio and television. For the vast majority of southerners born after World War II—even those raised in rural areas—a world of seeing by kerosene lamps instead of electric lights, of working mules instead of driving tractors, of drawing and carrying water instead of turning on faucets, and of depending on a cash crop instead of a paycheck was one they experienced only through the reminiscences of their parents. Although further cultural transformation would be wrought through the civil rights movement, the transition of the South toward structural congruence, that is, conformity, with the rest of the nation had become statistically apparent by the 1950s.[2]

By the 1960s, the tide of industrialization and urbanization had swept over the southern landscape to such an extent that some social scientists began to ring the death knell for the region's cultural distinctiveness. John C. McKinney and Linda B. Bourque, for example, examined regional differences in several structural characteristics, including the proportion of the population that was urban,

---

2. Thomas H. Naylor, "Priorities in the Development of the South," in *Group Identity in the South*, ed. Harold F. Kaufman, J. Kenneth Morland, and Herbert H. Fockler (Starkville: Mississippi State University Press, 1975), 209; Gastil, *Cultural Regions of the United States*, 182–83; Thomas D. Clark, *The Emerging South* (New York: Oxford University Press, 1968), 3–9; Ray Marshall, "The Economy: Industrialization and Labor Organization," in *Group Identity in the South*, ed. Kaufman, Morland, and Fockler, 76–77.

the ratio of agricultural to nonagricultural workers, the distribution of the population in various occupational and industrial categories, per capita income, and
educational attainment. These indicators showed a clear structural convergence.
Indeed, their data suggested that since the 1930s the South had changed more
rapidly than the rest of the nation, and that although differences between the
South and the non-South remained, the South would integrate rapidly into a national social system. Although McKinney and Bourque did not argue that all of
the traits that traditionally distinguished the South would disappear, they suggested that similarities between what southerners and nonsoutherners did and
how they lived would increasingly level the differences in how they thought and
felt.[3]

McKinney and Bourque's research did not examine attitudes and values directly. Thus it remained an article of faith that change in the material organization of southern life had transformed, and would continue to transform, the
South's cultural superstructure to conform with that of the rest of the nation.
Nevertheless, their central conclusion of structural convergence has been supported in other studies over the last two decades. For example, recent ecological
studies of the metropolitan structure of the United States show the South to be
increasingly functionally linked into a national metropolitan system. Interest-
ingly, the growth rate of southern (and western) metropolitan areas has tended
to exceed that of the North for three decades. Also, there have been some almost
paradoxical consequences of the economic expansion of the urban South. By
1990, the relatively younger southern (and western) metropolitan areas showed
the lowest levels of, and largest decreases in, black/white residential segregation.
Moreover, this changing and expanding infrastructure apparently has created
lower employment inequality between blacks and whites in the labor markets of
the South and West.[4]

Although it is indisputable that the South has undergone dramatic structural
transformation since the 1940s, evidence supporting the hypothesis of its regional cultural distinctiveness has continued to emerge throughout this period.
In 1973, for example, Harold G. Grasmic assessed the persistence of traditional-

---

3. John C. McKinney and Linda Brookover Bourque, "The Changing South: National Incorpo-
ration of a Region," *American Sociological Review* 36 (June 1971): 399–412.

4. Ibid.; David R. Meyer, "Control and Coordination Links in the Metropolitan System of Cities: The South as a Case Study," *Social Forces* 63 (December 1984): 349–62; Michael D. Irwin and
John D. Kasarda, "Air Passenger Linkages and Employment Growth in U.S. Metropolitan Areas,"
American Sociological Review 56 (August 1991): 524–37; William H. Frey, "Migration and Depopulation of the Metropolis: Regional Restructuring or Rural Renaissance?" *American Sociological Review* 52 (April 1987): 240–57; Reynolds Farley and William H. Frey, "Changes in the Segregation of
Whites from Blacks During the 1980s: Small Steps Toward a More Integrated Society," *American Sociological Review* 59 (February 1994): 23–45; Samuel Cohn and Mark Fossett, "Why Racial Employment Inequality Is Greater in Northern Labor Markets: Regional Differences in White-Black Employment Differentials," *Social Forces* 74 (December 1995): 511–42.

ism in southern attitudes and values and found little evidence that structural changes had eroded them significantly. Similarly, John Shelton Reed has argued that the regional distinctiveness of the South persists, despite the effects of increasing modernization. Reed and Lewis M. Killian used an ethnic analogy of southern culture and identity to argue that southerners, much like other ethnic and minority groups, continue to participate in an identifiable culture.[5]

As would be true of any demographic group in a pluralistic society, we should not expect traditionally southern characteristics to be completely absent among nonsoutherners or uniformly present among southerners. Rather, to the extent that the South remains a culturally distinct region (i.e., a regional subculture), we can expect that historically southern attitudes and values will be more prevalent, or will have greater intensity, among southerners than among nonsoutherners. In this regard, previous research suggests that the South differs from the non-South with respect to at least four measurable cultural dimensions: more favorable attitudes and value orientations toward the use of violence; more conservative political attitudes; more conservative racial attitudes; and more conservative religious attitudes and orientations toward religion, morality, women's roles, and the family.

Since well before the Civil War, observers have remarked on the southern penchant for violence. The favorable value orientation of the use of violence as a mechanism of dispute resolution seemed to pervade not only interpersonal conflicts but also attitudes toward foreign policy and, of course, interregional disputes. But the southern orientation toward violence should not be interpreted as endorsing random, criminal violence or as valuing violence in all situations. Rather, it has a distinctive defensive character. Whatever the historical roots may have been, this cultural trait has continued to appear in identifiable ways in southern life. Homicide rates involving personal disputes between friends, acquaintances, and family members have remained higher than in other regions. Ownership and use of the means of violence—firearms—is higher and more equitably distributed throughout the social structure and between sexes in the South than in the non-South, and there is a greater approval of, and willingness to use, guns for defense. The indicators of this dimension include attitudes toward a law requiring a permit to own a gun, personal violence experiences, and gun ownership.[6]

5. Harold G. Grasmic, "Social Change and Modernism in the American South," *American Behavioral Scientist* 16 (July–August 1973): 913–33; John Shelton Reed, *The Enduring South: Subculture Persistence in Mass Society* (Lexington, Mass.: Lexington Books, 1972); Reed, *One South: An Ethnic Approach to Regional Culture* (Baton Rouge: Louisiana State University Press, 1982); Reed, *Southerners: The Social Psychology of Sectionalism* (Chapel Hill: University of North Carolina Press, 1983); Lewis M. Killian, *White Southerners* (Amherst: University of Massachusetts Press, 1985).

6. Vandiver, "The Southerner as Extremist," 43–55; Jo Dixon and A. J. Lizotte, "Gun Ownership and the Southern Subculture of Violence," *American Journal of Sociology* 93 (September 1987):

That the structure of politics has changed in the South is apparent. Jim Crow is dead, rural dominance has eroded, the Democratically controlled Solid South has become permeable to Republican infiltration, and two-party politics has appeared in southern state and local campaigns. Yet the question remains whether these changes reflect a transformation in southerners' political attitudes or instead result from a move by the Republican party to capitalize on the unchanging quality of southern whites' political orientations. Indeed, the apparent regional convergence in political attitudes and perceptions of political issues may as easily be interpreted as the product of southern continuity in the face of a changing non-South. So, although party loyalties may have fluctuated, there is evidence that underlying political views may have remained stable or, at least, may not have changed to the extent that shifts in party alliance might imply. The stands of individuals on specific political issues and their expression of conservative beliefs are therefore likely to be better indicators of regional continuity and change than is party affiliation. Southern conservatism appears to be captured particularly in the orientations of southerners to such issues as government spending in various areas (including defense and welfare), or whether they consider themselves to be liberal or conservative, as well as their attitudes toward the roles of homosexuals and communists in the community.[7]

Racism, racist attitudes, and racial identity have been said to constitute the "cardinal tests" of a southerner. Certainly the South has been considered by its antagonists to be "the" racist region, as shown by the fact that the Voting Rights Act and its renewals applied only to southern states. Race and politics have been inseparable in the South since Reconstruction. Indeed, as both white and black southerners are quick to point out, this has been true wherever blacks have appeared in significant numbers in America. Nonetheless, even with the "reshaping" of southern politics (with the Republican flavor described above), race and racial issues remain a central feature of southern political campaigns and elec-

---

383–405; Reed, *Southerners;* Gastil, *Cultural Regions of the United States;* William B. Bankston, Roberta L. St. Pierre, and H. David Allen, "Southern Culture and Patterns of Victim-Offender Relationships in Homicide," *Sociological Spectrum* 5 (1985): 197–211; Lin Huf-Corzine, Jay Corzine, and David C. Moore, "Southern Exposure: Deciphering the South's Influence on Homicide Rates," *Social Forces* 64 (June 1986): 906–24; James Wright, Peter Rossi, and Kathleen Daly, *Under the Gun* (Chicago: Aldine, 1983), 106–7; Robert L. Young, "Gender, Region of Socialization, and Ownership of Protective Firearms," *Rural Sociology* 51 (June 1986): 169–82.

7.   Robert P. Steed, Laurence W. Morland, and Tod A. Baker, "Searching for the Mind of the South in the Second Reconstruction," in *The Disappearing South?: Studies in Regional Change and Continuity,* ed. Steed, Morland, and Baker (Tuscaloosa: University of Alabama Press, 1990), 125–40; John Shelton Reed, Foreword to *The Disappearing South?* ed. Steed, Morland, Baker, vii–xii; Jack Bass and Walter De Vries, *The Transformation of Southern Politics: Social Change and Political Consequences Since 1945* (New York: Basic Books, 1976); Bruce A. Campbell, "Patterns of Change in the Partisan Loyalties of Native Southerners, 1952–1972," *Journal of Politics* 39 (August 1977): 730–61; Joe R. Feagin, "Civil Rights Voting by Southern Congressmen," *Journal of Politics* 34 (May 1972): 484–99.

tion strategies, even if they no longer appear overtly in candidates' statements. Here regional differences, at the level of individual attitudes toward race and race relations, will be examined. We expect traditionally southern attitudes to be indicated among whites who say that they would object to their children attending a racially integrated school, refuse to vote for a qualified black candidate, oppose busing to achieve racial balance in schools, favor a law to prohibit interracial marriage, support segregation of the races in housing, or live in a segregated neighborhood.[8]

The last dimension of southern distinctiveness considered here is attitudes toward religion, morality, women's roles, and the family. Overwhelmingly Protestant, southern religion has had a distinctive regional quality. As Gastil notes, "Wherever there are southern Baptists, there is southern culture." Whether referring to the evangelical sects or the institutionalized denominations, however, most observers agree that southern identity has been bound intimately to religion. To an extent, southern religious identity has been forged in a defensive stance. The fundamentalism, antievolutionism, creationism, anti-Catholicism, and pro-temperance features that have characterized southern religion are well documented and rooted in southern nativism. Consequently, in the process of distinguishing themselves symbolically, southerners have reputedly endorsed a stricter code of private morality revealed in greater disapproval of premarital, extramarital, and homosexual sex; a stronger approval of temperance; a greater disapproval of divorce; opposition to abortion; more frequent church attendance; a stronger membership identity with their church; and greater likelihood of belonging to fundamentalist Protestant denominations.[9]

Although attitudes toward women's roles constitute another dimension of the cultural boundaries of the South, the degree to which the stereotypical characteristics of the "southern lady" have ever described anything but a small portion of southern women is questionable. Derived from an antebellum ideal, the description of the southern white woman as "a submissive wife whose reason for being was to love, honor, obey, and occasionally amuse her husband, to bring up his children and manage his household" is probably rooted more strongly in twentieth-century novels and media images than in nineteenth-century reality. Reality for the majority of southern white women was far removed from any ro-

8. Reed, *Southerners;* Earl Black and Merle Black, *Politics and Society in the South* (Cambridge, Mass.: Harvard University Press, 1987), 293–316; Thomas F. Eamon, "The Militant Republican Right in North Carolina Elections: Legacy of the Old Politics of Race," in *The Disappearing South?,* ed. Steed, Morland, and Baker, 156–73.

9. Reed, *Southerners,* 29; Gastil, *Cultural Regions of the United States,* 53; Kary D. Smout, "Attacking (Southern) Creationism," in *Religion in the Contemporary South,* ed. O. Kendall White, Jr., and Daryl White (Athens: University of Georgia Press, 1995), 59–66; Gary W. McDonogh, "Constructing Christian Hatred: Anti-Catholicism, Diversity, and Religion in Southern Religious Life," in *Religion in the Contemporary South,* ed. White and White, 67–78; Joseph R. Gusfield, *Symbolic Crusade* (Urbana: University of Illinois Press, 1963).

mantic ideal, before and after the Civil War and into the industrializing South of the twentieth century. Even so, the southern emphasis on family solidarity and the woman's place in it does seem to have originated in long-standing values of an agrarian elite. Traditionally, southern attitudes toward women have included a stronger belief in a division of labor in which women undertake primary responsibility for domestic and child-rearing tasks, disapproval of women working outside the home, and unwillingness to vote for a qualified female candidate for president.[10]

We selected indicators of these perceptions to determine to what extent these attitudes characterize southerners, and if they do, whether they have changed over time. Working from the cumulative data file of the 1972–94 General Social Surveys, we selected three time periods in which to examine southern distinctiveness: 1972–74, 1983–85, and 1994. These periods were chosen because they postdate the major pieces of legislation resulting from the civil rights movement and approximate the beginning, middle, and end of a two-decade period of rapid structural change in the South. Whenever possible, we used data for 1972, 1985, and 1994. When indicators were unavailable for these years, one of the other years for that period was substituted. To measure the four conceptual dimensions outlined above, which serve as our dependent variables, we chose indicators from the GSS that were available for at least one year in each of the three focal time periods.[11]

Because the GSS does not include state codes, a measure of our central independent variable, region, was constructed from census regional classifications. A series of dummy variables representing the New England, Middle Atlantic, East North Central, West North Central, Mountain, and Pacific regions was created, along with a dummy variable that combined all these regions into a single non-South category. The South, which serves as our reference category in all analyses, includes residents of the South Atlantic, East South Central, and West South Central regions. This procedure allows comparison of southerners to residents with specific nonsouthern regions and an aggregated group of nonsouthern regions.[12]

10.   Anne Firor Scott, *The Southern Lady: From Pedestal to Politics, 1830 to 1930* (Chicago: University of Chicago Press, 1970), 4; J. Wayne Flynt, "Folks Like Us: The Southern Poor White Family," in *The Web of Southern Social Relations*, ed. Walter J. Fraser, Jr., R. Frank Sounders, Jr., and Jon L. Wakelyn (Athens: University of Georgia Press, 1985), 225–44; Rupert B. Vance, "Family and Work in the South," in *Group Identity in the South*, ed. Kaufman, Morland, and Fockler, 17–32.

11.   The 1972–74 surveys used a form of block quota sampling. Multistage area probability samples were drawn above the block level, and quota sampling (with quotas for sex, age, and employment) was used at the block level. The 1983–85 and 1994 surveys used stratified, multistage area probability samples of clusters of households. In both cases, the samples were drawn from the noninstitutionalized, English-speaking adult population in the continental United States.

12.   The regions are classified as follows: New England includes Maine, Vermont, New Hamp-

To ensure that the effects of region are net of sociodemographic characteristics, the race, gender, age, marital status, education, and family income of respondents were controlled in all equations. Race was measured white (1) and nonwhite (0).[13] Gender was measured male (1) and female (0). Marital status was measured with a series of dummy variables. The first contrasted separated, widowed, and divorced individuals (1) with others (0); the second contrasted never married individuals (1) with others (0). The reference category was married. Education and age were measured in years. Family income was measured in dollars: we recoded the GSS income categories to their midpoints. Rural/urban residence was also controlled. Urban areas were classified as all areas within a Standard Metropolitan Statistical Area (Metropolitan Statistical Area (SMSA [MSA]), including suburbs; small cities were areas not within an SMSA (MSA), with a population between ten thousand and fifty thousand; and rural areas were all areas with less than ten thousand population.

To determine whether the South remains distinctive on the four conceptual dimensions, we performed, for each dimension, an analysis that proceeds in two stages. In the first stage, we developed our dependent variables. When possible, we used factor analysis to combine these indicators into a scale or scales (using factor scores), which then became our dependent variables.[14] Factor analysis is a statistical procedure that allows the development of measures of a construct. It yields a factor or factors that tap some aspect or aspects of the construct—in a sense, it identifies clusters of similar indicators of an underlying construct. For

---

shire, Massachusetts, Connecticut, and Rhode Island; Middle Atlantic includes New York, New Jersey, and Pennsylvania; East North Central includes Wisconsin, Illinois, Indiana, Michigan, and Ohio; West North Central includes Minnesota, Iowa, Missouri, North Dakota, South Dakota, Nebraska, and Kansas; Mountain includes Montana, Idaho, Wyoming, Nevada, Utah, Colorado, Arizona, and New Mexico; Pacific includes Washington, Oregon, California, Alaska, and Hawaii. The South includes Delaware, Maryland, West Virginia, Virginia, North Carolina, South Carolina, Georgia, Florida, the District of Columbia, Kentucky, Tennessee, Alabama, Mississippi, Arkansas, Oklahoma, Louisiana, and Texas. Because we include in the southern category some states that are not normally classified as southern (e.g., Delaware and Maryland), our test of the hypothesis of cultural distinctiveness is more conservative than it would be if these states were excluded.

13. We exclude nonblack nonwhites from these analyses.

14. Our goal was to use factor analysis to create a factor score for each of our conceptual dimensions for each period (e.g., to produce a factor score for race for 1972, 1985, and 1994). The timing of questions precluded the estimation of a single factor analysis for each dimension in any of the three periods (in some cases, groups of questions within a conceptual domain were asked in different years; in other cases, they were asked in the same year but were placed on different ballots and therefore were asked of different respondents). We therefore grouped the indicators for each dimension, based on the years for which data were available, and performed separate factor analyses for each group of indicators. In all cases, we used principal components factor analysis with squared multiple correlations as the initial communality estimates. With the exception of two cases for which no factor analytic solution was possible, we regressed the factor scores from these analyses on respondents' region of residence and a series of control variables.

Table 1.
Effects of Region on Attitudes
Toward Law Requiring Permit to Own a Gun[a]

Independent Variable	1972		1984		1994	
	Model A	Model B	Model A	Model B	Model A	Model B
New England[b]	−.887*	—	−.963**	—	−.309	—
Middle Atlantic[b]	−1.616**	—	−.810**	—	−.591**	—
East North Central[b]	−.230	—	−.445*	—	−.013	—
West North Central[b]	.034	—	−.253	—	−.113	—
Mountain[b]	1.026**	—	.464	—	.399	—
Pacific[b]	−.411	—	−.159	—	.241	—
Non-South[c]	—	−.407**	—	−.367**	—	−.048
Intercept	−.730	−.844	−.868	−1.031	−1.440	−1.546
η^2_v[d]	.092	.049	.072	.055	.067	.057

[a] Logistic regression coefficients; equation includes controls for age, marital status, education, gender, rural/urban residence, income, and race. Each coefficient represents the magnitude and direction of difference between a given regional category (e.g., New England) and the South. For example, a negative coefficient for the New England region indicates that New Englanders express less support for these laws than southerners do. * indicates that this difference is significant at the .05 level, and ** indicates that this difference is significant at the .01 level.

[b] Dummy variable for region of residence; reference category is the South.

[c] Dummy variable for aggregate non-South category; reference category is the South.

[d] Proportion of qualitative variance explained; see Jay Magidson, "Qualitative Variance, Entropy and Correlation Ratios for Nominal Dependent Variables," *Social Science Research* 10 (June 1981): 177–94.

example, it may produce a factor that taps most strongly the degree to which respondents favor the right of women to have abortions and less strongly their attitudes toward sexuality. In some cases, it was not possible to produce a factor analysis solution for a set of indicators. When that occurred, we predicted separately the individual indicators of a given dimension.

Tables 1–16 present the results of both stages of this analysis. When factor analyses were performed for a given dimension, we first present a table describing that analysis (e.g., Table 1). We then present the results of a regression analysis in which we compare the attitudes of southerners to those of nonsoutherners (e.g., Table 2). Thus in the example above, the regression analysis allows us to compare the degree to which southerners, as opposed to nonsoutherners, support this set of attitudes (e.g., primarily attitudes toward abortion and, to a lesser degree, attitudes toward sexuality). When no factor analysis solution was possible, we present only one analysis: a regression analysis that compares the attitudes (or behavior) of southerners with those of nonsoutherners.

Beginning with the violence dimension, our indicators are designed to tap both attitudes and behaviors related to gun ownership and experiences of personal violence. Because analyses of our three indicators failed to produce a factor analytic solution (identify a factor), we analyze them separately. Table 1 shows that there has been some change in the attitudes of southerners, relative to those of nonsoutherners, over these three time periods regarding laws requiring a permit to own a gun. In 1972, southerners were more likely than residents of

Table 2.
Effects of Region on Whether Respondents
Report Having Been Struck by Another Person[a]

Independent Variable	1972		1984		1994	
	Model A	Model B	Model A	Model B	Model A	Model B
New England[b]	.096	—	.043	—	−.054	—
Middle Atlantic[b]	.008	—	.079*	—	−.117	—
East North Central[b]	.018	—	.073*	—	−.005	—
West North Central[b]	−.022	—	.027	—	.074	—
Mountain[b]	.149**	—	.035	—	−.118	—
Pacific[b]	.135**	—	.106**	—	−.024	—
Non-South[c]	—	.044	—	.067**	—	−.040
Intercept	.283	.280	.501	.507	.699	.701
R²	.214	.202	.183	.181	.208	.198

[a] Ordinary least squares regression coefficients; pattern of results for region is unchanged for logistic regression coefficients. Equation includes controls for age, marital status, education, gender, rural/urban residence, income, and race. Each coefficient represents the magnitude and direction of difference between a given regional category (e.g., New England) and the South. For example, a negative coefficient for the New England region indicates that New Englanders are less likely than southerners to have been struck by another individual. * indicates that this difference is significant at the .05 level, and ** indicates that this difference is significant at the .01 level.

[b] Dummy variable for region of residence; reference category is the South.

[c] Dummy variable for aggregate non-South category; reference category is the South.

the New England and Middle Atlantic regions to express opposition to such laws; they were also more likely than members of the aggregate non-South category to oppose them. But they were less likely to do so than residents of the Mountain region. The latter finding may reflect the traditional importance of guns in the culture and history of the Mountain states, as well as the strong conservative political orientation that has existed in many of them.

This pattern held true in 1984, except that the East North Central residents were also less likely than southerners to oppose a gun law in this period and the South/Mountain comparison was no longer significant. By 1994, only one regional difference remained significant and the significant difference between the South and the aggregate non-South category had eroded. Thus southerners were less distinct in their attitudes toward gun laws in 1994 than they were in 1972. Comparison of means for this variable between southerners and nonsoutherners across the three time periods indicates that nonsoutherners have grown more tolerant of gun ownership. This finding shows that although the difference between the South and the non-South has diminished, this pattern does not reflect a diminution of the symbolic importance of the right to own guns in southern culture. Rather, it reflects a shift in attitudes of nonsoutherners, which is probably driven by increased fear of crime.

Diminishing southern/nonsouthern differences can also be found in reports of experiences of personal violence (Table 2). In this case, though, the differences that existed in the early periods contradict our expectations. In 1972, residents of the Mountain and Pacific regions were more likely than southerners to report

Table 3.
Effects of Region on Whether Respondents Report Having a Gun in Their Home[a]

Independent Variable	1972		1984		1994	
	Model A	Model B	Model A	Model B	Model A	Model B
New England[b]	−.313**	—	−.169**	—	−.158**	—
Middle Atlantic[b]	−.372**	—	−.176**	—	−.219**	—
East North Central[b]	−.105**	—	−.099**	—	−.009	—
West North Central[b]	−.097	—	−.121*	—	−.055	—
Mountain[b]	−.007	—	.111	—	−.085	—
Pacific[b]	−.148**	—	−.072	—	−.121**	—
Non-South[c]	—	−.183**	—	−.101**	—	−.102**
Intercept	.536	.508	.387	.352	.417	.429
R^2	.183	.144	.169	.154	.168	.153

[a] Ordinary least squares regression coefficients; pattern of results for region was unchanged with logistic regression coefficients. Equation includes controls for age, marital status, education, gender, rural/urban residence, income, and race. Each coefficient represents the magnitude and direction of difference between a given regional category (e.g., New England) and the South. For example, a negative coefficient for the New England region indicates that New Englanders are less likely than southerners to report having guns in their homes. * indicates that this difference is significant at the .05 level, and ** indicates that this difference is significant at the .01 level.

[b] Dummy variable for region of residence; reference category is the South.

[c] Dummy variable for aggregate non-South category; reference category is the South.

that they had been struck by someone, and in 1984, residents of the Middle Atlantic, East North Central, and Pacific regions were more likely to do so. Residents of the aggregate non-South category were also more likely than southerners to report that they experienced personal violence. But by 1994, these differences had disappeared. The pattern for 1972 and 1984 is not necessarily inconsistent with the traditionally southern orientation toward violence. Because that emphasis is primarily defensive rather than random, it should appear only in certain contexts and should not necessarily entail high rates of personal violence experiences.[15]

The final measure of this dimension is whether respondents report that they own a gun (Table 3). The results show that in 1972, southerners were more likely than residents of the New England, Middle Atlantic, East North Central, and Pacific regions and than residents of the aggregate non-South category to report that they owned guns. By 1984, this pattern held for all regions except the Pacific, and now residents of the South were also more likely than residents of the West North Central region to report that they owned guns. By 1994, significant differences between residents of the South and the New England, Middle Atlantic, and Pacific regions and the aggregate non-South category remained. These findings are interesting, particularly in light of our findings for attitudes toward gun law permits. Although southerners were no longer more likely than nonsoutherners to oppose laws requiring gun permits by 1994, they were still more likely to own guns themselves. Examination of means for southerners and nonsouth-

15. Reed, *Southerners;* Gastil, *Cultural Regions of the United States.*

Table 4.
Factor Analyses of Racial Attitude Indicators

Attitude	1972	1985	1994
Toward sending child to school with half of opposite race	.829	.771	.852
Toward sending child to school with few of opposite race	.613	.539	.534
Toward voting for qualified black for president	.548	.447	.307
Toward busing	.152	.138	.105
Eigenvalue	1.386	1.103	1.116

Table 5.
Effects of Region on Factor Scores, Racial Attitudes[a]

	1972		1985		1994	
Independent Variable	Model A	Model B	Model A	Model B	Model A	Model B
New England[b]	−.639**	—	−.244**	—	−.204*	—
Middle Atlantic[b]	−.493**	—	−.105	—	−.057	—
East North Central[b]	−.253**	—	−.117	—	−.044	—
West North Central[b]	−.395**	—	−.068	—	−.144	—
Mountain[b]	−.473**	—	−.121	—	−.098	—
Pacific[b]	−.601**	—	−.107	—	−.020	—
Non-South[c]	—	−.454**	—	−.119**	—	−.075
Intercept	.565	.559	−.120	−.128	.059	.089
R[2]	.152	.135	.070	.068	.030	.028

[a] Ordinary least squares regression coefficients. Equation includes controls for age, marital status, education, gender, rural/urban residence, income, and race. Each coefficient represents the magnitude and direction of difference between a given regional category (e.g., New England) and the South. For example, a negative coefficient for the New England region indicates that New Englanders express less support for the attitudes tapped by this factor than southerners do. * indicates that this difference is significant at the .05 level, and ** indicates that this difference is significant at the .01 level.

[b] Dummy variable for region of residence; reference category is the South.

[c] Dummy variable for aggregate non-South category; reference category is the South.

erners across the three time periods shows a slight increase in the rate of non-southern gun ownership and a slight decrease in the rate of southern gun ownership (possibly because of immigration). Thus although the non-South has moved closer to the South in its attitudes toward gun ownership permits, its rate of gun ownership has not yet approached that of the South. This is consistent with the fact that gun ownership rates were already high in the South and very low in the non-South.

One of the most salient aspects of the South's cultural notoriety has been racial attitudes. The first group of indicators of this dimension included attitudes toward sending one's children to a school where (1) a few children and (2) at least one-half of the children were of the opposite race; whether respondents indicated willingness to vote for a qualified black candidate for president; and attitudes toward busing. Our factor analyses of these indicators for 1972, 1985, and 1994 yielded one factor in each case (Table 4). Each factor taps most strongly attitudes toward integrated schools. When we use these factors as dependent variables

Table 6.
Effects of Region on Attitudes Toward Segregated Neighborhoods[a]

Independent Variable	1972		1985		1994	
	Model A	Model B	Model A	Model B	Model A	Model B
New England[b]	−.523**	—	−.340**	—	−.423**	—
Middle Atlantic[b]	−.290**	—	−.147	—	−.141*	—
East North Central[b]	−.208*	—	−.093	—	−.090	—
West North Central[b]	−.314**	—	.039	—	−.111	—
Mountain[b]	−.576**	—	−.309**	—	−.292**	—
Pacific[b]	−.563**	—	−.347**	—	−.251**	—
Non-South[c]	—	−.361**	—	−.176**	—	−.183**
Intercept	2.850	2.861	1.831	1.826	1.453	1.511
R²	.151	.140	.158	.146	.138	.130

     [a] Ordinary least squares regression coefficients. Equation includes controls for age, marital status, education, gender, rural/urban residence, income, and race. Each coefficient represents the magnitude and direction of difference between a given regional category (e.g., New England) and the South. For example, a negative coefficient for the New England region indicates that New Englanders are less likely than southerners to support the right of whites to exclude blacks from their neighborhoods. * indicates that this difference is significant at the .05 level, and ** indicates that this difference is significant at the .01 level.
     [b] Dummy variable for region of residence; reference category is the South.
     [c] Dummy variable for aggregate non-South category; reference category is the South.

(Table 5), we find that southerners were significantly more conservative than residents of every other region in these racial attitudes in 1972 and that there was a significant difference between southerners and members of the aggregate nonsouthern category. But by 1985, southerners differed significantly only from residents of New England, although the aggregate South/non-South difference remained significant. By 1994, only the South/New England difference remained, and it was slight. Thus southerners and nonsoutherners have come closer in their attitudes toward school integration and busing. Examination of means on the factor across the three time periods indicates that southerners' attitudes have become less conservative over time.

     Turning to our remaining race indicators, we were unable to produce a factor analytic solution (factor) for our measures of attitudes toward interracial marriage and the right of whites to live in segregated neighborhoods and our behavioral measure of whether respondents live in a neighborhood with residents of the opposite race. We therefore used these measures as separate dependent variables. Table 6 shows a decline (across our three time periods) in southern distinctiveness in attitudes toward segregated neighborhoods. Although southerners were distinct from residents of all other regions in this attitude in 1972, they differed only from residents of the New England, Mountain, and Pacific regions in 1985. In 1994, these differences remained, and the Middle Atlantic residents also diverged from southerners. The South/non-South comparison reveals significant differences in the predicted direction across all three time periods, however. Comparison of mean attitudes between southerners and nonsoutherners across

Table 7.
Effects of Region on Respondents' Reports of Living in Segregrated Neighborhoods[a]

	1972		1985		1994	
Independent Variable	Model A	Model B	Model A	Model B	Model A	Model B
New England[b]	−.522	—	.072	—	.906**	—
Middle Atlantic[b]	−.168	—	.137	—	.281	—
East North Central[b]	−.356	—	.313	—	.814**	—
West North Central[b]	.711*	—	.155	—	.484**	—
Mountain[b]	−.028	—	.662**	—	.475**	—
Pacific[b]	−.427*	—	−.540**	—	.218	—
Non-South[c]	—	−.211	—	.115	—	.526**
Intercept	1.000	.934	−1.943	−1.892	−1.823	−1.788
η_v^2,[d]	.101	.089	.135	.120	.113	.105

[a] Logistic regression coefficients. Equation includes controls for age, marital status, education, gender, rural/urban residence, income, and race. Each coefficient represents the magnitude and direction of difference between a given regional category (e.g., New England) and the South. For example, a negative coefficient for the New England region indicates that New Englanders are less likely than southerners to live in segregated (all-white) neighborhoods. * indicates that this difference is significant at the .05 level, and ** indicates that this difference is significant at the .01 level.

[b] Dummy variable for region of residence; reference category is the South.

[c] Dummy variable for aggregate non-South category; reference category is the South.

[d] Proportion of qualitative variance explained; see Jay Magidson, "Qualitative Variance, Entropy and Correlation Ratios for Nominal Dependent Variables," *Social Science Research* 10 (June 1981): 177–94.

the three time periods shows that southern attitudes have moderated somewhat: the proportion of southerners holding the most extreme position has decreased.

Our next indicator of this dimension is whether respondents reported that they actually lived in an all-white neighborhood. The results for this measure (Table 7) are particularly interesting, both because they show increasing rather than decreasing distinctiveness of southern attitudes and because the nature of the distinctiveness that emerges across these three time periods contradicts our predictions. In 1972, southerners differed only from residents of the West North Central and Pacific regions on this behavioral measure. As predicted, southerners were more likely than residents of the Pacific region to state that there were no blacks living in their neighborhoods, but West North Central residents were more likely than southerners to report that their neighborhoods were exclusively white. The South/Pacific difference held in 1985, but by then white residents of the Mountain region were more likely than white southerners to live in an all-white neighborhood and the South/West North Central difference had disappeared. In 1994, white residents of every region except the Middle Atlantic and Pacific were more likely than white southerners to state that they lived in a neighborhood that had no blacks and, for the first time, a significant South/non-South difference emerged. Thus by 1994, regional differences emerged that contradict our predictions.

Findings for southern attitudes toward interracial marriage (Table 8) are more consistent with our expectations. In 1972, residents of every region except

Table 8.
Effects of Region on Attitudes Toward Interracial Marriage[a]

Independent Variable	1972		1985		1994	
	Model A	Model B	Model A	Model B	Model A	Model B
New England[b]	−.824**	—	−1.036**	—	−1.383**	—
Middle Atlantic[b]	−.802**	—	−1.298**	—	−.745**	—
East North Central[b]	−.554**	—	−.971**	—	−.360	—
West North Central[b]	−.505*	—	−.792**	—	−.885**	—
Mountain[b]	−.119	—	−1.376**	—	−1.330**	—
Pacific[b]	−.998**	—	−1.449**	—	−1.492**	—
Non-South[c]	—	−.681**	—	−1.120**	—	−.860**
Intercept	1.077	1.041	−2.090	−2.124	−1.975	−1.850
η_v^2 [d]	.198	.192	.256	.253	.191	.183

[a] Logistic regression coefficients. Equation includes controls for age, marital status, education, gender, rural/urban residence, income, and race. Each coefficient represents the magnitude and direction of difference between a given regional category (e.g., New England) and the South. For example, a negative coefficient for the New England region indicates that New Englanders express less support for laws against interracial marriage than southerners do. * indicates that this difference is significant at the .05 level, and ** indicates that this difference is significant at the .01 level.

[b] Dummy variable for region of residence; reference category is the South.

[c] Dummy variable for aggregate non-South category; reference category is the South.

[d] Proportion of qualitative variance explained; see Jay Magidson, "Qualitative Variance, Entropy and Correlation Ratios for Nominal Dependent Variables," *Social Science Research* 10 (June 1981): 177–94.

the Mountain were less likely than southerners to say that they favored laws prohibiting interracial marriage. In 1985, residents of every nonsouthern region were less likely than southerners to do so, and this pattern held in 1994 for every region except the East North Central. Significant differences exist (in the predicted direction) between southerners and the aggregate nonsouthern category across all three time periods. As social distance theory would predict, then, attitudes toward interracial marriage appear to be converging more slowly across regions than attitudes regarding residential segregation. Some regional differences persist in both of these attitudes, though. The same is not true for our behavioral measure—reports of living in a segregated neighborhood. There, the traditional regional pattern has eroded. More important, the proportion of southerners who live in segregated neighborhoods has decreased in both an absolute and a relative sense across these three time periods. This is consistent with demographic findings, which show residential segregation to be lower in the South than in the non-South.[16]

To analyze our third indicator of southern distinctiveness, conservative political attitudes, it was again necessary to divide the measures into two groups. The factor analysis of our first group of indicators, which included all of our measures of attitudes toward government spending and the liberal/conservative

16.   Cohn and Fossett, "Why Racial Employment Inequality Is Greater in Northern Labor Markets," 511–42.

Table 9.
Factor Analyses, Indicators of Political Attitudes (Part I)

Attitude	1972	1985	1994
Government spending on racial issues too high	.560	.597	.601
Government spending on cities too high	.496	.525	.604
Government spending on environment too high	.439	.398	.391
Government spending on education too high	.429	.321	.461
Government spending on health too high	.417	.460	.502
Government spending on welfare too high	.351	.462	.325
Conservative political views	.281	.126	.317
Government spending on drug control too high	.281	.427	.514
Government spending on crime too high	.277	.336	.452
Government spending on foreign aid too high	.179	.208	.092
Government spending on space exploration too high	−.037	−.213	−.192
Government spending on arms too high	−.153	−.200	−.177
Eigenvalue	1.526	1.757	3.826

Table 10.
Effects of Region on Factor Scores, Political Attitudes (Part I)[a]

Independent Variable	1972 Model A	1972 Model B	1985 Model A	1985 Model B	1994 Model A	1994 Model B
New England[b]	−.258*	—	−.197	—	−.310**	—
Middle Atlantic[b]	−.185*	—	−.204	—	−.170*	—
East North Central[b]	−.129	—	.034	—	−.209**	—
West North Central[b]	−.172	—	.085	—	−.108	—
Mountain[b]	−.054	—	.116	—	−.163	—
Pacific[b]	−.063	—	−.091	—	−.084	—
Non-South[c]	—	−.139**	—	−.045	—	−.167**
Intercept	−.544	−.559	−.857	−.900	−.892	−.911
R^2	.149	.145	.105	.092	.139	.136

[a] Ordinary least squares regression coefficients. Equation includes controls for age, marital status, education, gender, rural/urban residence, income, and race. Each coefficient represents the magnitude and direction of difference between a given regional category (e.g., New England) and the South. For example, a negative coefficient for the New England region indicates that New Englanders express less support for the attitudes tapped by this factor than southerners do. * indicates that this difference is significant at the .05 level, and ** indicates that this difference is significant at the .01 level.
[b] Dummy variable for region of residence; reference category is the South.
[c] Dummy variable for aggregate non-South category; reference category is the South.

scale, produced a single factor (Table 9). The factors generally tap most strongly attitudes toward government spending on race, cities, and the environment in each time period. When we use this factor as a dependent variable (Table 10), we find modest differences between the South and other regions which seem to decline in 1985 and then to increase somewhat in 1994. In 1972, southerners expressed significantly more support for the attitudes tapped by this factor than New England and Middle Atlantic residents did, indicating stronger opposition to most forms of government spending and higher levels of political conservatism. Significant differences were also found between southerners and the aggregate nonsouthern category. In 1985, these differences disappeared. In 1994,

Table 11.
Factor Analyses, Indicators of Political Attitudes (Part II)

Attitude	1974	1985	1994
Would not allow homosexual to speak in community	.821	.762	.816
Would not allow homosexual to teach in local college	.792	.751	.731
Would not allow communist to speak in community	.718	.674	.641
Would not allow communist to teach in local college	.588	.625	.469
Eigenvalue	2.161	1.989	1.831

Table 12.
Effects of Region on Factor Scores, Political Attitudes (Part II)[a]

	1974		1985		1994	
Independent Variable	Model A	Model B	Model A	Model B	Model A	Model B
New England[b]	−.256*	—	−.380**	—	−.419**	—
Middle Atlantic[b]	−.327**	—	−.337**	—	−.240**	—
East North Central[b]	−.191**	—	−.219**	—	−.207**	—
West North Central[b]	−.257**	—	−.096	—	−.289**	—
Mountain[b]	−.196	—	−.166	—	−.332**	—
Pacific[b]	−.264**	—	−.187**	—	−.350**	—
Non-South[c]	—	−.246**	—	−.228**	—	−.282**
Intercept	.256	.252	.752	.724	1.147	1.203
R^2	.313	.311	.256	.250	.194	.190

[a] Ordinary least squares regression coefficients. Equation includes controls for age, marital status, education, gender, rural/urban residence, income, and race. Each coefficient represents the magnitude and direction of difference between a given regional category (e.g., New England) and the South. For example, a negative coefficient for the New England region indicates that New Englanders express less support for the attitudes tapped by this factor than southerners do. * indicates that this difference is significant at the .05 level, and ** indicates that this difference is significant at the .01 level.

[b] Dummy variable for region of residence; reference category is the South.

[c] Dummy variable for aggregate non-South category; reference category is the South.

though, the pattern of results mirrored that of 1972, except that a significant difference appeared between residents of the South and East North Central regions. These findings suggest that southerners remain more conservative—particularly in their attitudes toward government spending—than nonsoutherners, but these differences are primarily confined to the Northeast and Middle Atlantic regions.

Regional differences for our second group of political indicators are more pronounced. Our factor analysis of attitudes toward a community speaker who was a communist or who was a homosexual and toward a college professor who was a communist or a homosexual again produced one factor for each year (Table 11). The factors tap most strongly attitudes toward homosexuals, but all four indicators loaded (are represented) strongly. Our regression analyses for these factors (Table 12) identify strong differences between southerners and nonsoutherners in these attitudes. In 1974, southerners were more conservative than residents of all other regions except the Mountain on this measure. All of these

Table 13.
Factor Analyses, Indicators of Attitudes Toward
Religion, Morality, the Family, and Women's Roles (Part I)

Attitude	1974	1985	1994
Opposed to abortions for poor women	.768	.775	.820
Opposed to abortions for single women	.751	.775	.809
Opposed to abortions for women who want no more children	.751	.785	.810
Opposed to abortions for rape victims	.580	.607	.638
Opposed to abortions of defective fetuses	.570	.632	.654
Opposed to abortions when woman's health is endangered	.479	.494	.526
Frequently attends religious services	.450	.520	.478
Strong religious affiliation	.422	.503	.435
Opposed to homosexual sex	.335	.412	.426
Opposed to extramarital sex	.316	.364	.242
Fundamental religious affiliation	.213	.230	.273
Eigenvalue	3.247	3.709	3.826

differences except the South/West North Central remained significant in 1985. But in 1994, southerners were more conservative than residents of every other region on this measure. Thus southern differences in attitudes toward homosexuals and communists seem to be more distinct than attitudes on such issues as government spending. This pattern is not surprising: spending issues represent a more "instrumental" form of politics and tend to be much more class-based than attitudes toward homosexuals and communists, which tend to be symbolically and culturally based.

Our final conceptual dimension taps attitudes toward religion, morality, the family, and women's roles. The first group of indicators for this dimension included attitudes toward abortion (six indicators), frequency of church attendance, strength of religious affiliation, attitudes toward extramarital and homosexual sex, and the fundamentalism of respondents' affiliations. Our factor analyses of these indicators produced one-factor solutions (Table 13). Although there is slight variation in the structure of the factors across the three periods, all of them tap attitudes toward abortion most strongly, followed by strength of religious affiliation and attitudes toward sexuality. Table 14 shows that southerners were more conservative in their attitudes on these issues in 1974 than residents of the non-South, but this pattern largely owed to significant differences between the South and residents of the Middle Atlantic, West North Central, and Pacific regions. Differences between the South and the Middle Atlantic and Mountain regions appeared in 1985, although there was no significant South/non-South difference at this point and the direction of the South/Mountain difference contradicted predictions. But the South/non-South difference reappeared in 1994, when southerners were more conservative than residents of the Middle Atlantic, Mountain, and Pacific regions in these attitudes. Thus although differences

Table 14.
Effects of Region on Factor Scores, Attitudes Toward
Religion, Morality, the Family, and Women's Roles (Part I)[a]

Independent Variable	1974		1985		1994	
	Model A	Model B	Model A	Model B	Model A	Model B
New England[b]	−.140	—	−.214	—	−.085	—
Middle Atlantic[b]	−.348**	—	−.273**	—	−.230**	—
East North Central[b]	−.016	—	.011	—	.062	—
West North Central[b]	−.260*	—	.133	—	−.046	—
Mountain[b]	−.075	—	.405**	—	−.356**	—
Pacific[b]	−.413**	—	−.142	—	−.351**	—
Non-South[c]	—	−.198**	—	−.042	—	−.149**
Intercept	.746	.752	.826	.776	.642	.699
R[2]	.115	.093	.102	.075	.095	.076

[a] Ordinary least squares regression coefficients. Equation includes controls for age, marital status, education, gender, rural/urban residence, income, and race. Each coefficient represents the magnitude and direction of difference between a given regional category (e.g., New England) and the South. For example, a negative coefficient for the New England region indicates that New Englanders express less support for the attitudes tapped by this factor than southerners do. * indicates that this difference is significant at the .05 level, and ** indicates that this difference is significant at the .01 level.

[b] Dummy variable for region of residence; reference category is the South.

[c] Dummy variable for aggregate non-South category; reference category is the South.

Table 15.
Factor Analyses of Indicators, Attitudes Toward
Religion, Morality, the Family, and Women's Roles (Part II)

Attitude	1974	1985	1994
Toward women taking care of home, men taking care of country	.590	.624	.620
Toward premarital sex	.515	.512	.460
Toward voting for qualified woman for president	.504	.506	.524
Toward women working outside the home	.403	.250	.312
Regularly spends evenings in a bar	.375	.432	.344
Toward divorce laws	.105	.020	−.007
Eigenvalue	1.181	1.156	1.086

waned somewhat in the 1980s, they remained distinct in 1994, with southerners continuing to demonstrate a more conservative orientation than nonsoutherners on these issues.

Our factor analyses of the second group of indicators of this dimension (attitudes toward women's primary roles, premarital sex, voting for a woman for president, women working outside the home, and divorce laws and reports of the frequency with which respondents spend an evening in a bar) again produced a single factor for each time period (Table 15). These factors tap least strongly attitudes toward divorce laws. Our regression analyses (Table 16) show consistent differences between southerners and nonsoutherners in these attitudes and behavior, but different regions seem to account for those differences across the three time periods. In 1974, southerners were significantly more conservative

Table 16.
Effects of Region on Factor Scores, Attitudes Toward
Religion, Morality, the Family, and Women's Roles (Part II)[a]

Independent Variable	1974		1985		1994	
	Model A	Model B	Model A	Model B	Model A	Model B
New England[b]	−.054	—	−.309**	—	−.135	—
Middle Atlantic[b]	−.270**	—	−.318**	—	−.073	—
East North Central[b]	−.096	—	−.214**	—	−.087	—
West North Central[b]	−.100	—	−.084	—	−.138*	—
Mountain[b]	−.241**	—	.099	—	−.200**	—
Pacific[b]	−.155*	—	−.205**	—	−.216**	—
Non-South[c]	—	−.154**	—	−.190**	—	.132**
Intercept	−.032	−.016	.284	.252	.051	.070
R^2	.331	.324	.296	.280	.206	.202

[a] Ordinary least squares regression coefficients. Equation includes controls for age, marital status, education, gender, rural/urban residence, income, and race. Each coefficient represents the magnitude and direction of difference between a given regional category (e.g., New England) and the South. For example, a negative coefficient for the New England region indicates that New Englanders express less support for the attitudes tapped by this factor than southerners do. * indicates that this difference is significant at the .05 level, and ** indicates that this difference is significant at the .01 level.

[b] Dummy variable for region of residence; reference category is the South.

[c] Dummy variable for aggregate non-South category; reference category is the South.

than residents of the Middle Atlantic, Mountain, and Pacific regions in these attitudes. In 1985, they differed significantly from New England, Middle Atlantic, East North Central, and Pacific residents, and in 1994, they differed only from West North Central, Mountain, and Pacific residents. Thus Tables 14 and 16 show that attitudes toward abortion and related issues remain more distinct than attitudes toward sexuality, divorce, and women's roles.

Our results leave little doubt that a distinctive worldview continues to characterize southerners. This distinctiveness remains most evident in their continued emphasis on violence, their political views, and their attitudes toward religious and moral issues and the family and women's roles. Within these domains, issues for which we failed to find continued southern distinctiveness are particularly informative. The results show that the convergence that has occurred in these areas owes more to a changing non-South than to a transformed southern culture.

The conceptual domain in which the greatest convergence was found, race-related attitudes and behaviors, provided the most interesting results. Although racism traditionally has constituted the "cardinal test" of a southerner, its centrality in demarcating southerners from nonsoutherners appears to have waned. Attitudes toward issues related to school integration and voting for a black for president and toward segregated neighborhoods appear to have moderated in the South, with the former appearing to change more than the latter. Although southerners continue to distinguish themselves from residents of other regions in their disapproval of interracial marriage, they are more likely than nonsoutherners to report that they live in integrated neighborhoods.

This last finding is particularly interesting. In the rural South, residential seg-regation was virtually nonexistent—one could argue that informal and formal mechanisms of social control were sufficiently effective to obviate the need for physical separation of the races in housing. Because our results show that in-creased urbanization in the South is not bringing with it increases in residential segregation, they suggest that southerners are not turning to segregation as these other forms of social control disappear.

Thus these results suggest that, to a large degree, the transformations wrought by the civil rights movement and the legislation that followed in its wake may have had a greater impact on southern attitudes and behaviors than such structural changes as urbanization, increased education, and a rise in per capita income. With few exceptions, though, the attitudes of southerners in the other dimensions we examined remain distinct. We can therefore find little evi-dence that structural convergence has brought with it a decline in southern cul-tural identity.

Suggested Readings

The authors of the essays in this collection have provided substantial documentation in their notes that will introduce scholars and students to more extensive readings. In addition, anyone who embarks on the study of the South since World War II should first consult George Brown Tindall, *The Emergence of the New South, 1913–1945* (Baton Rouge: Louisiana State University Press, 1967); Numan V. Bartley, *The New South, 1945–1980* (Baton Rouge: Louisiana State University Press, 1995); Dewey W. Grantham, *The South in Modern America: A Region at Odds* (New York: HarperCollins, 1994); and David R. Goldfield, *Promised Land: The South Since 1945* (Arlington Heights, Ill.: Harlan Davidson, 1987). An extensive bibliography that covers many of the subjects in this collection of essays can be found in William J. Cooper and Thomas E. Terrill, "The South: A Bibliographical Essay," *American Studies International* 31 (April 1993): 42–88. Other essential studies include James C. Cobb, *The Most Southern Place on Earth: The Mississippi Delta and the Roots of Regional Identity* (New York: Oxford University Press, 1992); Jack Temple Kirby, *Rural Worlds Lost: The American South, 1920–1960* (Baton Rouge: Louisiana State University Press, 1987); and Lionel J. Beaulieu, ed., *The Rural South in Crisis: Challenges for the Future* (Boulder: Westview Press, 1988); Don A. Dillman and Daryl J. Hobbs, eds., *Rural Society in the United States: Issues for the 1980s* (Boulder: Westview Press, 1982); Jacqueline Jones, *The Dispossessed: America's Underclasses from the Civil War to the Present* (New York: Basic Books, 1992); and Robert L. Hall and Carol B. Stack, eds., *Holding on to the Land and the Lord: Kinship, Ritual, Land Tenure, and Social Policy in the Rural South* (Athens: University of Georgia Press, 1982). For a brief eclectic study of the twentieth-century

South see Pete Daniel, *Standing at the Crossroads: Southern Life Since 1900* (New York: Hill and Wang, 1986).

Scholarly literature that will help the student compare the rural with the urban South include two studies by James C. Cobb: *Industrialization and Southern Society, 1877–1984* (Lexington: University Press of Kentucky, 1984) and *Selling of the South: The Southern Crusade for Industrial Development, 1936–1980* (Baton Rouge: Louisiana State University Press, 1982). See also Gavin Wright, *Old South, New South: Revolutions in the Southern Economy Since the Civil War* (New York: Free Press, 1986); Melvin L. Greenhut and W. Tate Whitman, eds., *Essays in Southern Economic Development* (Chapel Hill: University of North Carolina Press, 1964); Calvin B. Hoover and B. U. Ratchford, *Economic Resources and Policies of the South* (New York: Macmillan, 1951); and Allen Batteau, ed., *Appalachia and America: Autonomy and Regional Dependence* (Lexington: University Press of Kentucky, 1983).

Other important studies on southern economic development with an emphasis on the concept of Sunbelt include Carl Abbott, *New Urban America: Growth and Politics in Sunbelt Cities of the South* (Chapel Hill: University of North Carolina Press, 1981); Bernard L. Weinstein and Robert E. Firestine, *Regional Growth and Decline in the United States: The Rise of the Sunbelt and the Decline of the Northeast* (New York: Praeger, 1978); Thomas A. Lyson, *Two Sides to the Sunbelt: The Growing Divergence Between the Rural and the Urban South* (New York: Praeger, 1989); and David C. Perry and Alfred J. Watkins, eds., *The Rise of the Sunbelt Cities* (Beverly Hills: Sage, 1977). See also David Goldfield's *Cotton Fields and Skyscrapers: Southern City and Region, 1607–1980* (Baton Rouge: Louisiana State University Press, 1982) and *The City in Southern History: The Growth of Urban Civilization in the South* (Port Washington, N.Y.: Kennikat Press, 1977).

Background on the agricultural history of the twentieth-century South can be gained by consulting Pete Daniel, *Breaking the Land: The Transformation of Cotton, Tobacco, and Rice Cultures Since 1880* (Urbana: University of Illinois Press, 1985); Gilbert C. Fite, *Cotton Fields No More: Southern Agriculture, 1865–1980* (Lexington: University Press of Kentucky, 1984); and Theodore Saloutos, *Farmer Movements in the South, 1865–1933* (Berkeley: University of California Press, 1960). More specialized studies include Thomas A. Campbell, *A Moveable School Goes to the Negro Farmer* (New York: Arno Press, 1969); Harry Crews, *A Childhood: The Biography of a Place* (New York: Harper & Row, 1978); John Leonard Fulmer, *Agricultural Progress in the Cotton Belt Since 1920* (Chapel Hill: University of North Carolina Press, 1950); Ruth Holland, *The Forgotten Minority: America's Tenant Farmers and Migrant Workers* (New York: Crowell-Collier, 1970); Theodore Rosengarten, *All God's Dangers: The Life of Nate Shaw* (New York: Knopf, 1975); James H. Street, *The New Revolution in the Cotton Economy: Mechanization and Its Consequences* (Chapel

Hill: University of North Carolina Press, 1957); R. Douglas Hurt, *Agricultural Technology in the Twentieth Century* (Manhattan, Kans.: Sunflower University Press, 1991); and Joseph J. Molnar, ed., *Agricultural Change: Consequences for Southern Farms and Rural Communities* (Boulder, Colo.: Westview Press, 1986). For an introduction to the role of women in agriculture, see Ann Rosenfeld, *Farm Women: Work, Farm, and Family in the United States* (Chapel Hill: University of North Carolina Press, 1985); Carolyn E. Sach, *The Invisible Farmers: Women in Agricultural Production* (Totowa, N.J.: Rowman and Allanheld, 1983); Judith Z. Kalbacher, *A Profile of Female Farmers in America,* USDA, Rural Development Research Report 45, 1985; and Wava G. Haney and Jane B. Knowles, *Women and Farming: Changing Roles, Changing Structures* (Boulder, Colo.: Westview Press, 1988).

Further studies of race relations in the rural South should begin with David R. Goldfield, *Black, White, and Southern: Race Relations and Southern Culture, 1940 to the Present* (Baton Rouge: Louisiana State University Press, 1990); Aldon D. Morris, *The Origins of the Civil Rights Movement: Black Communities Organizing for Change* (New York: Free Press, 1984); Harvard Sitkoff, *The Struggle for Black Equality, 1954–1992* (New York: Hill and Wang, 1993); and Hans A. Baer and Yvonne Jones, eds., *African Americans in the South: Issues of Race, Class, and Gender* (Athens: University of Georgia Press, 1992). An introduction to liberal and conservative views on segregation can be found respectively in James McBride Dabbs, *Who Speaks for the South?* (New York: Funk & Wagnalls, 1964), and William D. Workman, *The Case for the South* (New York: Devin-Adair, 1960). More specialized studies include Orville Vernon Burton and Robert C. McMath, Jr., ed., *Toward a New South? Studies in Post–Civil War Southern Communities* (Westport, Conn.: Greenwood Press, 1982); William H. Chafe, *Civilities and Civil Rights: Greensboro, North Carolina, and the Black Struggle for Freedom* (New York: Oxford University Press, 1980); Richard A. Couto, *Ain't Gonna Let Nobody Turn Me Round: The Pursuit of Racial Justice in the Rural South* (Philadelphia: Temple University Press, 1991); Chandler Davidson and Bernard Grofman, eds., *The Quiet Revolution: The Impact of the Voting Rights Act in the South, 1965–1990* (Princeton: Princeton University Press, 1994); John Dittmer, *Local People: The Struggle for Civil Rights in Mississippi* (Urbana: University of Illinois Press, 1994); Adam Fairclough, *Race and Democracy: The Civil Rights Struggle in Louisiana, 1915–1972* (Athens: University of Georgia Press, 1995); James F. Findlay, *Church People in Struggle: The National Council of Churches and the Black Freedom Movement, 1950–1970* (New York: Oxford University Press, 1993); Robert Hamburger, *Our Portion of Hell: Fayette County, Tennessee, an Oral History of the Struggle for Civil Rights* (New York: Basic Books, 1973); and Amelia Wallace Vernon, *African Americans at Mars Bluff, South Carolina* (Baton Rouge: Louisiana State University Press, 1994).

For an excellent introduction to race relations and education, see Richard Kluger, *Simple Justice: The History of "Brown v. Board of Education" and Black America's Struggle for Equality* (New York: Knopf, 1976). See also Jack Bass, *The Orangeburg Massacre* (Macon, Ga.: Mercer University Press, 1884); Howell Raines, *My Soul Is Rested: Movement Days in the Deep South Remembered* (New York: Penguin Books, 1983); and Clayborne Carson, *In Struggle: SNCC and the Black Awakening of the 1960s* (Cambridge, Mass.: Harvard University Press, 1981). Any study of race relations in the South must include works on Martin Luther King, Jr. For an introduction to this subject, see David J. Garrow, *Bearing the Cross: Martin Luther King, Jr., and the Southern Christian Leadership Conference* (New York: William Morrow, 1981), and Taylor Branch, *Parting the Waters: America in the King Years, 1954–1963* (New York: Simon and Schuster, 1988).

Anyone who embarks on the study of women in the rural South should consider the following general studies: David M. Katzman, *Seven Days a Week: Women and Domestic Service in Industrializing America* (New York: Oxford University Press, 1978); Alice Kessler-Harris, *Out to Work: A History of Wage-Earning Women in the United States* (New York: Oxford University Press, 1982); Barbara Mayer Wertheimer, *We Were There: The Story of Working Women in America* (New York: Pantheon Books, 1977); Jacquelyn Dowd Hall, *Revolt Against Chivalry: Jessie Daniel Ames and the Women's Campaign Against Lynching* (New York: Columbia University Press, 1993); and Eleanor Flexner, *Century of Struggle: The Woman's Rights Movement in the United States* (Cambridge, Mass.: Belknap Press of Harvard University, 1996). See also Sara Evans, *Personal Politics: The Roots of Women's Liberation in the Civil Rights Movement and the New Left* (New York: Knopf, 1979); Margaret Jarman Hagood, *Mothers of the South: Portraiture of the White Tenant Farm Woman* (New York: Norton, 1977); and Jacquelyn Dowd Hall et al., *Like a Family: The Making of a South Carolina Mill World* (Chapel Hill: University of North Carolina Press, 1987). Essential studies of working women include Dolores E. Janiewski, *Sisterhood Denied: Race, Gender, and Class in a New South Community* (Philadelphia: Temple University Press, 1985); Kathy Kahn, *Hillbilly Women* (New York: S. French, 1989); Mary Frederickson, *A Place to Speak Our Minds: The Southern School for Women Workers, 1927–1950* (Bloomington: Indiana University Press, 1990); and Victoria Byerly, *Hard Times Cotton Mill Girls: Personal Histories of Womanhood and Poverty in the South* (Ithaca: ILR Press, 1986). See also Orville Vernon Burton, *In My Father's House Are Many Mansions: Family and Community in Edgefield, South Carolina* (Chapel Hill: University of North Carolina Press, 1985), and Jacqueline Jones, *Labor of Love, Labor of Sorrow: Black Women, Work, and the Family from Slavery to the Present* (New York: Basic Books, 1985).

The study of country music in relation to southern culture must begin with the works of Bill C. Malone: *Country Music, USA* (Austin: University of Texas Press, 1985); *Southern Music, American Music* (Lexington: University Press of Kentucky, 1979); *Singing Cowboys and Musical Mountaineers: Southern Culture and the Roots of Country Music* (Athens: University of Georgia Press, 1993); and edited with Judith McCulloh, *Stars of Country Music: Uncle Dave Macon to Johnny Rodriguez* (Urbana: University of Illinois Press, 1976). Other useful studies include Melton A. McLaurin and Richard A. Peterson, eds., *You Wrote My Life: Lyrical Themes in Country Music* (Philadelphia: Gordon and Breach, 1992); Paul Kingsbury and Alan Axelrod, eds., *Country: The Music and the Musicians* (Nashville: Country Music Foundation Press, 1988); Nolan Porterfield, *Jimmie Rodgers: The Life and Times of America's Blue Yodeler* (Urbana: University of Illinois Press, 1979); Colin Escott, *Hank Williams: The Biography* (Boston: Little, Brown, 1994); Peter Guralnick, *Last Train to Memphis: The Rise of Elvis Presley* (Boston: Little, Brown, 1994); Joe Klein, *Woody Guthrie* (New York: Knopf, 1980); Charles Townsend, *San Antonio Rose: The Life and Music of Bob Wills* (Urbana: University of Illinois Press, 1976); and Louis M. Jones and Charles Wolfe, *Everybody's Grandpa: Fifty Years Behind the Mike* (Knoxville: University of Tennessee Press, 1984).

Other related works include William Ferris, *Blues from the Delta* (Garden City, N.Y.: Anchor Press/Doubleday, 1978); Greil Marcus, *Mystery Train: Images of America in Rock 'n' Roll Music*, 2d rev. ed. (New York: E. P. Dutton, 1982); William Lynwood Montell, *Singing the Glory Down: Amateur Gospel Music in South Central Kentucky, 1900–1990* (Lexington: University Press of Kentucky, 1991); Neil Rosenberg, *Bluegrass: A History* (Urbana: University of Illinois Press, 1985); and Robert Cantwell, *Bluegrass Breakdown: The Making of the Old Southern Sound* (Urbana: University of Illinois Press, 1984).

Scholars have given religion in the South considerable attention. For an introduction to the subject, see Robert Wuthnow, *The Restructuring of American Religion: Society and Faith Since World War II* (Princeton: Princeton University Press, 1988); Sydney E. Ahlstrom, *A Religious History of the American People* (New Haven: Yale University Press, 1976); Vansau McCauley, *Appalachian Mountain Religion: A History* (Urbana: University of Illinois Press, 1995); and Charles R. Wilson, ed., *Religion in the South* (Jackson: University Press of Mississippi, 1985). See also two works by David Edwin Harrell, Jr.: *Varieties of Southern Evangelicalism* (Macon, Ga.: Mercer University Press, 1981) and *All Things Are Possible: The Healing and Charismatic Revivals in Modern America* (Bloomington: Indiana University Press, 1975), as well as two studies by Samuel S. Hill, Jr.: *Religion and the Solid South* (Nashville: Abingdon Press, 1972) and *The South and North in American Religion* (Athens: University of Georgia Press, 1980). Also see Hill's edited collection *Religion in the Southern States: A Historical Study* (Macon, Ga.: Mercer University Press, 1983). Ted Ownby provides an excellent introduction to this subject in *Subduing Satan: Religion, Rec-*

reation, and Manhood in the Rural South, 1865–1920 (Chapel Hill: University of North Carolina Press, 1990). William Martin's *A Prophet with Honor: The Billy Graham Story* (New York: William Morrow, 1991) examines the life of the South's most respected and successful evangelist.

The Baptists have been given extensive study. See Nancy Ammerman, *Baptist Battles: Social Change and Religious Conflict in the Southern Baptist Convention* (New Brunswick, N.J.: Rutgers University Press, 1990); Howard Dorgan, *Giving Glory to God in Appalachia: Worship Practices of Six Baptist Subdenominations* (Knoxville: University of Tennessee Press, 1987); John Lee Eighmy, *Churches in Cultural Captivity: A History of the Social Attitudes of Southern Baptists* (Knoxville: University of Tennessee Press, 1972); M. Jean Heriot, *Blessed Assurance: Beliefs, Actions, and the Experience of Salvation in a Carolina Baptist Church* (Knoxville: University Press of Kentucky, 1994); and Ellen M. Rosenberg, *The Southern Baptists: A Subculture in Transition* (Knoxville: University of Tennessee Press, 1989).

Important studies of the African American religious experience include Hans A. Baser and Merrill Singer, *African-American Religion in the Twentieth Century: Varieties of Protest and Accommodation* (Knoxville: University of Tennessee Press, 1992); Peter D. Goldsmith, *When I Rise Cryin' Holy: African-American Denominationalism on the Georgia Coast* (New York: AMS Press, 1989); C. Eric Lincoln and Lawrence H. Mamiya, *The Black Church in the African American Experience* (Durham: Duke University Press, 1990); and Walter F. Pitts, *Old Ship of Zion: The Afro-Baptist Ritual in the African Diaspora* (New York: Oxford University Press, 1993).

For specific groups and denominations, see W. J. Hollenweger, *The Pentecostals: The Charismatic Movement in the Churches* (Minneapolis: Augsburg, 1972); Leonard Dinnerstein and Mary Palsson, eds., *Jews in the South* (Baton Rouge: Louisiana University Press, 1973); Troy D. Abell, *Better Felt Than Said: The Holiness-Pentecostal Experience in Southern Appalachia* (Waco: Markham Press, 1982); Joel Alvis, *Religion and Race: Southern Presbyterians, 1946–1983* (Tuscaloosa: University of Alabama Press, 1994); Carol H. Greenhouse, *Praying for Justice: Faith, Order, and Community in an American Town* (Ithaca: Cornell University Press, 1986); Samuel S. Hill, *Southern Churches in Crisis* (New York: Holt, Rinehart and Winston, 1967); and Hunter James, *Smile Pretty and Say Jesus: The Last Great Days of PTL* (Athens: University of Georgia Press, 1993).

Scholars have also given extensive attention to the politics of the South. The place to begin remains V. O. Key, *Southern Politics in State and Nation* (New York: Knopf, 1949). More recent studies that also provide an introduction are Jack Bass and Walter De Vries, *The Transformation of Southern Politics: Social Change and Political Consequences Since 1945* (New York: Basic Books, 1976); Alexander P. Lamis, *The Two-Party South* (New York: Oxford University Press,

1988); and Earl Black and Merle Black, *Politics and Society in the South* (Cambridge, Mass.: Harvard University Press, 1987).

See also Numan V. Bartley, *The Rise of Massive Resistance: Race and Politics in the South During the 1950s* (Baton Rouge: Louisiana State University Press, 1984); Earl Black, *Southern Governors and Civil Rights: Racial Separation as a Campaign Issue in the Second Reconstruction* (Cambridge, Mass.: Harvard University Press, 1976); Chandler Davidson, *Biracial Politics: Conflict and Coalition in the Biracial South* (Baton Rouge: Louisiana State University Press, 1972); Steven F. Lawson, *In Pursuit of Power: Southern Blacks and Electoral Politics, 1965–1982* (New York: Columbia University Press, 1985); Neil R. McMillen, *The Citizens' Council: Organized Resistance to the Second Reconstruction, 1954–1964* (Urbana: University of Illinois Press, 1971); Louis M. Seagull, *Southern Republicanism* (Cambridge, Mass.: Schenkman, 1975); and George B. Tindall, *The Disruption of the Solid South* (New York: Norton, 1972).

The political power of the Christian Right can be studied in Robert C. Liebman and Robert Wuthnow, *The New Christian Right: Mobilization and Legitimation* (New York: Aldine, 1983) and Michael Lienesch, *Redeeming America: Piety and Politics in the New Christian Right* (Chapel Hill: University of North Carolina Press, 1993). The influence of race on southern politics can be seen in Donald R. Matthews and James W. Prothro, *Negroes and the New Southern Politics* (New York: Harcourt, Brace and World, 1966); and Edward G. Carmines and James A. Stimson, *Issue Evolution: Race and the Transformation of American Politics* (Princeton: Princeton University Press, 1989). See also Douglas Rose, ed., *The Emergence of David Duke and the Politics of Race* (Chapel Hill: University of North Carolina Press, 1992); and Dan Carter, *The Politics of Race: George Wallace, the Origins of the New Conservatism, and the Transformation of American Politics* (New York: Simon and Schuster, 1995).

The concept of southern distinctiveness remains a fascinating and important area for study. The leading scholar in this field of inquiry is John Shelton Reed. Students will find his books essential: *The Enduring South: Subculture Persistence in Mass Society* (Lexington, Mass.: Lexington Books, 1972); *One South: An Ethnic Approach to Regional Culture* (Baton Rouge: Louisiana State University Press, 1982); *Southerners: The Social Psychology of Sectionalism* (Chapel Hill: University of North Carolina Press, 1983); *Southern Folk, Plain and Fancy: Native White Social Types* (Athens: University of Georgia Press, 1986); *Whistling Dixie: Dispatches from the South* (Columbia: University of Missouri Press, 1990); and *My Tears Spoiled My Aim and Other Reflections on Southern Culture* (Columbia: University of Missouri Press, 1993). See also Carl Degler, *Place over Time: The Continuity of Southern Distinctiveness* (Baton Rouge: Louisiana State University Press, 1977); George B. Tindall, *The Ethnic Southerners* (Baton Rouge: Louisiana State University Press, 1976); and Clyde N. Wilson, ed., *Why the South Will Survive* (Athens: University of Georgia Press, 1981). For a differing opinion, see John Egerton, *The Americanization of Dixie: The Southernization of America* (New York: Harper's Magazine Press, 1974); and Charles B. Sellers, Jr., *The Southerner as American* (Chapel Hill: University of North Carolina Press, 1960).

Contributors

WILLIAM B. BANKSTON is professor of sociology at Louisiana State University. His major research interest is the sociology of crime and deviance, particularly regional and cultural variations in patterns of interpersonal violence.

ORVILLE VERNON BURTON is professor of history at the University of Illinois at Champaign-Urbana. He is the author of *In My Father's House Are Many Mansions: Family and Community in Edgefield, South Carolina* (Chapel Hill: University of North Carolina Press, 1985) and the editor of *Class, Conflict, and Consensus: Antebellum Southern Community* (Westport, Conn.: Greenwood Press, 1982) and, with Robert C. McMath, Jr., *Toward a New South? Studies in Post–Civil War Southern Communities* (Westport, Conn.: Greenwood Press, 1982).

JEANNE S. HURLBERT is associate professor of sociology at Louisiana State University. In addition to her study of regionalism and southern distinctiveness, she conducts research on the role that social networks play in the determination of stratified outcomes. Much of this work entails the collection of primary data through telephone surveys.

SALLY MCMILLEN is professor of history at Davidson College. She is the author of *Motherhood in the Old South: Pregnancy, Childbirth and Infant Rearing* (Baton Rouge: Louisiana State University Press, 1990) and *Southern Women: Black and White in the Old South* (Arlington Heights, Ill.: Harlan Davidson, 1992).

BILL C. MALONE retired as professor of history at Tulane University. He is the author of *Country Music, USA* (Austin: University of Texas Press, 1985); *Southern Music, American Music* (Lexington: University Press of Kentucky, 1979); and *Singing Cowboys and Musical Mountaineers: Southern Culture and the Roots of Country Music* (Athens: University of Georgia Press, 1993); and editor, with Judith McCulloh, of *Stars of Country Music: Uncle Dave Macon to Johnny Rodriguez* (Urbana: University of Illinois Press, 1976).

TED OWNBY is associate professor of history at the University of Mississippi. He is the author of *Subduing Satan: Religion, Recreation, and Manhood in the Rural South, 1865–1920* (Chapel Hill: University of North Carolina Press, 1990) and the editor of *Black and White Cultural Interaction in the Antebellum South* (Jackson: University Press of Mississippi, 1993).

WAYNE PARENT is associate professor and assistant chair in the Department of Political Science at Louisiana State University. He is the co-editor, with Huey L. Perry, of *Blacks and the American Political System* (Gainesville: University Press of Florida, 1995). He has also published in the *American Journal of Political Science, American Political Science Review, Social Science Quarterly,* and *Western Political Quarterly.*

PETER A. PETRAKIS is an assistant professor in the Department of History and Government at Southeastern Louisiana University.

DONALD L. WINTERS is professor of history at Vanderbilt University. He is the author of *Tennessee Farming, Tennessee Farmers: Antebellum Agriculture in the Upper South* (Knoxville: University of Tennessee Press, 1994); *Farmers Without Farms: Agricultural Tenancy in Nineteenth-Century Iowa* (Westport, Conn.: Greenwood Press, 1978); and *Henry Cantwell Wallace as Secretary of Agriculture, 1921–1924* (Urbana: University of Illinois Press, 1970). He has also served as president of the Agricultural History Society.

Index

.